MIDORI HAUS

MIDORI HAUS

Transformation from
Old House to Green Future
with Passive House

Chie Kawahara

HybridGlobal
PUBLISHING

Published by
Hybrid Global Publishing
301 E 57th Street, 4th fl
New York, NY 10022

Manufactured in the United States of America, or in the
United Kingdom when distributed elsewhere.

Kawahara, Chie
Midori Haus:
LCCN: 2017951463
ISBN: 978-1-938015-73-1
eBook: 978-1-938015-76-2

Cover design by Daniel Cook

Interior design by Medlar Publishing Solutions Pvt Ltd, India

Editing by Penny Hill

Photos by John Terry and Kurt Hurley

The purpose of this book is to educate and entertain. The author
and publisher shall have neither liability nor responsibility to any
person or entity with respect to any loss, damage, accidents or other
trouble arising from any information contained in this book. Readers
are advised to consult with licensed and/or certified professionals
for assistance with their projects. Mention of trademark, proprietary
product, or vendor does not constitute a guarantee or warranty
of the products by the publisher or author and does not imply its
approval to the exclusion of other products or vendors.

http://midorihaus.com/

To my green building mentors

Contents

Foreword

There are some who say that the Passivhaus, or Passive House system, is worshipped by a cult of data-obsessed nerds who design boxy buildings with no charm. One critic claimed, "Passivhaus is a single-metric, ego-driven enterprise that satisfies the architect's need for checking boxes, and the energy nerd's obsession with BTUs, but it fails the occupant." There are others who say it has become irrelevant; just add solar panels to the roof and net zero it out.

The story of the Midori Haus puts paid to these arguments. Passive House is a chapter in a much bigger story, one describing a journey to find and build a warm, comfortable, and healthy home that fits into the neighborhood. Passive House gives focus and direction (system thinking instead of à la carte ordering of features), but the end result is so much more than just an energy-efficient box.

Passive House consultant Bronwyn Barry has noted that "passive house is a team sport" of architects, engineers, and consultants, but the most important member of the team is in fact the client. And oh, what a wonderful, glorious client Chie Kawahara appears to have been: she and Kurt know what they want, do their research, fully participate in the process, and respect the people they are working with. They are thoughtful, considerate, and disciplined. Doing a complex renovation is a challenge and often the cause of marital disruption; Chie and Kurt handle it all with aplomb. Perhaps the book should be subtitled, "How to be a client," and handed out by architects before every project.

To many people, houses are nothing more than real estate, a store of financial value. It's one reason that healthy, green, and passive houses are relatively rare—there is not much of a financial return on such an investment. Midori Haus will deliver other kinds of returns—in comfort, health, resilience, security, and happiness. The investment that the owners made was much greater than just money; it required a big dose of time and intelligence.

The story of Midori Haus proves that in the end what matters is people, not product; that Passive House is not an end in itself but a means to an end—a beautiful, comfortable home that meets the needs and desires of the people inside it. It's about so much more than just data.

Lloyd Alter
Architect, Editor, Professor

1
Introduction

The house

When my husband and I first met Midori, she was almost ninety years old. With perfect posture and classic styling, we could see she had been a beauty in her prime. But her energy performance was on par with others of her vintage and she suffered from ailing systems that needed attention. Her previous caretakers were not big on cosmetic surgery nor the latest fashion trends. In that way we were lucky. We didn't have to undo things that had recently been done. As our real estate agent dryly said, Midori was relatively unmolested. Nevertheless, her subpar energy performance was a problem. We wanted her to be world-class again.

No, our Midori is not a person. There are cities, a liquor brand, musicians, women, trains, manga, and even a web browser named Midori. For us, though, Midori was an Arts and Crafts bungalow originally built in 1922 that had definitely seen better days. We liked how she felt and we had a vision for her remaining years. We wanted to preserve the timeless, classic beauty of her Arts and Crafts style while making her durable, resilient, and as energy efficient as possible. The word *midori* literally means green in Japanese, and we chose this for our house. The thought of combining super energy efficiency with century-old style intrigued us and we thought it would be an interesting transformation.

The owners

Just as Midori has gone through a transformation, so have we. My husband and I became the owners and orchestrators of this house transformation project. Neither of us had any experience in construction or architecture. We were happily living our simple life working in offices during the week and enjoying the outdoors of San Francisco Bay Area on the weekends. Embarking on a huge transformation project was the furthest thing from our minds until a nagging problem, which built up over time, reached a point in 2009 where I quit my job to address it.

It's a common problem that most people face: Where shall we live after getting married? We were in our late 30s when we got married in 2001. We each were comfortably set in our own places. Kurt owned a condo in Santa Cruz and I owned a condo in San Jose. Since his place was the larger of the two, I sold my condo and moved in with him. I moved by squeezing my greatly pared down immediate possessions into one bedroom he vacated for me. It felt like renting a room again. Even after we changed the title on the deed, I never felt a sense of ownership. Sure, it was nice, but the place was not mine. I'm sure he would have felt the same if he had moved in with me.

The solution to this problem was to move into a new place we both felt good about and where we could co-create a place together that reflected our personal values. We went on green home tours to get inspiration so we could envision a place that reflected our style and functional needs. We soon learned that the homes we liked had been heavily renovated or custom built. There was nothing green off the shelf on the market.

This book

This book is a narrative of our journey, written to provide the reader with the experience of transforming an old house. It's a dual transformation, for it's also about the transformation of the owners. Having gone through this experience, we can no longer look at houses the same way ever again.

This book is an extended case study told from the perspective of intrepid homeowners approaching the project as novices. Each chapter closes with a short list of lessons learned. Features and concepts are discussed in a non-technical way, as one homeowner would talk about their experience with another homeowner.

Photos, videos, and links are available in blogposts on http://midorihaus.com.

2
Choosing Our Place

We need a place

The notion of green building resonated with our core values, and we approached this project intending to build a new house from scratch at a new location. As we explored the real estate market, we clarified our search criteria by referring back to our personal values. This chapter explores how we chose where to live.

Green building seed

Our desire to live in a green home had been brewing for years. I can trace the planting of the seed back to 2003 when our friend, Karsten, fell in love with a ten-acre parcel of land on a hillside in the mouth of San Lorenzo Valley. The green building sirens were calling him to build his dream green home. Through the shrubs, weeds, and trees, he could see his sanctuary where he could commune with nature and have a house that made smart use of resources. Though the property had a distinct rural feel, it was less than three miles from downtown Santa Cruz, offering quick and easy access to town on a bicycle to eat, shop, and socialize.

Karsten did not need to use the entire ten acres, but the property owner was set on selling the entire parcel of land. Motivated to make his dream home a reality, our friend worked quickly to find partners—future neighbors—to go in on this deal. Karsten, an early adopter of Leadership in Energy and Environmental Design (LEED), was an accredited U.S. Green Building Council professional. He would talk about green building principles with so much enthusiasm that his passion was infectious.

When Karsten presented this idea to us, we looked at the piece of land he described. Buying so much land so close to downtown Santa Cruz for a price of a small house seemed like a dream. Back then we were rather naïve. Instead of doing due diligence with a soils report or researching zoning to see if the lot was buildable, we did silly things like driving out there late at night and sitting on a log to see if we would see the ghost lady that supposedly haunted the area. Getting caught up in Karsten's enthusiasm, we were convinced that we could do this project fast and cheap. Because we didn't know what we didn't know, we floated in a nice dream for a while. It was a perfect escape from the daily grind of managing projects and people.

Then one day Kurt said it didn't feel right. This deal had long-term consequences. It's not a cut-and-dried one-time deal because the interaction wouldn't end with the purchase of the land. The subdivided lots needed to form a homeowners association to build and maintain shared infrastructure such as a private road and a common well and water distribution system. As condo owners we were familiar with the good and the bad of HOAs. We'd learned that having a difficult personality in the mix could be miserable, and we didn't know much about the other owners. Investing more than $600,000 in land and infrastructure before we even had a chance to start building our house seemed like a lot of risk. If the working relationship with others was unknown, neighbors could turn the dream house into a nightmare. Much to Karsten's dismay, we heeded Kurt's intuition and pulled out of the deal.

Eventually Karsten found other partners and proceeded to build his green home. He had lots of cool ideas that were demonstrated in his house—living green roof, large south-facing windows with solar electric panels for awnings, using thermal mass to heat the concrete floor during the day and slowly releasing the heat at night to keep the house comfortable. There were low-flow plumbing fixtures to conserve water, and he carefully chose interior materials that avoided off-gassing toxic chemicals. He even had work parties where friends came together to help plaster his walls— a nice community gathering where people learned about green building and Karsten got free labor. Watching from the sidelines, we were quite envious. But we also knew we did the right thing. And Kurt was glad he listened to his gut. Yet once exposed to this green building idea, our yearning for a green, sustainable house carried on like a low-grade fever that never went away.

Yearning

Once infected by thoughts of living in a green home, symptoms of yearning lingered. For instance, the kitchen in our condo had no windows. I wanted to feel the connection to the outdoors when I was in the kitchen and not feel like I was in a cave.

The yearning was further reinforced by the home tours we went to. It's one thing to browse through pretty magazines or websites to see gorgeous examples of newly built homes with green features. Walking through a home gave us a visceral feel of what it would be like to occupy the space and imagine how happy we would be. Green home tours gave us a chance to meet the homeowners who manifested their dream home and graciously opened their doors for public tours. They were all too happy to share information about their house and answer our questions. What is this type of window/wall that opens in a folding fashion? How long did the project take? How much did it cost? How do you like the split-level counter height? Also the builder or the architect was usually present for these tours and we could grab their cards if we were impressed with them.

Back in 2004 I thought how strange it was to see the owner pleased to have spent only $300 per square foot on the downstairs renovation and $400 per square foot on the upper floor. The added expense of using a steel I-beam to provide structural support was clearly worth it to the owner, who wanted the open feel in the living area downstairs. That seemed like a lot of money to me and I thought surely we would do much better than that, especially after reading a book with case studies of green homes built in Colorado ($100 per square foot) or Texas ($175 per square foot). Never mind that I was deluding myself. I would eventually learn that real estate and construction prices are relative to the location. A house in a desirable area within commute distance of Silicon Valley would cost a lot more than out-of-state case studies from seven years ago. Costs for building a house are pretty high in Northern California, and $300 per square foot was not outrageous in 2010 compared to $800 per square foot for luxury homes.

For many years we would become giddy as we wandered through the homes of people who either built from scratch or remodeled their houses using green principles. We particularly liked the open, airy feel of a space that featured recycled or sustainably harvested materials, and that the electricity generated on their roof made their annual electric bills near zero. Events such as Solar Homes Tour and Open Architecture Tour featured homes in several counties in the Santa Francisco Bay area that showcased different elements of green. Like travelers in the desert viewing pictures of people drinking water, no amount of looking could quench our thirst.

Though the home tours kept us in a state of yearning, these outings served a valuable purpose of clarifying our preferences. It was reassuring to know that Kurt and I had similar taste: the clean look of modern architecture, almost minimalist but with nice accents, functional layout that was not too big, with a light and airy feel that conveyed triumph over clutter gremlins. We especially liked the indoor-outdoor connection where the indoors opened up to an outdoor area that extended to an outside entertainment space. It was also important that we agreed on what we didn't like: large houses on a small lot without gardening space, houses on a scary steep hillside, smell of man-made materials that triggered headaches, and space lacking functional use that could turn into default storage.

Early on I began to carry a medium-sized spiral-bound notebook to take notes on features we liked as well as list architects and builders that we were impressed with. This notebook lasted about five years, from 2003 to 2008, when thoughts of green building were a pleasant distraction from working as an information technology manager braving the daily grind of commuting over the Santa Cruz Mountains to Palo Alto.

Santa Cruz real estate

The city of Santa Cruz has a population of about 60,000 fitting into less than thirteen square miles. This is the county seat of Santa Cruz County, one of the smallest (geographically) and one of the oldest counties in California. This little county is squeezed into a strip of coastal land south of San Mateo County and west of Santa Clara County, Silicon Valley. During commute hours the principal route, Highway 17, is clogged with commuters who pay the price of driving on a congested, curvy highway through the mountains to have high-paying jobs and still live in a place close to redwood forests, beaches, and surfing spots in a mild, Mediterranean climate.

Santa Cruz is a city where about quarter of the population is made up of students attending the University of California at Santa Cruz, its classrooms nestled in a redwood forest or on hilltops with ocean views. These students face intense competition to live in the community after their sophomore year; their parents blanch when they see the local rental property prices. Santa Cruz also is a city where local organic farms supply the residents with fresh produce year-round at farmers markets on Wednesdays, Saturdays, and Sundays. It's a city where there are more than dozen wineries with tasting rooms. It's an extremely desirable place to live. Finding a reasonably priced, unbuilt lot that is in a walkable area in the city of Santa Cruz is a tall order.

But we did see a few unbuilt lots tucked away here and there while we rode our bicycles around town. Noting the cross streets and the addresses of nearby houses, we went to the County Assessor's office to look up the names and addresses of the owners of those parcels. Many seemed to be vacant for so long we figured the owners would be glad to have an eager, eco-friendly couple take it off their hands. So we crafted a profile of ourselves on a document complete with a photo of our beaming, smiling faces and listed our wonderful attributes and sent a letter asking each landowner if they would like to sell their parcel to us. Two people responded to our inquiry. One was not ready to sell and the other wanted more money when we got into discussing price over the phone. Other letters went unanswered.

We were actively looking in 2008 through 2010 when the real estate market around the country tanked. We thought we might find a good deal on the foreclosure list from Santa Cruz Record publication and the Santa Cruz County Tax Sale. The rationale was that if bank mortgages were going bust in record numbers, we would be able to pick up a property at a good price. The problem for us was that the real estate market was less affected by fore-closures in Santa Cruz than other places. Moreover we weren't the only ones looking for a good deal. Investors flush with cash on hand were also scouring the market and picked up properties faster than vultures pick up carrion.

Did we consider moving to another city or region? Sure, Kurt obliged me with a courtesy discussion of what it would be like to live in San Francisco. But he was pretty set on staying in Santa Cruz, and I understand that. Unlike most people I meet in California who migrated from other states or countries, Kurt is a native Californian—a fifth generation Californian on his mother's side. His father attended Santa Cruz High School, and his par-ents met on the beach in Santa Cruz. Kurt attended the University of California at Santa Cruz and got a physics degree. He further tuned his personal compass towards ethics as well as environmen-tal and social justice. Taking personal action to minimize harm to people and the environment reflects his personal values.

More evidence that Kurt was rooted in Santa Cruz—he bought a condo when he was twenty-seven years old and rented out rooms to help pay the mortgage. When I met him eight years later, he was happily living alone in his place furnished with all the nesting accouterments of his liking. While he appreciated the green building examples we'd seen, the pull of redefining the space we shared was not as strong for him as it was for me.

I've lived most of my life in apartments and condos, and having a house where I could design and build to my dreams seemed luxurious, and that's what mattered to me. The inner voice of the little girl who grew up in Kalihi, a district in Honolulu infused with the sweat of several generations of immigrants from different countries, kept saying, "It's too expensive and out of reach."

The belly ache from not having my own space and feeling the gap between the life at the condo and my ideal green home seemed to grow year after year, and it became intensified by the eye candy of green home tours. Although we were capturing good ideas, not having a place to implement these good ideas left us wanting.

Where do we want to live?

After seeing Karsten build his green home from scratch, we wanted to do our own version. A clean slate—what better way to articulate our own style and ensure that all the functions and green features we wanted were put in place? In 2008 we still did not have a piece of land to build a house on and decided it was time to shift our focus to searching for real estate.

We explored the question, "What problem are you trying to solve?" in the style of Jeopardy, the TV game show where the contestants guess the question given the answer. If the answer in real estate always is, "Location, location, location," then what are the problem(s)? Mostly it's things that cannot be changed by the homeowner such as the local climate, access to public transportation, what's in the soil, noise and air pollution, access to the city infrastructure, zoning, property tax rate, public school district, neighborhood character, shops, hills, and traffic.

We thought about trade-offs between one sweet spot and another. For example, there are many trade-offs between city life and country life. Near the city center the property prices are higher, but many places we go during the week are close by. A quick hop on the bike or a short drive will get us to grocery stores, restaurants, movie theaters, medical services, farmers markets, gas stations, coffee shops, bakery, hair salons, and more. Yes, there is heavier traffic and more air pollution in a city area than in a rural area. Conversely, additional driving time that comes with living in a rural area could be offset by having more privacy, land to grow food, maybe enough acreage to have a couple of horses or a hiking trail in our private forest. The place where people live should reflect their preferences and values. We valued walkability to shops and driving less.

With Santa Cruz being a small coastal city, the air quality is pretty good, so the mountain air doesn't offer much advantage for us. If we chose to be deep in the mountains, we'd have more land but we'd also need to build our own infrastructure services for water (well), sewer (septic system), and energy (either shipped in via propane or generated by diesel or solar electric). Once set up properly, living in a rural area offers self-sufficiency and independence. It also requires us to be a bit more hands-on with maintaining the infrastructure needed in day-to-day living that city folks simply plug into. Here again we leaned towards living in the city because we valued the lower maintenance option of being able to plug into the infrastructure rather than building them ourselves. My desire for an edible garden could be met in the city by selecting a location with a sunny backyard, as long as we didn't end up owning a large house on a postage stamp lot where the view from the window would be the neighbor's wall.

Knowing how important and expensive the location decision was, we progressed to doing a decent due diligence on our real estate search. To further clarify our ideal spot, we organized our list of criteria in a spreadsheet to compare the different properties listed on the online real estate website. It was comforting to me to see these properties compared side by side as if the spreadsheet score would ensure success. Giving weight to factors we valued, like sun exposure and walkability to coffee shops and restaurants while ignoring school district information, underscored the fact that we were a middle-aged couple with no kids.

Our criteria of walkability was important because it had a direct impact on our carbon footprint and relating to the community. If we lived in an area where we could walk to shops, restaurants, and movie theaters, we would feel more connected to the community and minimize the need to burn fossil fuel for driving. But this walkability created a unique challenge in our search for an unbuilt lot within the city limits of Santa Cruz.

The hardest part, we found, was not creating a massive list or an intricate list of criteria. The hardest part was sticking to the agreed on criteria and saying "no" to pretty properties when they didn't fully match our criteria. This was especially hard when I realized I had a certain timeline expectation lodged in my head. I wanted the entire project to be done within twenty-four months—from purchasing a property to construction completion. This two-year time boundary came from a promise I made to Kurt in 2008. I asked him, "Is it OK if I quit my job for two years to work on my dream green home project? I think we can find a place, build, and move within two years. Then I'll go back to work." He thought about it for a minute and said, "Yes." As time ticked on and the deadline I made up in my head approached, I found myself wanting to compromise and buy a non-ideal place just to have this phase be over with. Lucky for us Kurt is the disciplined one with uncompromising focus who stuck to our selection criteria and kept us on course.

In retrospect I can see how our work styles, skills, and strengths complemented each other. He honors his sense of personal values, logic, and reason and sticks to them. I honor the logic and rational process of analyzing the pros and cons too, but I am susceptible to making spot decisions to avoid the discomfort of emotional drama. He is quick to grasp scientific concepts and verbally articulate them. I write notes to remember what I heard. He nurtures relationship through conversation. I nurture relationship through food. I'm quick to start new things and slow to finish. Once started, he is quick to tie up loose ends.

This dream green home project had a feel of adventure. We were heading into something we didn't know much about, but we had faith that we would figure it out. Since we didn't have children, this co-creation of the house represented our baby—the biggest thing we've done together.

A mentor appears

We met Gary Ransone through Jon and Marty Fiorovich, a design-build firm in Watsonville. One of the houses they built in 2008 was on the Open Architecture Tour, an annual event organized by the local chapter of the American Institute of Architects, with the proceeds of the tour benefitting the local chapter of Habitat for Humanity. We were impressed with Jon and Marty's work creating a beautiful green home. Jon was the general contractor and his wife, Marty, was the architect. We visited them in their office to find out more about their services. At that time we had our eyes set on a 6,098-square-foot lot on the west side of Santa Cruz—one of the few open lots in a walkable area. When we told them about making an offer on the lot, Jon mentioned, "Why use a real estate agent? You can save money by having an attorney write up a letter to the seller and save on commission cost." Then he gave us Gary's number. So I called him and made an appointment.

Wearing a T-shirt and jeans with work boots, Gary seemed more like a construction guy than an attorney. He was. With a general contractor's license, Gary focused his law practice on construction law. When we described our project and told him that we wanted him to draft a letter, we found out that he also had a real estate license. What a rare combination—attorney, general contractor, and real estate broker all in one person.

"Rather than hire me as an attorney to draft one letter, why not hire me as your real estate agent?" he said. "Hmm," I thought. That was a win-win proposition. Rather than spend hundreds of dollars per hour in attorney fees, we could consult with him for "free" while we searched and looked at properties. He'd earn a nice commission, much larger than attorney fees, when we found the ideal place to buy. We'd rather pay a commission to someone who provided us with value-added service of construction consultation.

Thus began our relationship with Gary. If we had worked with just a real estate agent, we may have been pushed into a deal and close quickly so that the agent could collect their commission and move on to the next deal. But Gary was more interested in having happy clients for the long run. From the beginning he told us that the asking price for the land was too high. At $429,000 the asking price for the plot of land was much more than the median price of homes in California. On a square foot basis, this was thirteen times more expensive than the two and a half acres we were looking to buy with Karsten six years earlier.

Explaining the facts to us, the uninitiated, Gary said, "The first thing you need to do to contain the cost for your project is to keep the cost of the land as low as possible. If you buy the land at the asking price and build on that, you'll end up with higher property taxes for the life of the house. The property will end up costing close to about $800,000 by the time you're done with construction, and houses on that street aren't worth near that. You'll stick out like a sore thumb with your beautiful house and it will have a market value of less than what you put in."

"What would be a reasonable cost for land in that neighborhood then?" I asked.

"$200,000"

"Wow, that's less than half of the list price. Would they go for that?" asked Kurt.

"You need to keep your land cost low," said Gary.

While my mind told me that I knew this already, it had the gravity of authority when someone with experience and seasoned knowledge told us. The chatter from the inner critic protesting, "Oh, you can't low ball, it won't work," went away and brought the focus back to what was right for Kurt and Chie. Gary also knew that if we let our emotion run high so that we felt, "We've absolutely got to get this one," we would end up regretting it later when we may not have had enough money left to complete the project to our desire. He truly had our best interest in mind.

Following Gary's advice, we sent in a bid for $200,000 in October 2008 for the 6,098-square-foot piece of dirt bordered by three houses on a street parallel to the main thoroughfare. The seller countered the offer at $375,000. We volleyed $250,000 back. They signaled end of the game by reducing their counter offer by only $100. Oh, really? We were disappointed. We thought by having our super agent on our side the low-ball offer would get accepted through his sheer charm and negotiation skills. But it didn't. It's fortunate that we were not emotionally attached to the lot. If we had been, maybe we would have paid the $175,000 premium and built a house that was way more expensive than the other houses in the neighborhood and have been reminded of that every year as we paid our higher property taxes. Gary guided us to make sure we didn't end up with a heavy dose of buyer's remorse. It was a lesson in sticking to the discipline of containing cost, and we appreciated the lesson.

Shift to "remodel" from "build from scratch"

We continued to look at land for a full year after that lesson. However, the inventory of unbuilt lots in a walkable area was quite limited and it was just a matter of time before we shifted gears to looking at houses in the right location that could be remodeled. In a way that's more green than building a brand new house because remodeling reuses existing materials. For example, the utility connections are all in place. These connection costs are not trivial. In our area, it costs over $11,000 to install water service at a new house built on a vacant lot. Charges for the water meter and inspection are extra. Then there is the labor and material cost to trench and install the pipes and fittings, which may be another $10,000 depending on the distance between the house and the water main. That's just for water. Sewer, gas, and electricity each have their own connection fees and construction fees. So there are some savings from having existing infrastructure connections despite paying a slightly higher price for having a house on the lot.

Ideally, we would be remodeling a house that didn't have lots of recent improvements so that we could rebuild to our own taste and avoid waste. This is common in our area. Some home-owners in the affluent areas of Silicon Valley would not hesitate to replace items that are in perfectly good condition just because they don't fit the homeowners' taste. It's a funny and sometimes wasteful dance that people do to sell real estate. A homeowner getting ready to sell the house may make upgrades to their home in hopes of fetching a higher sales price. But if those upgrades don't match the taste of the affluent new owner, they would not even blink an eye before tearing out the recent improvements.

We learned that a way to avoid routing perfectly usable material and appliances to a landfill is to use the services of a deconstruction company like Whole House Salvage in San Mateo. They facilitate deconstruction of a home by organizing a public sale where anyone with the skill and desire to carefully deconstruct things can come in to buy the homeowner's discarded countertops, cabinets, windows, siding, bricks, appliances, and whatever can't be easily hauled off to the local charity thrift store. It's a win-win situation for bargain hunters and homeowners. Bargain hunters who relish finding good deals from salvage yards win and the homeowner gets a tax write off. Plus the local landfill operator wins because less waste is sent to the landfill. The appliances and materials, if they had feelings, would also be thrilled to have a second or third life. Living during times when the on-the-go lifestyle relies on disposable convenience and obsolescence is engineered into some electronic products, it feels good to increase the longevity of useful material.

Bidding wars during housing downturn

We got our first taste of investors pouncing on a juicy deal when we put in a bid for a 109-year-old Victorian. This house was a case study in neglect. Paint was peeling off on the exterior, and I found myself taking a gulp of fresh air outside before stepping in. There were layers of malodorous smells inside. The kitchen's cooking odors, decades thick, permeated the walls and the floor. That base odor was frosted with rat urine and feces, and accented with dust. Other rooms were less pungent, but the state of neglect was consistent throughout this old house. How did anyone manage to live here? This was not a house I wanted to live in. I kept thinking, "Can we go now?" as we viewed the house.

The eyes of Gary, our real estate agent, were gleaming. He could see things we couldn't. He had restored old Victorian houses before and could clearly envision the future of this house after it was gutted, cleaned up, and restored to its original beauty. All we could see was an ugly, old, stinky house, but his vision and enthusiasm won us over. And we trusted him. This 109-year-old Victorian house was on the market for little more than the price of the land in a walkable neighborhood. So we put in an offer.

The seller's agent received multiple bids. Our offer, which we thought was a solid, strong offer, was not accepted. "Oh..." was about all I could manage to say when we learned that we'd been outbid. At that time, the news was filled with foreclosure stories. What we'd just experienced seemed incongruent with what was going on in the rest our country. Kurt was furious for days. I was secretly relieved at not getting a place with a bunch of redwood trees that blocked light from a potential vegetable garden in the backyard.

After that disappointment, I returned to my usual routine of looking at email notifications from an online property search company that gave me a daily digest of properties fitting my search criteria. By looking at listings based on zip code, type of property, and price range, I monitored the pulse of the local real estate market. When I saw something that seemed interesting, I reached out to Gary and asked him to show us the place. "Wait a minute," you might say. "Isn't this the opposite of what real estate agents normally do? Aren't they supposed to do the search for you and present you with the properties?" True. But Gary isn't a typical real estate agent.

A month after we'd been outbid on the 109-year-old Victorian, we found ourselves sitting on the floor of a house on a slight hill with an ocean view. We were asking Gary questions and taking copious notes about what we could do to this house. It was built in the 1970s and had a great southern exposure, which brought lots of natural light into the space. We picked Gary's contractor brains on what parts of the house signaled red flags. He patiently answered our questions and spent two hours at the house with us. By now we'd figured out that the market in Santa Cruz was not as affected by the housing crisis that gripped the country, so we put in a strong offer $50,000 above the asking price with a fast close. We felt confident until we learned that ours was one of twenty-seven offers made on this house. The winning bid came in at $80,000 above the asking price. We were stunned. This was 2009 when the mortgage and banking crisis churned out foreclosures at a feverish pace, in the media anyway, but our local real estate market was not so soft. Feeling like a deflated balloon for the third time, we continued to look for the elusive property that would be our dream green house in Santa Cruz.

A month later we put in a bid on another 1970s house. This one had been recently renovated. The location was good, in the "banana belt" area on the east side of Santa Cruz where they had more sun than fog. A nice-sized yard that backed up into the alley was a bonus. The renovation they'd done was OK, but not exactly what we wanted. If we bought this house, we would be undoing some of their work, which is something we wanted to avoid. But this house, which met our other criteria, was on the market. Then something strange happened. The seller rejected our offer and pulled the house off the market. I suppose this wasn't meant to be. It had been two and a half years of active searching and we'd not found a house yet. I felt antsy.

Midori chose us

A month later we got a call from Gary about a house that might work for us. The house just came on the MLS real estate listing and it was the day before the weekend-long open house. It was in a good walkable location on a street parallel to one of the major traffic arteries in town. We wondered if the traffic noise would be a problem and if the church few doors down the street would create congestion on the weekends. We were cautious but decided to look at the house with an open mind.

Gary knocked on the door and an elderly man answered the door. He was friendly and allowed us to come in to take a look. From the curb it looked like a much larger house than the 1,574 square feet advertised on the MLS listing. Perhaps it was the generous porch and a double gable in the front that made the house look bigger than it was. The three-bedroom, two-bath house with a funky fake brick façade wasn't in tip-top shape. Stepping in we noticed the old house smell. Decades of gas furnace combustion, cooking and body odors, and stored papers and magazines fringed in yellow perfumed the interior. That was to be expected of a house built in the 1920s. Unlike the stinky Victorian house we were outbid on, this house *felt* good. Afternoon light bathed the dining room with beautiful warm sunlight that only an old, leaded, single-pane window can transmit. The buffet (a type of furniture, not a spread of food) below the windows of the dining room was original, built-in furniture. Bob, the elderly man who answered the door, mentioned that the original owner of the house had a furniture business in Santa Cruz back in the 1920s.

This home had been occupied by Bob's family for over fifty years. The lanky, white-haired man was gregarious and his stories of the house were punctuated with his dry sense of humor. He mentioned interesting tidbits about the house as we politely looked around. Other parts of the house didn't quite have the same pleasant, warm lighting as the dining room. Kurt attributed that to the insufficient lighting of various lighting fixtures around the house. The backyard was spacious and had mature apple trees and orange trees bearing lots of fruit. There appeared to be the remnants of a once-raised vegetable bed sticking out like a grave in the sea of grass and random volunteer plants. What I saw was a large south-facing yard to grow fruits and veggies to my heart's content.

We thanked Bob and went out the front door onto the large concrete porch, which could easily hold a dozen people for a porch party. We walked over to Gary's truck next to a fire hydrant decorated with rust and peeling paint. Standing on the sidewalk, we huddled to discuss what we just saw. "Well, it's got good bones. There is a lot of deferred maintenance, but you guys will be replacing those items so it's not a problem. What do you guys think?" asked Gary.

We each shared our first impressions. We were cautious. Having been outbid a number of times recently, we weren't going to set ourselves up for another disappointment. We were rather factual in our observation and, frankly, found nothing wrong with it. We concluded that this house met all of our criteria so we should make an offer to buy it from the old man. With a confirming gaze into our eyes and a quick nod, Gary moved into action. He suggested we ask Bob if he would be willing to sell the house to us now and take it off the upcoming open house. If this worked, it would greatly reduce the competition—we were still feeling the bruises from the recent bidding wars and snatching it before a formal open house would be an advantage. During our short visit through the house, Gary formed rapport with Bob by swapping stories of old times in Santa Cruz. While Bob told us about the people who owned the house before and histories of the area, Gary stoked the fire with his own personal connections to Santa Cruz area by sharing stories from his grandmother's days. Turning up the volume on his sincerity and charm dials, Gary knocked on the door again and asked Bob if he would be willing to sell the house to us now.

No sale. Bob wanted to go through with the open house. Crap. We were in the competition field again. After sleeping on this and focusing on intentions of having a good outcome, we met at Gary's office the next day to write up the offer. How much? What else can we offer that's valuable to the seller? "Well," said Gary, "Here's a guy who is selling the home that was in his parents' estate, and they had the house for over fifty years. He's looking forward to traveling across the country in his RV. Surely he'll need time to sort out the decades of stuff in his house. So maybe he'd appreciate a longer close rather than a fast one."

"Right," we nodded in agreement.

The house was priced at fair market value. This time we were not looking to buy the house for the price of the land. We agreed we could reuse the parts of the house that made sense rather than scrap it and build new. We'd been outbid numerous times so we needed a strong but sensible offer. Following a short pause that indicated the end of brainstorming, Gary asked, "How much would you like to offer?"

I closed my eyes and took a deep breath. Opening my eyes I slowly said, "Five, six, eight," looking straight at Gary. Kurt nodded. Instead of filling out the price I stated, Gary suggested we raise the offer price by seven thousand dollars and ask for a credit in an addendum to land at the price I stated. We thought that was clever. He filled out the offer price on the standard multi-copy California real estate form. "Let's offer him a 45-day close and leave it up to him to take as long or short time as he wants," Gary said. We agreed. After filling out the necessary blank spaces on the form, we signed the offer and wrote the deposit check. Leaving Gary's office we were neither exuberant nor worried. Having been through the emotional ups and downs with the previous four properties, we were somewhat guarded in our expectations and did not allow ourselves to get too hopeful. Whatever was meant to happen would happen.

The message we got the next day sank in slowly. "Congratulations," said Gary cheerily on the other end of the line, "They've accepted your offer." It took a few heartbeats for guarded anxiety to change into disbelief and finally to relief. I stammered thanks and probably asked some questions about the next steps before we hung up. Then Kurt and I looked at each other and exhaled, breathing out the anxiety and past disappointments. The search was over. The house, Midori, chose us.

Past caretakers of Midori

When we found her in 2010, Midori'd had relatively few caretakers in her eighty-eight-year life. The original owner of the 1922 craftsman-style house was a furniture dealer named Frank Chapman. In the archives of our local newspaper, the *Santa Cruz Sentinel*, a 1923 article described him as a co-owner and a manager of a furniture store at the northwest corner of Pacific Avenue and Cathcart Street. He was a member of the chamber of commerce and was an astute businessman who had increased the store's business by 50 percent, attracting customers from as far as San Francisco to the north and Hollywood to the south. With Frank being a furniture dealer, there was no doubt he had some say in the selection of wood used in the house. People visiting the house would admire and appreciate the built-in furniture in the dining room.

As they ran a hand down the wood used in the dining room buffet, some would say it was Philippine mahogany and others would say African mahogany or perhaps a type of eucalyptus. Even the carpenters and furniture makers would continue making guesses as they inspected the French door that separated the dining room from the living room. We still don't know the type of wood for sure. Sadly, less than six months after the Sentinel article appeared, Frank Chapman was dead at age 56.

The next owner, Arthur D. Wirt, who was a former petroleum engineer for Standard Oil in Kern County, lived at the house from 1926 to 1946 and planted the two apples trees in the backyard. He was involved in the search for crude oil in Santa Cruz. Life here in Santa Cruz would have taken a different course if they actually found oil.

After Arthur D. Wirt passed away in 1946, a former real estate agent, Fred Garrison, bought the house and made some changes. He covered up the redwood lap-siding, which had been painted in a reddish brown color reminiscent of a country farm, with a sheet of asphalt that gave the look of brick. Brick was the signature style of bungalows in Chicago in those days and perhaps he wanted that look but didn't want to spend the money to redo the entire house using real brick. The left-over faux-brick sheets were used to cover up the walls of a shed next to the garage. To further add value and to bring revenue to the property, he added two small rooms to the bedroom in the southwest corner of the house. The tiny kitchenette had an exterior door and was furnished with a sink, Kelvinator refrigerator, and a small one-burner gas stove. The bathroom was just big enough to have a small shower in one corner, a toilet in the other, and a sink that had a view of the backyard through a double-hung window. When the door to the hallway of the main house was walled off, this three-room corner unit made a perfect rental. Several math teachers who taught at Santa Cruz High School, just few blocks away, made use of the corner rental unit.

After Fred Garrison died in 1953, his widow Hattie continued to live there for nearly a year before selling the house to State Farm Insurance agent Robert Lemmon in November 1954. When Robert and Mary Lemmon moved in with their five children, the walled-off bedroom that had been a rental unit became part of the house again. The O'Keefe & Merrit gas stove that had a wood burner on the side was in the kitchen when the Lemmons moved in and was still there when they moved out. The home's gas water heater was in the kitchen. A brick fireplace was on the east wall of the living room. This was badly damaged during the 1989 Loma Prieta earthquake and was removed. Bricks from the chimney that originally exhausted the fumes from the gas stove in the kitchen also fell during the magnitude 6.9 earthquake. The Lemmons stuccoed over the fake brick siding and painted it baby blue, yet kept the fake brick siding in the front. When Mary passed away in December 2009 she was the record-holder for living the longest at the house Frank Chapman built—fifty-five years. We bought the house from her eldest son, Robert Lemmon Jr., trustee of the Lemmon Living Trust.

Despite being full of deferred maintenance and having poor energy performance, we liked Midori. She had charm and character in her simple ways. The warm afternoon sunlight that filled the dining room made me feel cheerfully calm. Bungalows and craftsman style homes can have a bit of heavy, old library-like feel with columns, half walls, and dark wood wainscoting. But Midori didn't feel heavy. She had well-crafted woodwork from the 1920s—the baseboards, the French door between the living room and the dining room, and trims framing windows. Doors in the living room and dining room were made of beautiful wood stained in a color of lightly brewed tea. The original woodwork gave just enough accent to give it a warm tone, and she seemed to be telling us, "Keep me this way." So the aesthetic direction was set early on—retain the look and feel of the Arts and Crafts style.

Due diligence

For the next forty-five days we busied ourselves with due diligence, looking over the seventy-plus-page packet from the seller consisting of termite report, flood zone report, leaking underground storage tank, and a few other reports. The contingency period after the acceptance of the offer was when we could back out of the transaction if the obligatory stack of paper provided by the seller's real estate agent raised a concern. Gary went over and beyond what a typical real estate would do and visited the building department at the City of Santa Cruz to look up building permit records to see if the small addition containing a bathroom and a kitchenette was legit or not. This was a precautionary step to see if we would run into permitting issues when we submitted our plans for the remodel. It would be a lot of hassle if the 1940s addition had not been permitted, putting us in a red tag situation where we would have to pay fines for something someone did to the house before we were born. The exact data was not available due to records being lost during the big flood of 1955 that covered the downtown area with six feet of water. But the tax assessor's office had a record of the property's value going up in 1947 due to the addition that was made. "Good," we thought, "We won't be red tagged."

Gary wanted us to have the property boundaries confirmed and have the records "clean" by confirming the mutual easement on the property boundary. This was prompted by the presence of a duplex garage and a shared driveway with the neighbor to the west. "They're nice people," Bob Lemmon said of the next-door neighbors Patrice and Bob Keet. The property boundary and easement became important because, as Gary explained, "You'll never know if the next owner of the house will be as nice as Patrice and Bob." Their beautiful Dutch Colonial style house next door was easily the largest and most expensive house on the block. This ensured that our house would not stick out as the most expensive house on the block after the remodel. Since we had previously entertained buying in neighborhoods that Gary characterized as "the height of ordinary," this neighborhood was a strong improvement.

On a gray and foggy morning typical of Santa Cruz summer, Michael Beautz, the surveyor, came out with his assistant lugging instruments. To determine property boundaries, he first looked at the sidewalk for bronze-colored metal markers fixed in the pavement on the east boundary of the property. Surveyors used these markers to delineate the property boundaries and those in the business of determining property boundaries relied on these tell-tale signs made by their brethren. Referring to the written description of the property in the title document filed at the county records office, Michael measured sixty-five feet from the metal marker. It landed right in the middle of the driveway we shared with Bob and Patrice. So far so good.

One thing Michael noted during the visit was that the width indicated on the tax assessor's property map was incorrect. The property lines were drawn in the right place but the label indicating width measurement was short by three feet. He asked if we wanted him to go to the tax assessor's office to have this corrected. Basically it entailed showing them the map and the descriptive text of the property and pointing out the discrepancy on the map and having them change it. Since he had the working relationship with the people at the county building, we asked him to do so.

While the surveyors were out at the house with the equipment, we had them measure the slope of the driveway from the curb to the garage door at the end of the driveway. We were told that the backyard flooded during heavy rain because the ground was lower there. Sure enough, the paved driveway sloped down 1.5 inches over a span of sixty feet, directing rainwater from the sidewalk to flow down into the garage. We put this information in our back pocket since we planned to repave the driveway when the house construction was done.

The termite report that came with the seller's package indicated spots where there was damage from termites as well as other causes. Apparently the termite people do more than inspect for termites. There was little damage, nothing to be alarmed about. Still rather than rely solely on the seller's termite report, we decided to have our own home inspection done on our dime to get a second opinion of the house. Some folks might use the information from an independent inspection report to haggle a credit from the seller during the contingency period during escrow. But we did this more in the spirit of getting a second opinion before a major elective surgery.

Kurt found a home inspection provider in the quaint local yellow pages phone book. When the inspector came over to inspect the home, we looked over his shoulder as he walked around the house and made his notes, kind of like following a doctor around while they made diagnostic assessment. Again, nothing horrible showed up. The wiring was old (knob and tube) and the portion in the attic buried under the cellulose insulation was a fire hazard. Bob Lemmon told us that the cellulose insulation in the attic was done in 1994 through a utility rebate and that no other insulation had been added to the house. The inspector said the roof had ten to fifteen years of life left, but the galvanized plumbing should be replaced. He pointed out some cracks in the perimeter foundation that should be fixed.

Better than imagined

Eventually the forty-five-day escrow period passed and we signed the papers and paid the balance of the escrow at the title company. We were scheduled to pick up the keys to the house from Bob on the first Saturday in October in 2010. "There is a neighborhood block party going on that day if you guys want to join the pot-luck," Bob told us in an email. Really? This means we have neighbors who enjoy block parties and we get to meet them all at once.

We loved this idea. Ever since we'd been to a neighborhood block party at a friend's house in San Jose, we had a bit of a block-party envy. Now we would get to live in a neighborhood where we would close down the street and spend time in the middle of the street eating food and playing games with our neighbors. This was more than we expected of our new neighborhood. On the day we received the house keys from Bob, we felt welcomed into the community as we chatted with each new neighbor we met and broke bread.

As we met our new neighbors we told them that we were planning to do a "green" remodel and apologized in advance for the construction commotion. Several neighbors were into zero-waste and they appreciated our intention to go green. Plus their property values would go up when the ugliest house on the block got a makeover. We didn't meet our shared driveway neighbors at the block party but when we did, they were so happy to have us as their new neighbor. Patrice and Bob invited us over to an informal barbecue dinner and proved to be fun and gracious hosts. A few days later we were taking an early evening stroll when Lisa flagged us down. She was having wine on the porch of Claire and Wendy's house and invited us to join them. It was a comfortable porch where the warmth of the day lingered into the evening. "I've never lived in such a neighborhood before," said Kurt when we joined the porch party, "We look forward to having porch parties ourselves!"

So we started our green home journey with the idea of building a brand-new green house but instead we would be creating a house that was much greener. We would reuse the parts of a house built eighty-eight years earlier, such as framing, foundation, roof, nice woodwork, and built-in furniture. What could be greener than that?

What we learned in choosing our place

These things worked well for us during the property search phase:

❖ Having written property-selection criteria based on personal values. This helped us focus our real estate search as well as communicate with the real estate agent. See example at: http://midorihaus.com/site_selection/

❖ Sticking to the property-selection criteria. This meant saying "No" to places that almost fit.

❖ Listen to gut feelings.

❖ Trust that the right place will show up. Don't be discouraged when your offer isn't accepted.

❖ When purchasing a fixer-upper it's helpful to have a general contractor review the property before making the offer.

3
Setting A Building Energy Limit

Setting an energy limit shifted our focus

We couldn't look at houses the same way again after we learned about the internationally recognized performance-based energy standard in construction called Passive House (*Passivhaus* in German). This chapter covers how we learned about Passive House and how it shifted our green home focus to energy.

Our mindset before Passive House

Early on we thought green building consisted of different green components: something that used resources efficiently so that we didn't end up consuming everything and leaving nothing for future generations; something that protected our health so that we didn't get sick from breathing toxins or allergens; something that reduced waste and pollution so that future generations (and ours) could enjoy clean air, clean water, and nature.

In 2003 I visited the home of Kristen and Mark Sullivan in Capitola. Their house is an example of a green home designed using passive solar principles that reflect carefully chosen green building components: exterior walls made of straw bales (agricultural waste product), which provide good insulation; floors made of a concrete and fly ash (industrial waste product) mixture, which provides mass for capturing and releasing heat from the sun; recycled tiles in the kitchen and bathroom; electricity generated from the sun using photovoltaic panels on their roof; an arbor covered with grape leaves for summer shading; various native plants in their landscape that needed little water; and landscape irrigation provided by rainwater collected in a large tank. I also found it refreshing to learn that the Sullivans hired a female general contractor in an industry dominated by men.

This was my first exposure to a green home, and it left quite an impression on me. In addition to the home being healthy for its occupants and the planet, it embodied a lifestyle I longed for—a bright and airy living room that seamlessly transitioned to the patio through a sliding glass door to a beautiful garden that attracted birds and bees. I liked the Sullivan's solar systems for heating water and creating electricity.

I used to think, "Why not install photovoltaic (PV) panels on the roof to generate electricity from the sun and be done with it?" Solar energy is green, right? We could generate all the electricity we used in our home and sell some back to the utility so that at the end of the year our electricity bill would be near zero. It would probably pay back in about twelve years. I wondered why someone would go through the extensive calculation and install lots of insulations and perform extensive air sealing to save energy. It seemed to me that PV was easier and better. Eventually we learned that it depends on how you frame the problem.

The problem we were trying to solve was not solely about getting the electricity bill to zero. We wanted to live in a house that was comfortable and healthy. Covering the roof area of a ninety-year-old house with PV would not make it comfortable and healthy. The single-pane, double-hung windows had gaps in the seams that let in cold air during the winter and hot air during the summer. The uninsulated walls would conduct heat quickly, making the inside hot during the summer and cold during the winter. We'd once booked a vintage 1920s house through Airbnb in a similar coastal climate in central California. The house had PV, but no insulation and no air conditioning. At the height of summer, this charming house was uncomfortable. That was a nice getaway, but lesson learned: PV by itself might lower the energy bill, but it won't make the house comfortable.

To make Midori healthy so that we could breathe clean air, we knew we had to pay attention to the air quality inside the house. Sure, we'd use non-toxic paint, but what about the unintended air that comes through the cracks in walls? Mold, along with natural gas that didn't burn off in the furnace, were wafting up through the floor. We were also concerned that gaps wide enough to let bugs and rodents in, created by generous openings to allow plumbing through the walls and floor, would invite critters to track in bacteria and leave their excrement.

Clearly, the walls and floors needed to be fixed up, but how? We'd seen a lot of approaches with different materials that were green in different ways. The Sullivans used straw bale walls, representing a choice to reuse agricultural waste material over non-renewable conventional material. Karsten used insulating concrete form (ICF) blocks, a modular wall assembly that has good energy performance. A former coworker used structured insulated (SIPS) panels, another type of wall assembly that has good energy performance that can be installed quickly with minimal waste. We saw some Earthship homes featured in green building books that had walls made out of old tires filled with dirt, which looked perfect for creating an off-grid sustainable home. Some homes used recycled jeans for wall insulation, another way of diverting and reusing consumer waste.

Interior walls can come in different types too. Midori has lath and plaster. Many interior walls are made of gypsum boards (also known as drywall or sheetrock). Our friend, Mary Kay, used a brick wall as one of her interior walls to provide mass for heating and cooling much in the same way the Karsten's concrete floor did. Having a vertical mass (brick wall) rather than a horizontal mass (concrete floor) was so intriguing to us that we latched on to this idea for a while until several people gently coaxed us out of this idea because they felt it was not suitable for Midori. The opportunities for reusing material, avoiding waste, and employing systems that manage heating and cooling seemed vast and fascinating.

Neither of us had any training or experience in architecture and construction. As our knowledge of home construction and building science grew, everything that used to seem mundane and ordinary was now cast in a new and fascinating light. What shall we choose?

Had we tried to use all of the neat ideas we gathered, we might have ended up in a hodgepodge of different styles, materials, and techniques that probably would not have worked well together. Without a guideline or a theme, the likelihood of Midori being an odd, incoherent patchwork was high. Having lots of ideas seemed really good until the choices become somewhat confusing. Of all the choices out there, we had to figure out which was the best for us. But we didn't yet know how to choose.

Unexpected mentor

Our first breadcrumb to guide us out of the mire of too many good green building ideas came before we found Midori. In the spring of 2010 we thought it would be wise to get input from a green building consultant before we bought a place, so we reached out to Uwe Heine. Kurt liked Uwe's personal energy when we met him at a tour of his house he hosted as part of the green homes tours in the Bay Area. On a foggy spring morning he met us in a quiet residential area where an old house sat on an oddly shaped lot. We asked him if there were "greening" opportunities or red flags he could see about that house.

On the surface there was nothing profound in what he had to say—better windows, insulation, minimize air leaks, consider the shading from the trees. These all sounded mundane and pedestrian, perhaps because I was secretly hoping to get an insight into the latest tech gadget that makes green magic happen at the push of the button. Sadly, he offered no such gadget. The one thing that seemed to perk him up was discussing the Passive House Standard. Passive House? I thought back to the concepts we learned at Karsten's home and the Sullivan's home I said, "Oh, you mean like passive solar homes where you pay attention to the sun angles and use concrete floor to warm the space in the winter?"

Uwe, in his German accent, explained that it was easy to confuse the term because Passivhaus in German means passive buildings and is different than passive solar homes in the U.S. The Passive House Standard is not exclusive to single-family homes and has been successfully applied to other types of buildings such as schools, commercial buildings, and apartment buildings. Passive House is not an architectural style and it can apply to different types of buildings. In fact, there are over 30,000 Passive House buildings worldwide in places such as Belgium, Ukraine, Japan, China, Korea, Spain, Croatia, Norway, Canada, and in the USA.

Uwe told us that the origin of Passive House goes back to a super-insulated home in Canada built in 1977 by a group of Canadian researchers. It used very little energy because it was practically airtight and had superb insulation, not just thick but installed very well. Unlike passive solar homes, which were designed to have walls, windows, and floors to collect and distribute heat from the sun, the super-insulated home used very little passive solar heating. In fact, Uwe said, the super-insulation works so well that a home no longer needs a conventional furnace.

We were astonished that someone had built this home thirty years earlier, but disappointed to learn that there was not much interest in the super-insulated home the Canadians developed. At the same time in the U.S., solar energy tax credits had disappeared, and the Reagans even had the solar thermal panels removed from the White House. But the idea was not lost. A German physicist, Dr. Wolfgang Feist, took this concept, added to it, and coined the term Passivhaus to describe the energy modeling and construction method. The buildings didn't need conventional active heating and cooling systems. The first prototype was built in Germany in 1991. Today, homes built to the Passive House Standard use 80 percent less energy, and there are more than 30,000 buildings built to this standard around the world.

Uwe passed away in 2011, and we never had the opportunity to tell him, "We got it."

Crossing the threshold

We didn't immediately dive into Passive House research after our meeting with Uwe. Months went by. Then Passive House gently knocked on the door to remind us that it was time to take a look. We received an email from West Coast Green, an annual conference that featured lectures and workshops on green and sustainability topics.

When the West Coast Green email landed in my Inbox in August 2010, we were in escrow, waiting for the paperwork to be finalized with Midori. Scanning over the email I called out, "Hey Kurt, you remember the Passive House thing Uwe mentioned?"

"Yeah?" he called back from the living room.

"There's a half-day workshop about Passive House at the upcoming West Coast Green. Shall we sign up?"

"When is it?" he asked, coming into the kitchen. "And where?"

"Last Wednesday of September in San Francisco, Fort Mason Center."

"Hmm, OK, sign us up."

Fort Mason Center, a collection of century-old military buildings, is less than a quarter mile west of Fisherman's Wharf in San Francisco. Cold and utilitarian, the austere chairs and tables in the room made me sit up straight. The workshop was full of early adopters of Passive House—architects, builders, and home energy consultants—who were eager to learn more about the Passive House Standard.

The building and energy-modeling approach that gained respect and acceptance in Europe over the last twenty years was still nascent in the U.S. It delivered comfortable and healthy homes that were durable and ultra-energy efficient. In the San Francisco Bay Area, architect Nabih Tahan had built the first Passive House in California. In 2005 he remodeled his California Bungalow in Berkeley by applying his experience of working with low-energy buildings in Austria, where he'd lived for many years. There were perhaps two dozen houses built to the Passive House Standard in California, and more were under construction at the time we attended the workshop.

We were the only homeowners unassociated with the construction industry. How did we know we were the sole homeowner couple in the large room? During one of the question and answer sessions, Kurt raised his hand to ask a question and prefaced his question by identifying himself as a homeowner looking to remodel an old house. "Clients!" yelled someone from the other side of the room and a chorus of laughter assured us that we were welcome.

Then something wonderful happened. Chie and Kurt, ordinary homeowners, transformed into Passive House enthusiasts with a single realization: energy used to quickly adjust temperature, either to heat or cool a conventionally built house, can be eliminated if the shell of the building is constructed like a thermos. Keeping the indoor temperature constant and controlling ventilation could make our house comfortable and healthy. And we didn't have to wait for some new invention to come about or spend extraordinary amounts of money to achieve a radical reduction in home energy.

The tools, techniques, and products to successfully build Passive Houses are available today. It requires the architect to use detailed modeling to guide the plans to hit the specific target for energy use. It requires the builder to pay careful attention to construction details and comply with the specific limit on air leakage. In other words, good design and good craftsmanship. This is Passive House.

During the workshop we reviewed case studies of homes in Northern California built to the Passive House Standard. They had results that would be approved by Goldilocks—not too hot, not too cold, but just right all year round and the homes used very little energy. That's nice, I thought. But do they look nice? I didn't want to live in place built with weird materials that didn't resonate with my taste. This concern was dispelled as I took in the presentations from the panel of Passive House contractors. They showed us nice houses that could easily be featured in *Sunset* or *Dwell* magazines. Phew!

In case studies, contractors highlighted different materials and details of their Passive House projects. Each construction team paid special attention to insulation—what types of materials they chose and the techniques used for installing them, even under the floor. Really? Under the floor? Up until this point I thought of insulation as the fuzzy stuff that got stuffed inside the wall cavity and sometimes sprinkled in the attic.

This approach to insulation made sense when I thought about it in the context of the house wearing the warm layers of clothing for me so I don't have to. We humans have a need to keep our body temperature around 98.6°F (37°C) and we do this by wearing or removing layers of clothing and turning on heating or air conditioning. Houses and buildings wear their version of clothing. How much clothing depends on the climate where the house is located. Unlike humans, who can easily peel off layers when we're hot and pile on sweaters and jackets when we're cold, houses have only one set of clothing for all seasons. Too little clothing results in using more energy to heat the house in the winter and cool the house in the summer. If I imagine myself standing outside for twenty-four hours, like my house is doing, I would wear a hat, jacket, and covered shoes. Although we live in a mild Mediterranean climate, the average overnight low temperature even during summer in Santa Cruz is in the mid-50s Fahrenheit (11–14°C). Midori had a very light hat (attic insulation), no sweater (no wall insulation), and was wearing flip-flops (or slippas as we say in Hawaii) instead of covered shoes (no floor insulation). Wouldn't you think wool lined boots would be even better especially in the winter? So the foam insulation installed under the floor is like the warm fuzzy liner in winter boots breaking the cold connection with the ground.

The builders who were presenting at the West Coast Green workshop showed pictures of how they've used foam insulation in the slab foundation and talked about minimizing thermal bridging. That was a new term I'd not heard before, but by the end of the workshop I thought of thermal bridging as the escape path for energy thieves—the highways that allow heat to move fast. The larger the escape path, the faster the energy thieves moved heat. Conventional construction practice doesn't focus on minimizing thermal bridging. In fact, the presentation made it sound as though the special skills of energy forensic investigators would be needed to even identify where these paths occur.

It's one thing to see a presentation on the theory of construction, but this was fascinating because the lessons learned from building a Passive House were shared by the builders who swung the hammers. They made it real by sharing the techniques and stories of how they'd overcome tricky problems to achieve excellent energy performance. Two houses presented by these builders were California bungalows built or remodeled to the Passive House Standard. That perked our ears up and we wondered could Midori, our 1922 bungalow, have the same energy performance?

"You know what I like about the Passive House approach?" Kurt said during one of the breaks. "It's brilliant systems-thinking." The green building certification programs we'd seen so far were like ordering a la carte from a restaurant menu: slap on a solar panel, get energy star appliances, get bigger windows to make use of day lighting, and so forth. Each component was green in its own way, but who knew if they would work together effectively to seriously reduce energy consumption. I didn't want to wait until after we lived in our house to find out if the mishmash of systems resulted in comfort and or heartburn. The Passive House Standard was geared towards achieving a very specific low-energy use with occupant comfort in mind. MY comfort in mind!

I liked the idea of running different what-if scenarios using the PHPP software to model the energy performance of the house. To me it was like business software system implementation projects I used to manage, and I knew it would be much cheaper to make changes during the design stage rather later in coding or post-production stage. For a person with a physics background like Kurt, Passive House made total sense. It confirmed our belief that energy efficiency needed to be designed from the beginning.

We sat together in silence as each of us explored in our minds the iteration of different scenarios—specifying different low-e coating for the windows, exterior shading, type and amount of insulation used, and the construction details to minimize thermal bridging. We had not used this software yet but I could imagine the precise calculation to achieve performance results in the way we've come to expect from German engineering.

By the end of the workshop we were convinced that the systematic whole-house approach to renovation was better than a mishmash of random green features for Midori. We didn't want Midori to end up like a technological Christmas tree where the shiny and pretty objects invite "oohs" and "ahhs" from the casual observer but have disappointing energy performance. We liked the fact that Passive House didn't lock us into a prescribed look and feel. It was architecture agnostic. It's been successfully applied to different types of buildings around the world including single family homes, apartments, commercial office buildings, schools, and even a prison.

Having a specific target drives focus

Like most conventionally built houses of her vintage, Midori was energy obese compared to the Passive House standard. She needed to go on a slimming program to be a Passive House.

When people go on a diet or fitness program, there often is a specific target they're trying to hit. The target could be something like "lose 30 pounds," or "reduce waist size by two inches," or "fit into a size eight dress," or "have a body mass index of 20." What are the equivalent targets for a house?

The ultimate measurement will be the utility bill and the experience of occupants living in the house. These measurements are not practical to iterate on because once the house is built, the homeowners are not going to tear down the wall and try a different technique to see if they can eke out more energy savings. The way to create comfort and super-low energy use is by using a software tool called Passive House Planning Package (PHPP). By entering the details of the planned construction, PHPP software will assess whether or not the approach is going to hit the target. There is an explicit target in the software tool of 15 kWh/m² (4.75 kBtu/ft²) per year for heating and cooling the house to the design tempera-ture (20°C or 68°F) and 120 kWh/m² (38 kBtu/ft²) per year for total *source energy* [read more about source energy and site energy in the next two sections] consumed at the house. If the entries made don't calculate out to the target numbers, try again.

I get that. Running various what-if scenarios using software makes sense. What I didn't get was what these numbers meant. I wasn't impressed when I first heard of 15 kWh/m² for heat-ing and cooling per year to keep the house at comfortable 68°F. Without context the impressive benchmark information can sim-ply breeze into one ear and escape from the other ear without the light bulb of comprehension turning on. It clicked for me when I saw the results from the case studies of homes built to Passive House Standard. Over and over these houses showed impressive results: 80 percent less energy use throughout the year than new homes built in the conventional way. It's pretty convincing when the source of the data is the utility bills and the logs of temperature data corresponding to the billing period, which showed that the house was indeed comfortable. It wasn't a case of vigilant people piling on sweaters and turning down the heat in the winter or liv-ing in a sauna during the summer for the sake of energy efficiency. They were just as comfortable, if not more, as people living in homes using 80 percent more energy.

How does Passive House target compare with average home energy use in California?

In 2009 the United States Energy Information Administration (EIA) collected and analyzed residential energy consumption across the country. This data puts the PHPP target in perspective. The aver-age household in California used 61.5 million Btu (18,023 kWh) of energy per year. The average U.S. household used about a third more energy, or 89.6 million Btu (26,259 kWh) per year.

So how does Midori, in the state we found her at the time of purchase, stack up against the California average? We used the utility bills the seller of the house shared with us for this baseline comparison. Midori used a total of 74.9 million Btu (21,938 kWh) of site energy in one year of which less than a quarter (4,881 kWh) was for electricity. This showed that her total site energy use was more than the California average. But her electricity usage was less than what average California homes used, which meant that her natural gas usage was way more than average. Given that she was a leaky old house with no insulation and heated using a furnace fueled by natural gas, it wasn't surprising that she was energy obese.

By the way, don't let the Btu and kWh figures faze you. Btu (British thermal unit) is a measure of energy used to raise the temperature of one pound of water by one degree Fahrenheit. While most countries around the world use the International System of Units (SI units), we use the imperial unit of measure in the U.S.

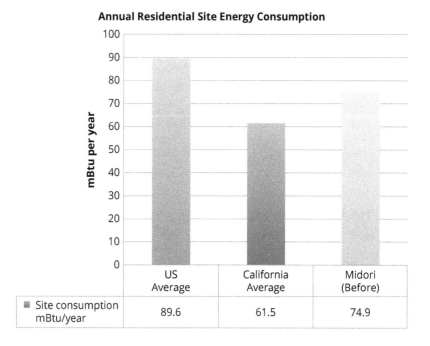

	US Average	California Average	Midori (Before)
Site consumption mBtu/year	89.6	61.5	74.9

Annual Residential Site Energy Consumption

To make an apples-to-apples comparison, they need to be in the same units and it's easily done by using online calculators. I'm grateful for these handy online calculators that pop up when I put "Btu kWh conversion" into an online search engine.

To compare the Passive House target with the U.S. averages in the EIA survey, look at the energy use intensity (EUI), which is a measure of the home's annual energy used per square foot. The average size of homes in the U.S. is 1,971 square feet and in California it's 1,583 square feet. Midori is about the size of an average California house. The annual *site energy* usage per square foot for Midori and an average California house are 47 kBtu/ft² per year and 39 kBtu/ft² per year respectively. The Passive House target for *source energy* is 38 kBtu/ft² or 120 kWh/m² per year. That may sound as though average California homes are somewhat close to the Passive House standard target, but it's not even close. Site energy and source energy are worlds apart.

Source energy

Whenever I hear the fundraising team on public radio inviting listeners to double their impact by donating when a matching gift sponsor is featured, I think of source energy. When I learned that there is an impact ratio of almost 1:3 between site energy and source energy, my desire for saving site energy increased. If I reduce the usage of electricity at my house by one unit, that translates into reducing up to three units of input energy at the power plant. My personal impact of saving energy at home is multiplied at the power plant. Less water used, less heat and carbon released into the atmosphere, and much less fossil fuel needed to create steam to turn the turbine at the power plant when I save energy at home.

Most of the energy loss happens at the power plant for electricity generation, but with natural gas the energy loss happens during delivery. About 10 percent of natural gas escapes into the air through leaks. Compared to the 200 percent loss for electricity generation, the energy loss from natural gas transportation seem minor, but it impacts climate change. Natural gas is twenty times more potent than carbon dioxide as a greenhouse gas.

Once I understood source energy, I appreciated the aim of Passive House to reduce the ongoing amount of natural resources extracted and burned. Once we could start living in a Passive House, we'd use only one-fifth the amount of energy to heat and cool the house for decades to come. I felt that was a significant personal contribution we could make: less fossil fuels extracted and less greenhouse gas created by electricity generation. The beauty of it was that we didn't need to change our behavior to make this permanent impact once the house was built.

Shifting from unconsciously guzzling ancient sunlight in order to make up the deficit in the clothing of the house to wisely sipping ancient sunlight with better clothing for the house—this is what Passive House enables us to do. I was struck by the concept of ancient sunlight in the opening chapter of Thom Hartmann's *The Last Hours of Ancient Sunlight*. Hartmann describes the energy resources we extract from the earth today as a product of sunlight and biological processes over millions of years. Coal, oil, and gas are the compressed decomposition of plants and animals that lived on earth that relied on the sun. It takes 300 to 400 million years for the current plants and animals to turn into fossil fuel. If we take out these fuel resources at a rate faster than we're creating them, we'll run out of fuel eventually. If we can reduce the need for ancient sunlight and make smart use of current sunlight, the energy from ancient sunlight will last longer.

According to the interactive map on http://www.eia.gov, most of the electricity generated in the Santa Cruz area is from a power plant that uses natural gas. Using published information from our electric utility for the electricity delivered to Midori, we assumed a factor of 2.6 to convert site energy to source energy. Therefore, the site energy of 39 kBtu/ft^2 for average California homes becomes source energy of 101 kBtu/ft^2 per year, and Midori's site energy of 47 kBtu/ft^2 per year becomes source energy of 122 kBtu/ft^2 per year. Passive House standard is 38 kBtu/ft^2 per year. That means Midori's energy appetite was 320 percent more than the Passive House target. She really needed to go on an energy diet!

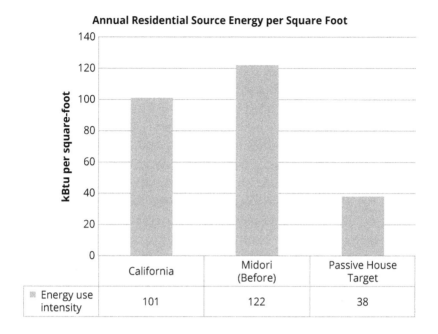

Annual Residential Source Energy per Square Foot

	California	Midori (Before)	Passive House Target
Energy use intensity	101	122	38

PHPP = energy diet plan

But not just any diet. For Midori we wanted something that was proven and had a comprehensive approach to look at the entire house as a system. If we simply applied all the cool ideas we learned along the way and randomly applied them, Midori may have ended up in the land of fine print where they say your actual mileage may vary. The Passive House approach is like having Midori eat less without feeling hungry because the comfort factor for the occupants is considered along with low energy use. It promised us radical energy reduction without discomfort.

Achieving the energy targets for Passive House required designing a house that was planned using the aforementioned software called Passive House Planning Package (PHPP) and having a contractor with good craftsmanship and attention to detail build the house.

The PHPP software calculated whether we met the Passive House target or not based on the details entered: climate data, orientation of the building, the size of window openings, types of materials and amounts of insulation, equipment used for water heating, airtightness of the house, number of people in the house, and much more. This software calculates how much energy will be used to heat and cool the house given the data entered. The focus is energy performance, and different construction materials can be used to meet the target. We could imagine the builder, architect, and the passive house consultant all sitting together and plugging in different values to the model and asking a bunch of what-if questions: "What if we use different material like polyiso for the exterior insulation rather than mineral wool?" or "What's the energy trade off if we use different low-e coating on the south facing windows to allow solar heat gain versus keeping all the coatings the same?" This software is pretty accurate. We learned that the tighter the house, the more accurate the energy forecast is.

The software platform is Excel, which I can manage decently, but we relied on the knowledge and experience of a trained consultant to run this software for us because we knew little about the details of architecture and construction. The learning curve would have exposed us to mistakes and frustration. It's much cheaper to do the what-if scenarios using software than having the builder build a wall and have to undo it.

Airtightness for comfort, health, and energy savings

We had a visceral appreciation for airtightness when we went to a backyard taco party just thirty-five miles away in San Jose. In the daytime, it was quite warm and people turned up in short-sleeved shirts and cute sundresses. But as soon as the sun went down, the wind picked up and on went jackets and hoodies. I was glad that I brought my puffy jacket because when it's cold and windy outside, it's more comfortable to wear a windbreaker over a sweater rather than layering sweaters. Houses are like this too.

When we found her, Midori wasn't comfortable during the winter because she didn't have a sweater or windbreaker on. She was also uncomfortable during a heat wave because her breezy outfit let air in and out quite freely. How breezy was it?

We measured Midori's airtightness level using a blower door test and she came in at twenty-three air changes per hour at 50 Pascals (23 ACH_{50}). This meant if a twenty mile-per-hour wind was blowing outside, the entire air volume of the house would be replaced twenty-three times in one hour even with all the doors and windows closed; 23 ACH_{50} meant if a winter storm wheezed constant cold wind at twenty miles per hour, the air inside Midori would turn over about every three minutes. If the furnace was used to heat the house, all the warm air would be going outside every few minutes with lots of energy wasted trying to keep the house warm. If she had an air conditioning unit, she would have wasted more energy trying to keep the house cool during a heat wave.

Airtightness plays a role in healthy indoor air quality. Through the various gaps and cracks present in a conventionally built house, dust, mold spores, pollens, and chemicals can freely pass and accumulate. Damp air and stale spaces allow bacteria to grow. When a person is constantly exposed to that, the body has an inflammatory response—hives, depression, anxiety, exhaustion, sinus infections, and other symptoms.

This is what the Hayward family experienced when they moved into their dream luxury home in 2008. It turns out there was a lot of mold in the crawlspace. The floors and walls separating their living space from the crawlspace did not protect them from the mold. Homeowner Bill Hayward discovered this when he did a simple test. Bill took a can of Lemon Pledge and a flashlight into the crawlspace. His wife, Adriana, stood inside the living space, and when Bill sprayed Lemon Pledge in the crawlspace, Adriana could smell it in the living space. This meant the mold in the crawlspace was just as easily traveling through the cracks in the floor and the walls. They moved out and their health symptoms went away. The Haywards share their experience through videos and information posted in their website http://haywardhealthyhome.com.

Measuring airtightness

We wanted to measure Midori's airtightness in her "before" state, so we had a home performance assessment specialist perform a baseline blower door test. The principle is like having a person step on a scale before starting a diet and fitness program.

The blower door is a set of equipment recognized by the bright red plastic sheet on a temporary frame that fits into the doorway. It has a round cutout fitted with elastic that snugly attaches to a large, variable-speed fan. And then it blows. The test measures the pressure difference between inside the house and the outside as well as the volume of air blowing in or out of the house. Some systems have a specialized automated test sequence to run a series of tests from a laptop computer, but we went with a simpler test.

Midori came in at 5,500 cubic feet per minute (CFM) at 50 Pascals (commonly written as 5,500 CFM_{50}), which is roughly 23 ACH_{50}. I'd heard that older homes typically fall in the range of 6,500 CFM_{50} to 8,500 CFM_{50}, so Midori's airtightness was on par with her peers. A typical new house built in California is assumed to leak at about 5 or 6 ACH_{50}. Midori was about four times leakier than brand new conventionally built houses. Our goal was not to be on par with a conventionally built house, but to far exceed it. We wanted her to be about ten times tighter than conventionally built new houses in California. The airtightness criteria for Passive House of 0.6 ACH_{50} seemed daunting. To pass the energy diet plan we set out for her, she needed to be thirty-eight times tighter than she was when we did the blower test.

Is this focus on airtightness absurd? Not in other countries. A European study conducted between 2007 and 2010 found seven countries had minimum requirements integrated into their building codes. Sweden, where the blower door test originated, specified 3 ACH_{50} airtightness in their building code for single-family homes decades ago. California has a building standards code, Title 24. Part 6 of this code specifies the energy efficiency standard. While it is a bit more stringent than the national standard, the 2013 code (current as of this writing) does not require a specific measurable target for air leakage. Though California seems to be leading the way for energy efficiency in the U.S., it's still way behind European countries.

Heat recovery ventilator

When I mentioned the airtightness criteria of Passive House, a friend asked me, "Wouldn't an airtight house smell funky after a while?" He's the not first person to ask this question. Airtightness is important if we want to be comfortable inside the house using as little energy as possible, but aren't there problems when the house is too tight? Aren't houses supposed to breathe?

A few decades ago the building science folks who focused on tight houses came up with a device that circulates fresh air throughout the house while recovering heat energy from the air inside the house. This appliance is called a heat recovery ventilator or HRV. This would be Midori's new respiratory system. (This will be discussed in detail in chapter 12.) Midori's respiratory system would consist of lungs (HRV body) and the blood vessels (HRV ducts) to move oxygen (fresh air) into the body parts (various rooms in the house) and remove carbon dioxide (stale air) and expel it out of the body (outside the house). Continuing with the human body analogy, Midori also would be wearing sweaters (extra layers of insulation) and a windbreaker (to be air tight) to keep us comfortable inside the house. These new systems meant the air inside the house would be fresh and comfortable—and also healthy because the air circulated through the house would be filtered. And to kick it up a notch, it made sense to use a heat recovery feature that reuses heat that is normally lost.

Passive House windows

Windows are an essential part of the "building envelope," which is basically like a beer cooler that keeps the drinks cold at a picnic when it's ninety degrees in the sun during the summer. In the winter the building envelope functions like the sleeve that pizza delivery folks use to keep the pizza warm. If the beer cooler or the insulated pizza sleeve had a window, it would transfer heat more rapidly than other parts of the containers. So glass windows are the weakest part of the building envelope, thermally speaking. Windows are relatively thin and will always transfer heat faster than the walls. Plus if windows are not designed, manufactured, or installed correctly, they can let air and moisture through the cracks and cause damage. Paying special attention to windows is not only important to meet the stringent Passive House target but also important for durability and comfort.

Passivhaus Institut in Germany came up with a windows certification program. This did two things. It made it easier for architects and builders to specify windows for their projects, and it had the effect of improving the quality of windows available on the market. Before we learned about the Passive House Standard, we thought double-pane windows with low-emissivity coating on the glass were pretty good. But now we know different. (Read more on Passive House windows in chapter 11).

Why bother?

Building a Passive House is a lot of work with a lot of fastidious details. Why bother? If the previous occupants of the house didn't get sick, how can the house make us sick? Why not just install solar panels to generate electricity to offset the energy use?

We wanted more than a lower utility bill. Our focus was to follow our values and do the "right" things that would last a long time. We wanted to use more current sunlight and less of the ancient sunlight. We wanted the air inside our house to be healthy. We wanted the house to be pretty and pleasant and we wanted to be comfortable living there. We wanted to demonstrate and show others that an old house can retain its charm and have excellent energy performance. We wanted everything to work together nicely and within our budget. Passive House represented the path to achieving this. Simply installing a bunch of PV panels on the roof without doing any of the other work did not.

It's not that we're opposed to using PV. Learning about Passive House clarified the sequence for us: First do the improvement on the building envelope. See how it performs. Then later add PV when we're ready to switch from gasoline vehicles to electric cars.

In the introduction to this book, I said that the most important thing we learned was to stick to our personal values, and that has guided us through buying a home and navigating options to make it green. Besides the personal benefits we'd enjoy by living in a Passive House, we set about on this renovation project to make a contribution to the greater community. Rather than wait for the government to institute regulations to curb greenhouse gas emissions to retard climate change, we wanted to reduce the greenhouse gas emissions that came from living in the house.

We took our first step in this direction in 2006 after hearing Al Gore's call to action to do something to reduce carbon emissions. We replaced my six-cylinder gasoline engine car that got an average of 19 mpg with a small hybrid car that got more than 40 mpg. That made a difference in my ninety mile daily commute to Palo Alto and back.

Switching from a gas guzzler to a fuel efficient car reduces the amount of fossil fuels extracted and pollution generated, and the same is true for pursuing this voluntary standard during the house retrofit. Buildings consume about 40 percent of the total energy in the United States, and 48 percent of that is used for space heating and cooling in the house. By applying the Passive House standard to our renovation, we could make a significant personal contribution to reducing our future energy consumption and thus reducing our carbon footprint.

Peeling the layers of onion

This journey felt like peeling the layers of an onion, solving one problem, which revealed the next layer to be solved. The onion seemed large at this point, and we knew we would come across more and more problems and even be wiping away tears along the way. Friends warned us that doing a home remodel was a test of relationship resiliency. One friend confessed, "My sweetie and

I get along great and we've been together for decades. But when we built our house, we almost killed each other and uncovered sides of each other we never knew." In fact, several people told us similar horror stories of happy couples driven to the brink of divorce during a house remodel. I worried whether we would suffer the same problems and whether our shared values would help us overcome the perils of remodeling.

There were so many unknowns. At this stage we didn't yet know exactly how Midori would look when the transformation was done. But we had faith in the building science behind the Passive House Planning Package and it was possible for an old house to target 80 percent energy reduction. If we kept our focus on energy reduction as the primary goal, we could get there.

Now that we had decided on a methodology, we would next need to find the people who could make the transformation happen.

What we learned in setting an energy limit

The Passive House Standard opened our eyes. Once we "got it" we couldn't look at houses the same way again. We learned these concepts right when we purchased a house that shaped our decisions.

❖ Gathering ideas and doing research was essential in the beginning. To move forward we needed a strategy for choosing which of the vast choices was the best for us.

❖ Choose a focus and simplify. There are many different "green" features in a house and trying to do everything all at once is overwhelming. We chose our focus to be energy efficiency and relied on the Passive House Standard to guide us.

❖ Using the Passive House Planning Package (PHPP) not only would allow us to dramatically reduce our household energy usage, it could also be applied during the design phase to explore different what-if scenarios for cost performance.

❖ Airtightness and insulation are analogous to the house wearing a windbreaker and a sweater on our behalf so that we can be comfortable in the house.

❖ Airtightness and a heat recovery ventilator can promote good air quality for health and comfort.

❖ Windows are an important component in Passive House to meet the energy target and for comfort.

4
Interviewing Architects, Builders, and Homeowners

We need a team

Now that we had a focus on Passive House, we needed to find people who could design and build one. We knew we needed a team of people, but we didn't know how to choose them, how long it would take, or how much it would cost. We asked a lot of questions to reduce uncertainty and gain confidence in choosing team members.

Importance of choosing the right team members

Gary advised us, "Be sure you can work harmoniously with the builder (general contractor) because you'll be married to him for a year." True. It's a given, he said, that surprises come up during construction despite good planning: unforeseen problems as contractors strip down the house, logistics delays, quality of materials, crew turnover, building inspection, and more. If we had to make a spot decision, we wanted a general contractor who was articulate, timely, and rational in presenting us our choices.

The relationship with the general contractor lasts a bit longer than the duration of the project. In most states contractors are required to warranty all the project work for one year. In some states like California, by operation of law, the contractor is also responsible for many structural and waterproofing defects that can arise for a period of ten years after the work is complete. This meant we needed to pick a contractor that we could work well with and who was likely to be around for years after the project was complete. We could see that picking a fly-by-night contractor just because he was a few dollars cheaper was not a very good idea.

Before we could hire a general contractor, we needed an architect. A gray beard I was talking to at a conference told me that in the old days, the architect played a primary role of keeping the project together because he or she was knowledgeable about the details of the various systems such as electrical, plumbing, engineering, and energy efficiency as well as being an expert on the design of the building. As various disciplines became more complex, the architect started to hire or consult with specialists such as structural engineers to provide drawings and details to make sure the house was structurally sound based on their calculations; mechanical engineers to design and size the heating, ventilation, and air conditioning systems; and energy consultants to perform calculations to make sure the design would meet the energy code. Therefore, to design a high-performance building today, we needed a team of experts. I began to appreciate that construction of a high-performance home is a team sport where specialists not only need to be competent in their field but also be team players.

We could have gone with a design-build firm and left it up to them to pick the people from their network. This choice makes the design-build firm the single point of contact accountable for the results. While it means paying more for project management services, we would only have one neck to choke if something went wrong. Had we been short on time due to demanding careers while raising a family, this approach would have been very attractive.

Or if we had the hard core do-it-yourself streak in us, then we could have gone down the owner-builder route and become our own general contractor and done everything ourselves.

We happen to fall in the middle of this spectrum. We knew our own strengths and limitations. We would actually be miserable swinging hammers and using power tools. We have neither the talent nor the experience, so we'd make unnecessary mistakes and it would take longer and the outcome would be questionable. On the other hand, we are quite good at doing research and asking questions. We knew that we could apply our respective career experiences in hiring people, team building, and managing projects to our home-building project. So our immediate task was to interview and select an architect and a Passive House consultant.

We planned to live in the house for many years. Perhaps this would be our forever house. We needed the right people working on the house to deliver our vision for Midori—transformation to a Passive House. We would push the envelope for energy efficiency to boldly go where nobody (locally) had gone before. Without specific Passive House experience, what was most important was their willingness to learn and their commitment and passion for green building. Just as important was their ability to communicate. No matter how brilliant or technically savvy the architect or the builder, we felt if we could not communicate with him or her easily, it would make a challenging project even harder and unnecessarily frustrating.

Who shall we work with?

A Yellow Pages search popped up about fifty architects and over one hundred general contractors in our little city of Santa Cruz. Reaching out to random people on the Yellow Pages didn't seem like a good approach. We needed to focus on green building expertise to make our search productive. We'd met Joe Fullerton, the green building specialist at the City of Santa Cruz building department, at the Santa Cruz Chamber of Commerce business fair when he was manning a booth at the fair to promote the city's Green

Building Awards program. Joe had developed this voluntary program to incentivize the permit applicant to implement green features in their building over and beyond the regulations.

Joe gave us a list of green building recipients from the 2009 Green Building Awards List. There were nineteen projects with fifteen different designers and eleven different builders. We also wanted to check out the people who were not on the list but who had been recommended by local friends who had recently done a remodel. We cross checked the names against member listings from various organizations that certify green building professionals such as Building Performance Institute (BPI), Build It Green (BIG), and United States Green Building Council (USGBC).

To shrink the list to a manageable size, I made the first cut based on my impression formed while reviewing their websites: Do they seem competent? Are they committed to green? Do they smell expensive? Do they seem approachable? I knew that a track record of having happy customers was an important criteria. Credentials and designations over and beyond the minimum license requirement were a bonus. I had made the mistake in the corporate world of once hiring someone with impressive credentials but who then fell short in important performance factors. To avoid making that mistake for our home project, I was committed to asking questions in an in-person interview and doing a thorough job of reference checks.

Asking questions

Kurt is the talker of the two of us. I feel more comfortable with email. So he picked up the phone to make appointments with the architects and builders I'd filtered from the list. We created a list of questions by synthesizing the questions listed in books such as *Green Building for Dummies*, *How to Plan, Contract and Build Your Own House*, and on various websites.

Some of the questions we crafted in the behavioral interview style would give us a feel for what it would be like working with them. For example, by asking, "Could you give us an example of a problem that came up in your project and how it got resolved?" we gave them a chance to tell a story to illustrate their problem-solving skills. Their answers would give us a sense of their problem-solving style as well as how they'd likely behave under pressure. Everyone is on good behavior during the interview. But when there are problems and things are stressful, we wanted to be partnered with someone who could rationally solve a problem rather than increase our stress. One of the builders we interviewed emphatically said that he would never work with a certain architect again. We asked him why.

"Because the last time I worked with him he lost it when we ran into a problem. He swore and berated me in front of others. It's not professional." Good to know. We didn't have that architect on our list and after that discussion, we wouldn't be talking to him for sure.

That conversation gave birth to one of my favorite questions, "What types of projects have you turned down or refused to do?" Most people pause and give a thoughtful response. The answer provides us with an insight into their boundaries and their personal standard of integrity. Answers like, "I would never work on a project where the house blocks the view from another property," might indicate sensitivity and respect for others, but it might also indicate the battle scars they have from getting beat up in public hearings before the permit was issued.

We collected brainstorming ideas as we interviewed people knowing that we didn't have to use all the ideas that popped up. One of the architects we interviewed lived a few blocks away from our house and knew that we were in the archaeologically sensitive zone. He advised us to expect to pay about $600 for the archaeology report required by the planning department to get a permit." OK, noted. Two other architects mentioned that a soils report (geotechnical report) is expensive (maybe $3,000) and hopefully we could avoid it. We mentioned to another architect that we wanted an indoor-outdoor connection for entertaining, but the living room and kitchen were not facing the backyard. "Why not pick up the house and rotate it 180 degrees?" he said. Hmm, interesting. (FYI, we didn't do that.)

One of our favorite phrases is, "It's about the patient," and it became our mantra. This phrase came from a local architect, Frank Phanton. He viewed the architect as the doctor and the house as the patient. Just as the doctor's responsibility is to look after the patient regardless of the drama going on in the emergency room, the architect keeps focus on the house regardless of the contractor, subs, or the homeowner squabbling over problems. Frank said he keeps his eyes on the patient and does what's best for the house. We liked that focus. We adopted Frank's mantra and repeated, "It's about the patient," when things got tense during the project. After all, it's not about being right or one person's opinion being more important than another. Neither is it about the architect proving a point. The mantra allowed all of us to have a common purpose. In the long run the house will outlive all of us and the more durable the house, the greener it is.

While interviewing architects and builders, we tested some of our pet ideas. We soon learned that a brilliant feature we saw at someone else's house could not be incorporated into Midori out of context. It is just as important to release a dissonant feature as it is to embrace an unfamiliar logical concept. We needed to do both to move forward. So we thanked the architects and builders for the interesting exploration and moved on.

Every once in a while we got a flash of an idea while brainstorming. Sometimes the ideas appeared brilliant, but here's one we're glad we let go: To stretch our budget, we thought we could tap into the energy and enthusiasm of bright architectural students. We thought maybe local colleges would welcome the opportunity to apply Passive House principles to a real live case study. Perhaps we could create a design contest to remodel our 1922 bungalow to the Passive House Standard and offer a small prize. Kurt called the UC Berkeley School of Environmental Design and found the timing wasn't right. In retrospect, we didn't have the experience and knowledge to judge the winning design, we wouldn't have been able to do the integrated design process, and without proper supervision, we may have ended up with creative musings that wouldn't work.

How much should we pay for an architect?

We asked our mentor, Gary Ransone, what he thought would be a reasonable architect's fee for our project. He factored in that the project was a remodel and not a new house, and that the housing market was in the dumps, so he recommended keeping the architect's fee at about $15,000. We put that number on the table when we interviewed architects to see how they would react. The response to this ranged from "workable" to "workable if you do the materials research" to "way under budget" because combined fees for architects, structural engineers, and other consultants typically would be 10 percent of the construction cost. I thought part of the architects' reaction reflected what else was going on in their business at the time. If they were busy with a large commercial project, a tiny $15,000 house remodel would seem like an irritation. If they truly wanted to have the Passive House experience under their belt, maybe they were willing to take a low budget project as an investment in their portfolio. Asking the question about their project load and naming a price of $15,000 gave us an insight into where they were in the continuum of willingness to do challenging work and whether we were the type of clients that are in their sweet spot. We wanted to have a good relationship with them and have the architect enjoy the experience of working with us too.

When we mentioned our desire to do Passive House, some architects signaled a soft no by saying, "Passive House is not suited for remodels." Some were curious and came up with an idea of building a whole new outer enclosure to ensure air sealing. Others were curious and wanted to take on the challenge. The number of Passive House buildings in Santa Cruz County in 2010 was zero. Our project presented an opportunity to be the first in the county to showcase this building approach. Willingness to learn and having a "can do" attitude was essential.

Having our list of questions kept the conversation on our terms. Our list is at the end of this chapter.

Interviewing homeowners

The best person to give information about the performance of a house is the person who lives in it. We found homeowners to be more than willing to share their experience and lessons from their house projects. They understood the value of the reference visit. The homeowners we visited were the beneficiaries of helpful others in their journey. They were now paying it forward by sharing their experience to those of us who were starting the renovation journey.

Visiting the reference homes was helpful in seeing the architect's design and the quality of the contractor's work. The experience of being in the house to see, smell, feel, and sense the place was priceless because physically being in the house gave us sensory information that would be impossible to get over the phone. We wanted to know: Does it have a feel of effortless flow as we walk through? Are the homeowners happy? What are the clever uses of space? What problems did they solve with the renovation? Did we feel relaxed or tense as we entered their space? Does the quality of interior finishes resonate with us? Are there ideas or inspirations that we want to replicate? Does it smell good?

As with the architect interviews, we went in with a list of prepared questions. Our intent with the homeowner interviews was to build rapport with the homeowners in the first few minutes so that they would volunteer information as if they were talking to a friend. This was the closest we would get to test driving the construction experience, and we wanted to know what it really was like. We wanted to be exposed to things we hadn't thought about. We weren't trying to ferret out dirt about the builder or the architect, but we wanted to know what "gotchas" were lurking around the corner in a recent construction project and maybe avoid making that mistake.

Building rapport is key to shifting the homeowner from the place of representing the work of a certain builder or architect to helping a fellow homeowner by sharing their lessons learned. Before getting into the "Where did you get those lovely tiles?" types of questions, I like to find out the context behind the remodel to understand why they did the remodel in the first place. I can easily judge a house or a feature based on assumptions in my head, but my interpretation could be completely off base. Plus, asking questions like, "What problems were you trying to solve?" or "What drove you to do the remodel?" opens the conversation in a way that allows the homeowner to tell their story. After asking such questions, we practiced active listening and then asked clarifying questions.

One of the houses we visited was in a lovely idyllic area. Built in 1953, it had a country barn feel to it. Cyndi told us that the house had been completely illegal. "See those big windows there?" She pointed to the framing around large pieces of glass covering a section of the wall from floor to ceiling. "The original house had a 'moment frame' made of 4 x 4 wood. It should have been made with steel." [A moment frame is a special type of framing designed to resist the horizontal forces when there is not enough room for the shear wall.] "This room had too much light. I wanted to see the sky, not the hill coming into the house. Most people want more natural lighting coming into their house. We had the opposite problem." Lesson learned: windows and lighting are like Goldilocks— not too much, not too little, but just right.

We noted that Cyndi had crystalized her vision by living in the house for four years to carefully identify what she liked and what she didn't. We were going into our remodel without living in the house. I wondered what we were missing if we did not live in the house first.

The homeowner stories were illuminating and interesting. One question that produced helpful insight was, "What advice do you have for us?" We asked this toward the end of the conversation in hopes of receiving their pearl of wisdom. They'd relived their remodel experience through the stories they told and were perfectly primed for imparting useful advice. Cyndi's timeless advice was, "When you reach the point where you think, 'I just don't care, do whatever,' that's exactly when you *do need to care*. Be sure to save a reserve of patience for that moment."

This advice was spot on. Later in our project I experienced moments when I felt exhausted, like hitting the wall at the twenty-mile mark running the marathon and the last 6.2 miles will take every ounce of grit I can muster. The difference between running a marathon for the first time and doing a major remodel for the first time is training. With a marathon I have a reasonable sense of what the race will feel like during the training runs. With a home remodel, we don't exactly practice picking out materials, interviewing people, building the house, or checking on the workmanship before embarking on the project. Preparation consists of summoning good intentions and gathering information and advice. But that's not the same as doing it. So we would simply have to learn by doing it.

While onsite visits are the best, pearls of wisdom are also revealed during phone conversations with homeowners. Krishna said, "Each subcontractor must be licensed and you need to like them." Yes, that is a practical advice. How would we go about checking the subs that the general brings in? Through Gary, we knew how to check the license of contractors in California: Go to http://cslb.ca.gov website to look up the contractor by their license number, their business name, or any of the names of the personnel in the company. Ask the general contractor for the names of the subs and look up their licenses too.

Another homeowner, Dina, said she was happy with the architect, but the contractor veered off the plan and their house got red-tagged. Yikes! Red-tagging is like getting a traffic ticket, getting caught doing something you weren't supposed to do. It occurs when the building department discovers a discrepancy between the approved plan and what was actually built.

One of the reference homeowners was also named Kurt. The remodel he did was his first experience and it went well for him. He told us to inspect construction carefully—daily—and to not settle if it's not what we wanted. This made sense. Vigilant daily inspection could avoid costly re-work in the future. This advice was taken to heart during our construction process by my husband, Kurt.

Integrated design

By the time we finished interviewing dozens of professionals and their references, we felt ready to make a decision, but we were having a hard time reconciling all the different advice. We wrestled with one conundrum in particular: How do we get competitive fixed bids from three contractors based on an approved plan set but still involve a contractor early on to ensure that the plan was cost effective and could be built practically? We felt stuck so we resorted to what we often did when we needed to get unstuck. "Let's call Dad," Kurt said, and I pressed Gary's number on my phone. We had started calling him "Dad" because Gary often had sage, fatherly advice. Since he's not much older than we are, we've never shared this nickname with him. I suppose the cat's out of the bag now.

Gary suggested we hire a builder as a consultant during the design phase. "Have him bill you on an agreed upon hourly rate and put in a 'Not to exceed' clause so that you cap the contract at say $2,000." He paused to let the thought sink in.

I thought that was brilliant.

That would allow us to still get competitive fixed bids from three contractors when the design was done. If we ended up choosing the same contractor to build our house, by then he would have gained familiarity with our project. "If you don't choose him, it's still a square deal because you paid him for his time. You weren't leading him on with the anticipation of getting the construction job," Gary said.

Being fair and square was important to me. Avoiding mistakes and keeping the cost low was important to Kurt. This was a win-win solution.

Architect selected

With Dad pointing us in the right direction, we got back on track evaluating and selecting the team members. We decided not to go with the design/build companies at this point because some of them would only engage if they got the entire job, and we weren't ready to select a builder. Next we reviewed the notes from the different architects we'd interviewed and noted the strengths and weaknesses of each individual. We scored them on three broad criteria: track record and commitment to green building (40 percent), experience with Arts and Crafts style (30 percent) and cost performance (30 percent). That narrowed the field down to six architects.

We talked with them again. This time we focused on chemistry, Passive House experience, and their physical location. Chemistry, especially their ability to listen to us and translate our desired outcome into a set of plans that would be interpreted by the builder, was important. Graham Irwin, the Passive House consultant we met at the West Coast Green Conference, was soon revealed to be our best choice to provide both Passive House consulting and architecture design services. He was the Passive House consultant for the O'Neil house in Sonoma, the first certified Passive House remodel in California, so he had good track record and credentials. He had a keen interest in our project because Graham also lives in a bungalow built in 1922. He had made several energy efficiency improvements to his house before he found out about the Passive House Standard. Had he known about Passive House when he bought his home, he said he would have done his improvements differently. Our bungalow presented a unique opportunity for him to have another shot at retrofitting a 1920s house to the Passive House Standard while preserving the original character.

The only problem we saw was that he was not local. Graham lived in Marin County in the cute little town of Fairfax, a two-hour drive to Santa Cruz. An onsite visit would cost us four hours of travel time. I'd worked with global teams on software implementation projects and knew we could collaborate through emails, phone calls, and online meeting applications for the design phase, but from that distance Graham couldn't monitor the work of the contractor during the construction phase and we would have to monitor the contractor's work ourselves. Still, we liked Graham's sense of humor, especially when he described the communication between the Passive House consultant and the architect: "I can talk to myself." Kurt also liked the fact that Graham had a physics degree so he could talk about building science without dumbing it down.

In 2010 there weren't many certified Passive House consultants in California, and we learned through our interviews that Graham had a very good reputation among his peers. Ideally we would have liked to hire local folks, but there were no certified Passive House consultants in Santa Cruz County. Perhaps one outcome of our project could be to raise awareness for Passive House in Santa Cruz County and build local talent.

Passive House design begins

Graham visited Midori Haus for the first time on November 17, 2010. First order of business was to draw up the as-built plans for the house, which would serve as the starting point for the new design. Graham walked around and took measurements to create the as-built drawing. "I think we can approach the insulation and air sealing from the outside," said Graham, "That way you can leave the interior walls undisturbed. And it will cost less." Great, this guy is thinking about achieving energy performance by re-using existing materials and keeping the cost down. I think Kurt must have said, "We have a limited budget," about a dozen times in our prior conversation. The message must have sunk in.

Graham's commitment to passive house showed in other ways. Two weeks before his first site visit we saw him at the California College of Arts in San Francisco where he was escorting Dr. Wolfgang Feist around the Bay Area. Dr. Feist, founder of Passivhaus Institut in Darmstadt Germany, is a physicist, not an architect. He approached energy efficiency by looking at the house as a system and had an idea to create a functional envelope where you can achieve a high level of comfort with very little energy consumption. He was presenting to a crowd of people assembled by Passive House California, a nonprofit organization that promotes Passive House through education. For the energy geeks, seeing Dr. Feist in person is like meeting the Dalai Lama. There was something special about listening to the founder talk passionately about Passive House twenty years after the very first prototype was built in Germany.

Dr. Feist opened his talk giving examples of energy efficiency in products such as lighting and computer display monitors where over time energy consumption dropped significantly (80 percent to 98 percent) with the release of new products and technologies. Then he showed that significant energy consumption drop applied to buildings too. When the very first passive house was built in Darmstadt, Germany it was monitored with sensors to measure energy consumption and comfort throughout the seasons. The data from 1991 to 2010 showed that average heating energy dropped by 90 percent while maintaining a comfortable temperature of 68°F (20°C). Since then many passive house buildings have been built. Note that Passive House Standard is not exclusive to single-family homes. It has been successfully applied to other types of buildings such as schools, commercial buildings, and apartment buildings.

One message from Dr. Feist that rang true for us was, "Do the refurbishment at the time when the building needs it, not just for energy's sake." This is exactly the condition we have with Midori.

Punted on other team members

We felt a sense of relief after deciding to work with Graham and did not fill out our "team roster" at that point. We figured the sales engineer from Zehnder would help us with the layout of the ventilation system. We had a vague notion of wanting to do solar thermal system but were not quite ready to pull in a specialist for that yet. Title 24, the California energy compliance calculation, seemed like something we would do as an afterthought when design was done because we figured we would exceed it anyway. At that time we didn't know we would need a structural engineer to do calculation on a load bearing wall. We figured these things will work out when the time comes. Looking back, the advice we would give ourselves in 2010 is continue to interview people and firm up the team player to do the mechanical engineering work.

What we learned in interviewing architects, builders, and homeowners

When in doubt, ask questions. We did a lot of that while learning about the stages and process of a house renovation project.

❖ Do the remodel at the time when the building needs it, not just for energy's sake.

❖ Hire people who are competent and smarter than you.

❖ Integrated design can be done without hiring a design-build firm. Hiring a contractor as a consultant during the design phase will ensure the plan is capable of being built and estimate known.

❖ Homeowner interviews are very useful. Reference calls are a must and site visits are even better.

❖ In retrospect, we should have interviewed and hired a mechanical engineer up front to have their full participation during the design phase.

❖ Ask insightful questions before hiring. See our list of questions at: http://midorihaus.com/questions_list/

Questions we asked architects and contractors

	Questions	Why we asked	Probing question(s)
1	Have you worked on a project of a similar scope? Please specify size (both cost and square footage), architectural style, and homeowners' intended outcome.	We wanted to work with someone with recent experience in a project similar to ours.	When was it? Where was it?
2	What are standard green building measures you include in all your projects?	Reveal if green building is part of their standard practice or not.	Can you give us a list?
3	Can you show and tell us about the features of past projects in your portfolio?	"Green" can be interpreted and expressed differently. See if their notion of green is appealing.	What features are you proud of?
4	Could you provide us with a reference list of your clients whose projects were similar to ours? Can we contact them?	Note how they handle the names and contact info. We appreciated the care they take in checking with the client first.	Can you describe their project?
5	Could you produce a design for $15,000 for a build budget of $250,000?	Set budget expectations up front. We chose these starting point numbers based on our research.	What would a project of this scope typically cost?
6	What is your current project load?	If they're really busy we may not get enough attention for our project.	
7	What's been your experience with working with green building consultants?	We needed Passive House approach integrated into the design, not as an afterthought.	
8	What types of projects have you turned down or refused to do?	See what boundaries they have for risk, ethics, and comfort.	Why did you turn them down?
9	Could you give an example of a problem that came up in your project and how it was resolved?	Reveal problem-solving skills.	

Questions we asked homeowners

	Questions	Why we asked	Probing question(s)
1	Where is the house? Are there any unique features?	Gauge similarity to our project.	Was your project a new construction? Addition? Remodel?
2	When was the project done? How long did it take?	Different circumstances during boom or bust of housing market.	What was the market condition?
3	Why did you choose this architect or contractor?	Reveal selection criteria.	Who else did you consider?
4	What challenges did you face? How were they resolved?	Learn from others' experience.	Gain insight to architect or contractor's problem-solving skills.
5	What went smoothly?	Validate skills.	What were their strengths?
6	Did the project complete on time, on budget?	Estimate accuracy.	What surprises did you encounter?
7	How involved were you in the process?	Gauge if the homeowner project management preference is similar to ours.	How did the architect or contractor communicate with you?
8	After living in the house for x years how are the systems and quality of materials holding up?	Gauge performance over time.	What about the workmanship? Are the energy bills what you expected?
9	If you were to do this over again, what would you do differently? What would you do the same? Do you have any advice for us?	Lessons learned and advice.	

5
Designing for Lifestyle and Budget

Specifying within constraints

We worked with Graham to write up our specifications. At that time, we knew having detailed specification would help us achieve the results we wanted and save us from excessive headaches. What I didn't see at that time was the implicit boundaries or constraints we had. These constraints guided us down a path of seeing creative opportunities rather than picking out and settling for a collection of routine rule of thumb choices. Unlike the blank slate we had at the beginning of our real estate search, we were proceeding down a funnel of constraints to shape Midori to our intentions in the design phase. In Midori's transformation design, we focused within the multi-faceted constraints by:

- Honoring the original Arts and Crafts style
- Observing regulations

- Heeding data from health and safety diagnostics
- Using space well to meet the lifestyle we envisioned
- Embodying our personal values
- Navigating kitchen design to solve problems
- Applying the principles of Integrated Design
- Ensuring we could afford the vision with detailed estimate.

Arts and Crafts style

Midori gave us a reason to learn about the style of the home that we now love. Midori is a bungalow from the 1920s dressed in the Arts and Crafts style. We wanted to keep her that way: understated elegance of stained wood shaped with care to show off the workmanship of the craftsman; careful attention to design detail; respect for the natural beauty of the wood.

I didn't know that the charming Victorian homes in the Bay Area had fallen prey to mass production of architectural flair of that time and were ostentatiously embellished with bric-a-brac. It was a relief to learn that the Arts and Crafts style of the late nineteenth century and early twentieth century was a reaction against this. The Arts and Crafts movement was the call to simplicity that honored the skills of the craftsman, an emphasis that comes from Japanese woodwork. This resonated with us.

Had you asked me what Arts and Crafts style was a decade ago I would have thought you were asking me about some school program that was being cut from the school district's education budget. Likewise, the term "bungalow" seems to have slightly different meanings and is interpreted differently around the world. Originally used to describe a single story house with a wide veranda in India in the Bengal style, the California bungalow is a one or one-and-a-half story house with a gable over the main portion of the house. The low-pitched roof is supported by large brackets at the broad eaves. The exterior siding may be of wood shingles or horizontal clapboard siding. Porches are spacious. Porch gables are supported by squat posts atop cement piers (like Midori) or on chunky river boulders.

Windows of that era had multiple panes patched together to cover a large opening. This was done to overcome the difficulty of creating a single large piece of glass and the creative result of patching together different glass pieces was another aspect of Arts and Crafts style we had come to love. Midori didn't have the multiple-pane feature, but we wanted her to have that period look (it's called a muntin pattern) on the windows to fit in with the rest of the neighborhood.

That feature, missing on the outside, was found on the inside of the house. The buffet built into the entire length of the dining room had rectangular glass doors for the display cabinets flanking the sideboard. The muntin patterns on these reflected the typical pattern we saw in our neighborhood windows: two rows of small glass panes about the size of paperback novel gave just enough interest to the glass door comprised of one large piece of glass about three feet tall. We appreciated the integrity and beauty of materials displayed in the built-in furniture. While some of our neighbor's houses' walls were lined with wainscoting that extended three or four feet from the floor, Midori had none. We liked our walls with a simple six-inch-wide stained baseboard as an accent. Wainscoting would have made the room feel heavy and darker, and the living room wasn't big enough to warrant that look. The other feature missing in Midori was a fireplace. The original brick fireplace came down during the 1989 Loma Prieta Earthquake and the prior owners chose to remove it rather than repair it.

The Arts and Crafts style gave us the theme and aesthetic direction early on. It was a welcomed constraint because it prevented us from making random design choices. It was either period correct or not. It kept things simple. The beauty of transforming our 1920s bungalow to something ultra-green is that Passive House is architecture-agnostic. It can be applied to any style of architecture, including Arts and Crafts.

When we bought the house in 2010, there were charming features from the original bungalow in the kitchen. The built-in furniture in the kitchen had a deep flour bin below the counter of the hutch. There was the California-cooler, not the cocktail drink but a narrow vertical built-in cabinet next to the kitchen door.

The shelves of the cooler were made of metal mesh racks that allowed air to circulate through the different levels. It drew cold air from the outside through a vent near the floor and allowed warmer air to escape to the outside through a vent near the ceiling. No insulation in the walls could be called a feature of the era because the building codes in the 1920s, if there were any, didn't require it. There was a gas furnace in the crawlspace as well as a wall furnace to provide heat. We imagined these would turn on even in the summer as the temperature dropped as the fog rolled in.

History and regulations

Back in 1907 the two-block area of our neighborhood was known as Corona Heights. Most lots on our street were 50 feet wide and 120 feet deep. By 1912 someone combined the four lots in the middle of the street and redivided them into three lots so that each lot was slightly larger. Our lot is the middle one. The lot to the east is slightly smaller and the lot to the west is slightly larger. Frank Chapman, the original owner of Midori, must have been on good terms with his neighbors, the Rowlands, because the shared driveway is laid out exactly on the property line with mutual easement on the Tax Assessor's map. The shared duplex garage at the end of the driveway suggests the owners got along well and the building codes were different back then because it sits very close to the back fence, something that won't fly with the city's planning department today. When the Rowlands built their house in 1912 (ten years before Midori), they built their house as far west as they possibly could without being on the property of the other neighbor.

To help us explore the limits of the building code setback and our neighbor's comfort level, Graham drew up a couple of different plans. One plan was to have a small deck outside the kitchen facing the driveway to create a little indoor-outdoor connection and have a place to barbecue. The other plan extended the edge of this deck and the 1947 addition (master bathroom and closet) much closer to the driveway, up to the legal limit. To make sure there were no snags for creating the deck plan, Kurt called the city's planning department. We were told that because our lot is over 5,000 square feet and the house is under 3,000 square feet, a planning permit was not needed. As for extending the master bathroom and closet out toward the driveway, we chose not to do it. It was within code, but to do so would cut into the width of our shared driveway. Our neighbors Patrice and Bob were concerned about hitting their fence or our house while backing out of the driveway.

Home inspection report

Midori was due for upgrades. This was made apparent by the home inspection we ordered during the escrow period when we bought the house. Essentially, Midori was a ninety-year-old patient facing major surgery. We needed proper assessment of her current state to see if special attention would be required for her transformation. We hired a home inspector to do a complete physical exam of Midori. The home inspector didn't mind us tagging along like hospital interns and asking questions. We were curious about Midori's condition and observed the process intently as she got her physical exam.

Our inspector, Dennis, moved around the house taking notes and photos. He examined the termite damage that was disclosed in the termite report we'd read in the inch-thick real estate packet we originally received. Dennis said the termite damage to the floor could be removed and patched, and the white oak floor in the living room and the dining room was in good shape and could be refinished. Moving on to the dining room, he noted the buffet and said, "Leave the built-in furniture on this wall intact." Great. We quite liked the built-in furniture and intended to keep it.

There were visually obvious items like the old knob-and-tube electrical wiring (which is a fire hazard) which needed to be upgraded to code-compliant wiring. Plumbing was a mix of metal pipes: copper in some parts and galvanized pipes in others. We knew there was corrosion in the pipes because when we turned the water on in the bathtub, it ran brown. An old, abandoned wastewater pipe in the crawl space was just hanging like a large piece of stalactite bitten off by a monster. The original house had a brick chimney that went all the way up through the attic. Bricks had fallen during the 1989 Loma Prieta earthquake, but most of the structure still existed behind the wall and could cause more damage in a violent earthquake. This needed to be removed.

There were other dangers, including a live wire running overhead between the main house and the detached garage in the back. This electrical hazard needed to be removed. The posts and piers holding up the floors in the crawl space had signs of water pooling under the house. We would need to put proper drainage in place. The roofing looked to be about fifteen years old so it had some life left. Often roofing is redone at the time of solar panel installation to tie the warranty together, so we considered re-roofing the southern portion of the roof before putting up solar panels. Homes of this era may not have the sill plates anchored to the foundation, and there were a couple of cracks in the foundation that needed to be fixed.

By the time his forty-page inspection report came, we knew that Midori was way overdue to have all of her systems replaced. Although the physical exam report contained a long list of stuff that needed fixing, it wasn't alarming as it was in line with homes of this age. Nothing horrible showed up.

Asbestos test

"Nothing horrible" is relative when you know you're going to gut and replace entire walls. Looking up at the ceiling Dennis said, "Those popcorn ceilings have asbestos and you should have them remediated by a licensed asbestos professional. You may want to hire an asbestos inspector who can take samples and have them tested. You'd be surprised where you find asbestos." Noted.

We knew that asbestos was a fire retardant used in various building materials and products. Its use dates back thousands of years to earthenware pots and cooking utensils. A thousand years ago King Louis IV of France would delight his dinner guests by throwing a tablecloth into the fire to clean it. Since it was made of asbestos fiber, it never burned, but the food scraps did. In the nineteenth century, asbestos was used in diverse applications such as ceiling insulation, fire retardant coating, flooring, fire retardant cement, drywall, pipe insulation and more. In the 1970s it was banned in the United States as breathing asbestos causes serious lung damage. Because she was built in 1922, it's no surprise that Midori would have asbestos.

Just as we get blood analyzed at a lab before surgery, Midori was about to get some lab work too. Kurt contacted Asbestos Inspectors, Inc. to schedule an inspection. A middle-aged woman showed up with her son to take samples from various parts of the house. I was surprised to see where she took the samples from: window putty, paint on various surfaces, roofing material, countertop, stucco siding, attic insulation, vinyl floor tile, and more. The divot marks left from the sampling were pretty deep. Good thing we weren't planning on keeping the tiles and countertop surfaces.

The asbestos inspector sent multiple samples from twenty-six locations to the lab for analysis, and the lab report showed the contents of various layers from each sample. It was detailed and tedious work. No wonder the asbestos inspection cost more than the home inspection! We paid a total of $1,423 for the asbestos inspection. When we looked at the report, we learned that the bulk of the cost was from lab fees. Even more expensive was the remediation fee. At the end of the twenty-three-page inspection report were estimates from two certified and licensed asbestos abatement companies. Both were around $15,000 to remove and dispose of asbestos properly.

Most of the samples were free of asbestos, but we were surprised to learn where asbestos was detected. It was not detected in the white and tan vinyl floor tile or the black and white floor tile, but the gray-pink vinyl tile contained 8 percent chrysotile (white asbestos, the most common type). The popcorn ceiling contained 5 percent, the off-white plaster contained less than 1 percent, the window putty contained 2 percent, and the roof mastic contained 10 percent.

The big question was how to deal with asbestos so that it didn't harm the workers doing construction while also making sure that we wouldn't breathe in traces of asbestos left over from construction when we move in. Our concern for health and safety didn't make the high price tag easier to swallow, but we decided to hire a certified asbestos abatement company to remediate this toxic substance in a responsible manner.

Lead-based paint test

Lead-based paint is another test we subjected Midori to. In the past lead has been added to paint to speed up drying, increase durability, and maintain a fresh appearance. It is now recognized as a health hazard that causes nervous system damage, stunted growth, and kidney damage. When we had Midori inspected for lead-based paint, the inspector took photos utilizing a special camera that was able to detect lead in the various layers of paint.

Of the 270 images taken, 63 percent of the surfaces contained lead-based paint and these surfaces need to be handled in a manner consistent with California regulations during demolition and salvage. The cost of this inspection was about half as much as the asbestos inspection. Later we gave this report to the contractor to deal with painted surfaces containing lead responsibly. Thank goodness we didn't have to fork out a large sum to remediate this like we did with asbestos.

Radon test

While we were on a roll detecting various toxic substances around the house, we did a radon test. Radon gasses are naturally present in soil, rocks, and sometimes water. This colorless, odorless gas is the second leading cause of lung cancer after smoking. Concentration of radon varies from region to region and we live in an area that is known to have moderate concentrations. We bought a kit from the local hardware store and followed instructions on the package to expose the canister in the house and shipped the container to the lab. When the report came back, we were relieved to see no radon was detected accumulating in the house.

Air quality

Indoor air quality is important for health and comfort, especially in an airtight house. In a way living in a passive house is like being inside of a refrigerator—well insulated and tightly air sealed. I don't smell the food odors from outside the refrigerator, but if I store leftover takeout food seasoned with lots of garlic in the fridge, my nose will be assaulted the next time I open the fridge. The tight house can amplify the smell of what we bring into the house. Even if mechanical ventilation is used in a passive house to provide adequate oxygen for the occupants, a stinky smell can hang around for a while, especially if the rate of off-gassing is faster than the rate of air being extracted out of the house. The source of the malodorous smells or noxious fumes may be carpets, furniture, paint, or particles clinging to clothing. We knew that there were chemicals and carcinogens in paint mixture and glue used to bond cheap furniture. This was the time to be diligent about specifying what we didn't want to bring into the house.

People know a lot about outdoor pollution, but indoor air pollution is also an issue. Wanting the best possible indoor air quality, we looked first at using zero-VOC paint to reduce the airborne carcinogens in the house. The U.S. Environment Protection Agency cites a number of carcinogens in the chemicals used in paint. VOC, or volatile organic compounds, have a very low boiling point. For example formaldehyde, a known carcinogen, evaporates at a very low temperature of –2°F. I wonder how many of us have sat in rooms painted with regular paint breathing in this cancer-causing agent that can off-gas for a number of years? If you're wondering what formaldehyde smells like, just walk into a nail salon that uses nail polish containing formaldehyde.

Other materials we paid attention to included wood pressed products such as particleboards, plywood, and fiberboard. We paid attention to the interior walls after learning about the problems with certain drywalls manufactured in China. Reports from the CDC covering cases between 2001 and 2008 traced the source of headaches, eye irritation, difficulty in breathing, and other health problems to reactive sulfur gasses coming out of certain drywalls (also known as sheetrock and gypsum board) manufactured in China. Unlike furniture that can be moved around easily, walls are permanent fixtures in the room. Best to get it right at the beginning.

Avoiding bad stuff and feeling overwhelmed

When it comes to indoor air quality (IAQ), there is a lot to consider, but with so much and information from manufacturers not being easily accessible, this can feel overwhelming. To add to the sense of overwhelm is the sheer volume of information online. At times websites, social media feeds, blogs, radio, commercials, and advertisements all seem to conspire to change behavior through fear. Some "stories" are just urban legends. Some are simply sensational pieces with iffy science behind them. And some stories have important information that will impact us in a significant way. Which advice do I heed?

Some days when I found myself reading about what toxin du jour to avoid, I noticed I was reaching a point of information fatigue. I wondered, "Is this what Cyndi meant by reserving patience?" We had not even begun construction and I was feeling annoyed by the choices we needed to make.

Yes, I wanted to avoid health hazards. Yes, I wanted to reduce carbon emissions. Yes, I wanted to use water sustainably. Yes, I wanted to minimize waste and reuse materials. Yes, I wanted to vote with my dollars to buy materials from companies that were socially responsible. Yes, I wanted to source materials to promote local businesses. Yes, I valued durability. Yes, I wanted comfort too.

But I thought: Can I have all of this without spending a fortune? Would I feel good about it? I hoped so. There were so many facets to examine when specifying materials. I think this is what Jacquie must have meant when she said, "$15,000 design fee is doable if clients do the materials research." With a crushing amount of information to evaluate, how would we ever choose the right stuff? The specification work could have been simplified somewhat had we known about the "Red List," a list of specific chemicals to avoid in home construction and furnishing, and used that rigorously.

Clarifying values

I put a blank sheet of paper on the kitchen table.

"What are we doing?" Kurt asked cautiously.

"We're going to brainstorm."

He looked askance. "Don't we need a white board?"

"This will have to do." If I can get teams through brainstorming meetings at work, I can get my husband through this. "Here's a pen. Just write down all the things that are important to you that you want for the house."

"But I don't think—"

"Just write without thinking, without judgment, anywhere on the sheet of paper." I would do the same with my pen.

"OK?" I checked his expression for acquiescence. "Ready? Go!"

In two minutes we filled the paper with words—clean water, example demonstration, longevity, be happy, IAQ, aesthetics, rebate eligibility, and so on.

Having emptied our heads by transferring our thoughts onto the paper, I surveyed the sheet with satisfaction. I pulled out colored highlighters. "You know, we could group these into several categories."

"Okay, these could be grouped into costs," Kurt said while circling the words longevity, rebate eligibility, and cost effectiveness with the orange marker.

I was getting into this. "We can further group them into initial implementation cost and on-going costs. I think it's important to distinguish the two." I used a yellow highlighter to circle consumables and run costs.

Then we used a green highlighter to identify the items that made us feel happy. Blue was for items related to Passive House. Red marked items in the big tent representing values, including sustainability and re-use. Some items had double or triple circles. We did this exercise not so much to rank and order them to feed into some selection algorithm, but simply to have a conversation about them. Writing and seeing printed words anchored our thoughts and ideas we had discussed.

We were glad to be pretty much aligned with what was important and how they related to each other. We saw how valuable it was to have this discussion before we'd have to decide on something under time pressure.

Gaining insights by spending time in the house

We gained useful insights by having parties and by camping in the house during the design phase. One outcome was a decision not to do a "great room" layout where the space between the kitchen, dining room, and living room opens up to one big space. It's a popular trend seen in magazines, and several people urged us to do it. We chose not to after having a dinner party. We were taken with the pleasant feeling of being hugged by the room when we closed the doors. This, unbeknownst to us then, turned out to be one of the best decisions we made. We also liked the layout of the rooms, meaning we didn't have to dramatically change the framing of the house.

One night we slept in our sleeping bags in the back room of the house.

"How's your throat?" Kurt asked me the next morning.

"OK, I guess," I replied, looking at the canary of the family. "How's yours?"

"It feels a bit scratchy, and I don't like the smell."

I sniffed the air. "The old house smell?"

"It's like the walls are emitting decades of combustion byproducts from the furnace and the gas stove."

That led to a discussion about keeping the interior walls, imbued with the smells of generations of people living there. Graham had mentioned keeping the inside walls intact and doing the insulation from the outside by replacing the siding as a way to limit scope and contain cost. But we needed to improve the indoor air quality because Passive House is a really tight house and we wanted to breathe comfortably. Taking down all of the interior walls would make it easier to do the wiring, ducting, and plumbing. We decided it would be worth it to pay a bit more for new interior walls for our health and comfort.

What will we do in each room?

The experience of camping out at the house convinced us not to officially move into the house until the remodel was done. But camping out made it easier to imagine what we would do in each of the rooms and how it would feel to spend time there. We asked ourselves, "What's our lifestyle, room by room?" We did a walk-through.

We started out at the front door on Midori's generous porch facing the street. This could hold a dozen people lounging around with a glass of beer or their favorite drink in hand, engaging in conversation. We liked our vision of porch parties and decided to keep the solid concrete porch as it was, maybe with new patio furniture to make the space more inviting.

We walked from the porch into the living room, which is a good-sized space that seemed ideal for entertaining. It was much larger than what we had in our condo, which felt cramped with any more than the half-dozen people we'd invite over for slide show parties. Midori's living room could comfortably fit a dozen people for future slide show parties.

Kurt envisioned setting up the spacious living room so he could listen to music on his old-school stereo. He earmarked the four corners for his large speakers, and in the space between the window and the main door, he imagined his hi-fi stereo system consisting of tube amplifier, CD player, tape player, and topped with a turntable. A vintage Silvertone, a hand-cranked phonograph, came with the house. Set in a tall cabinet trimmed with flowery flourishes, the Silvertone could add to the old-school look and feel.

When Kurt and I walked into the formal dining room to consider our lifestyle and what we would do there, we both looked at the built-in furniture and said, "That stays!" The built-in furniture defines the space. It would be perfect for displaying the collectible porcelain that had been cooped up in storage.

The dining room table would comfortably sit eight people, a nice size for entertaining. And, as we found out when we did have a dinner party, closing the French door and the door to the kitchen made the room feel cozy. It didn't at all have the stuffy feeling of a formal dining room, maybe because it had such a nice view of the front yard, and we planned to sit there regularly.

We stood together spinning ideas for the kitchen. We both enjoyed preparing and eating food, and we wanted to cook together without getting into each other's space. I wanted to bake regularly. I also wanted to preserve the bounty of apples in our backyard and get into canning. We knew we'd be grilling meat, veggies, and fish on the outdoor barbecue, so having easy access to the outdoor barbecue would be nice.

We discussed other ways we would physically move in the space. We wanted a place to easily land the bags of groceries when we came home from the store. Hooks for coats and hats near the landing spot would be nice, too, and a pantry to easily put away grains, sugar, noodles, cans, and jars would be great. Considering our lifestyle, we wanted a phone in the corner of the kitchen with notepad and paper and then next to the phone, some built-in organization furniture to avoid cluttering the countertop with mail, magazines, and to-do lists.

Midori had a hallway that connected the living room with the three bedrooms and a bathroom. It seemed a great space for storage and book shelves. If we had a clothes washer and dryer tucked away in the hallway closet, we'd want to make part of the hallway a laundry prep and sorting area. Built-in furniture would assist with that. We could store laundry supplies, towels, linens, and a lot more in built-in storage in the hallway.

Two of the bedrooms of this three-bedroom house would be his and hers office spaces. Kurt and I stood in the doorway of his future office. In the cabinets and drawers he saw ample built-in storage for his various collections. He wanted a clean, tidy look while he sat at his desk to work.

I wanted my office to be a multi-purpose room and got excited about installing Craftsman-style built-in furniture.

"I want my desk facing the window overlooking the backyard," I said. Kurt nodded as I shared more and more ideas. The closet in the room would allow me to tuck away my sewing machine and supplies. My flute and the sheets of music would be on a stand in the corner to remind me how much I enjoy playing. On the rare occasion when we had friends or family stay with us, we could pull down a Murphy bed to convert the space into a guest bedroom. This arrangement would give us both an office and accommodate visitors without having to expand the house with an addition.

By mutual agreement, the master bedroom would be a quiet place for sleeping, reading, and intimate moments.

"No phones, no TV, no computers," Kurt insisted.

"Maybe we'll do some stretching or foam rolling to manage sore muscles from cycling or running," I suggested.

"OK," Kurt mused. "I can do push-ups, sit-ups, and hand-weight exercises here rather than in the living room." We'd finally have space to do all that.

Kurt asked, "What about the walk-in closet?"

I blinked. "It's a place to store our clothing and get dressed. Let's not use this space to store random stuff we can't fit anywhere else. That's what the garage storage will be for." This made me realize that we had an underlying intention of honoring a clutter-free tidy aesthetic throughout the house. I smiled inwardly. "Very Midori," I thought.

The master bathroom was next to the walk-in closet. It was in such bad shape that we enjoyed showing it to our friends for the shock factor. The small corner shower was decorated with multicolored rust and mold and had more than its life squeezed out of it. The toilet rocked lightly as we sat on it and invoked the fear of falling through the termite-eaten floor. But even with these drawbacks, we could envision the space we wanted. Rather than create a large, luxurious master bathroom with a period-correct claw foot bathtub, we chose to keep it small and functional. We just needed to have a toilet, shower, and a sink for morning and evening routines. Our priority was easy maintenance. But I confess: I did yearn for a luxurious soak in hot water up to my chin, but a large Japanese-style tub was not going to fit in the master bathroom.

The other bathroom stood at the end of the hall, and it would be for visitors. It looked like it had been updated a few years earlier, and it was serviceable. The built-in dresser was functional, but it didn't exude historical charm like the built-in furniture in the dining room. It just took up space. The bathtub and shower was clean and in working condition. It had a hand-grip rail, the type seen in homes of the elderly. The bathroom had a sink on a pedestal, and it also was serviceable. Above the tub was a cavernous cabinet that could store years' worth of toilet paper and supplies. We decided to keep the sink, bathtub, and cabinet just as they were. The bathroom would probably come in handy if we had to pre-wash clothing before we put it in the clothes washer. It would be convenient to have the sink close by the washing machine when we need to wash away oils from poison oak we sometimes pick up from hiking or running through trails.

After our "envisioning walkthrough," we felt confident that the existing footprint of the house and the layout of the rooms mostly worked. The kitchen needed to be revamped along with the master bathroom and master closet. The hallway closet needed to be expanded to create the small laundry and utility room. The rest of the rooms (living room, dining room, hallway, and the three bedrooms) worked. We would keep them the same shape and size. For just the two of us the house, at 1,574 square feet, was plenty big. With the addition of the large deck facing the backyard and a smaller deck facing the driveway, we had the indoor-outdoor connection we'd always wanted to make the place feel bigger.

Designing the kitchen

The original kitchen was a galley kitchen. A swinging door separated the dining room and the kitchen. The door to the hallway provided easy access to the kitchen from the other rooms. A third door separated the kitchen and the small mudroom. It was a small space with lots of doors and the layout didn't meet our needs.

The functional problem we were trying to solve in the kitchen was, "How do we cook together without getting into each other's way?" We both like food and enjoy cooking. The times we've tried to cook in the same space at the condo we've found ourselves fighting over the sink. So having two sinks in the kitchen was non-negotiable. I love to bake and bring cake, cookies, and lemon bars to meetings and parties. We wanted the happy feeling of hanging out with people in the kitchen during a party while using the space efficiently with smaller appliances and effective storage.

Besides looking at magazines, websites, and books for kitchen ideas, we took a weekend class at the local community college to learn about kitchen design. We learned about the work triangle of placing the cooktop, fridge, and the sink in a triangle to facilitate easy flow for cooking. We applied the concept of a work triangle to brainstorm different layouts of the kitchen, but none of them made our hearts sing. We salivated over the images in *The New Bunga-low Kitchen* by Peter LaBau that combined the classic look and feel of the bungalow done with modern appliances and materials. We thought, "How do we make it work for us in a galley kitchen with three doors?"

The answer was, "Don't keep galley kitchen with three doors!" Change the footprint to make it work. Graham sent us a drawing of the kitchen concept he came up with. While Kurt and I held fast to the constraint of keeping the door between the kitchen and the hallway, Graham sealed it up, creating the space for a sink. Kurt and I also tried to work within the constraint of having a separate mudroom and a kitchen with a wall and a door. Graham kept the function of the mudroom by the kitchen door by putting in a bench with cabinet and coat hooks, but he knocked down the wall between these rooms and combined it into a larger space.

Graham created a breakfast bar counter with a generous L shape where one end was connected to the cabinets and the other end was open. "You want to protect yourself in the kitchen," he said. "People naturally congregate in the kitchen during parties and can get in the way of food prep. With this layout you can still talk to them on the other side of the counter while you tend to your kitchen tasks." This layout did make our heart sing.

We continued to get ideas and inspiration by visiting other peoples' places and kitchen showrooms. One such inspiration was from our friends Paul and Flora in Seattle. Having sold their beautiful, custom-built house in Santa Cruz a few years earlier, they continued their vibrant life in Seattle. Flora, an artist and a wonderful cook, prepared pasta while we admired her kitchen and asked her about her most recent remodel experience. "We got a deep sink because they contain splashes better, and dirty dishes disappear in a hurry if you need them to," Flora explained, as I scribbled down the name of the sink, "Kraus," in my notebook. Next to the sink was a tiny dishwasher only eighteen inches wide. "This Miele dishwasher is great. It's the perfect size and does a good job." Flora asked if we'd been to the Miele showroom in San Francisco. She said they have cooking demonstrations to show their appliances in action. "It's free and since it's not a sales office, you don't feel pressured to buy anything," Flora added. We signed up for the next Master Chef class scheduled on their calendar.

Visit to the appliance showroom

The design center is located near the intersection of Highway 101 and Interstate 80 in San Francisco. It's in an industrial area with various galleries, showrooms, and stores that feature home furnishings. The design choices come alive when visitors see, touch, and smell the furniture, carpets, window treatments, artwork, appliances, and more.

The Miele showroom is tucked away at the end of an old warehouse building. The main item of interest for us was the induction cooktop that uses a magnetic field to heat the cooking vessel directly, bypassing the two-stage heat transfer typical of an electric resistance cooktop. Although we have both enjoyed cooking with gas for over twenty years, we have been leaning toward an induction cooktop ever since we learned about indoor air quality issues with gas combustion appliances. After browsing http://theinductionsite.com, we knew how it worked and what the benefits were, but we'd never seen one in action.

The Miele Master Chef demonstration class was two hours long. There were twelve students watching two friendly ladies demonstrating the Miele appliances by making a four-course meal for us to enjoy at the end of class. The atmosphere made it feel like being in a friend's kitchen rather than being in a class-room as the ladies explained features as they cooked. The induction cooktop was very responsive. When Rebecca turned down the temperature setting, we saw an instantaneous response in the pan sautéing the vegetables. This settled our anxiety about electric cooking appliances having a slow response. The downside of the induction cooktop was that we'd need new cookware. Rebecca said, "Induction cooktops only work with pots and pans with iron in them." I was concerned, and shot Kurt a look. "We can check using a magnet," Kurt whispered. "If the magnet sticks we can use the pot or pan." Since we had a set of cast iron skillets, we wouldn't have to replace too many pans, and maybe the magnet would stick to a few others.

After we finished the delicious four-course meal Emma made on the induction cooktop, we looked at ovens. A traditional oven burns natural gas (or wood) or it uses electric resistance to raise the temperature of the oven cavity. Since we wanted to eliminate the use of natural gas inside the house, we were interested in an electric convection oven.

The convection oven is a bit more efficient than a traditional electric oven because a fan circulates the warm air within the oven cavity and heats the food faster and more uniformly. A steam oven is even more efficient than a convection oven because steam is used to heat the food. This notion of steam being more efficient than air didn't click for me until I was invited to visualize sticking my bare hand into an oven. Would I stick my hand into an oven with an air temperature of 200°F? Yes. Would I do the same if 200°F oven was full of steam? No, it would scald me. Hence, using steam I could cook food at a lower temperature and that saves energy. They showed us that steam adds moisture during cooking. No more dry cakes. Kurt leaned over and said, "That's nice, but do we really need it?" The coconut rice dish prepared in the steam oven answered that question. "Wow, I can make rice in the oven!" Rice cooker appliance is not needed. Another benefit is preserving food. Setting up a water bath for canning is a hassle. A steam oven eliminates this cumbersome water bath setup. I was hooked.

It may seem premature to be looking at kitchen appliances at the beginning of the design phase. I've always thought that since appliances are installed toward the end of the construction, it could be decided then. True, the actual make and model of the dishwasher, cooktop, oven, and the fridge could be decided later if we could live with the openings and dimensions allowed for it. If for some reason we fell in love with a refrigerator that was a different dimension than what was in the kitchen layout plan, we'd be faced with a decision to redo the countertop and cabinet placement and size or settle for a fridge that fit into the space. We didn't have to buy the appliances yet. We just had to choose the model so that cabinet and countertop dimensions could be finalized on the plan.

Looking at finishes

Just as we looked at appliances during the design phase with the intention of buying them later toward the end of the construction phase, we also looked at finishes. These are items on the interior exposed surfaces such as tile backsplashes, towel racks, flooring, closet systems, countertops, trims around doors and windows, interior doors, and other items attached to the building. Things like flooring make a difference in indoor air quality and cost. The more specific we could get with the finishes, the more accurate the overall construction estimate would be, so we spent some time clarifying what we liked and updated the specification document.

We knew we wanted to reuse the existing baseboards and trims. In the dining room and the living room we wanted to keep the look of natural wood in the bungalow style. We asked to reuse what was practical and find other wood to match in the case where a window size change made existing trim unusable. We also chose to reuse the interior French door between the living room and dining room as well as the bedroom doors and knobs. The bedroom doors weren't valuable pieces of history but were functional, and we liked the aged patina on the metal around the glass door knobs.

Marmoleum is a flooring product that is true to the vintage of the house. It is a brand name for a linoleum product made from linseed oil. The durable, easy-to-clean flooring has a vintage marbled look and comes in many different colors, which can be cut and arranged to form a striking design. We spent quite a bit of time hanging around at greenspace, a local retail store that furnishes homeowners and contractors with healthier materials that have a lower footprint on the earth. Lydia, the store owner, has a background in kitchen design and is passionate about green. She is a trusted resource in the community for those seeking paint, flooring, bedding, cleaning products, tile, countertops, and other products that are aligned to her sustainability values. She also hosts events at her store, showing films or featuring a panel of contractors discussing green aspects of their practice.

While we did online research on materials and got a good idea of what we wanted to choose, being able to touch and feel the sample material made a difference. It made it real for us. Lydia would allow us to "check out" sample pieces the same way the library would allow you to check out a book. We would take those sample pieces to the house and look at them in different light—dull, foggy morning light, late afternoon low-angle light, and fluorescent light at night. What looked good in the store may have a different feel at home. We noted our first choices (2498 Willow Green for the master bathroom and 2607 Marble White for the hallway bathroom) in my notebook after viewing them in different light conditions.

Integrated design and initial estimate

Once the general layout and a draft of the specifications were done, we asked Taylor Darling of Santa Cruz Green Builders to give us an estimate of what this design would cost us. We met Taylor a month after we finalized the contract with Graham. Initially we didn't reach out to the company because they seemed rather young when we checked out their website. Our impression was correct: Taylor was born the year Kurt graduated from college. Born and raised in Kauai, Taylor exuded the friendly feel of the Hawaiian islands. He has a bachelor's degree in political science from the University of California at Santa Cruz and chose to express his environmental beliefs through the construction business. Often general contractors will use subcontractors for common trades like plumbing and electrical work, but he does it himself. He and his business partner Spencer Keenan have a talented and dedicated crew. Their first and foremost criteria for hiring an employee is that they are a good person. We liked that.

Word of mouth and testimonials won us over. Our friend Dave raved about them. Dave had recently had his house built by Santa Cruz Green Builders. It embodied many different green elements and it was a green builder's dream project. Taylor showed interest when we told him that we were pursuing the rigorous Passive House Standard and we wanted to hire him as a consultant during the design phase to have him provide a builder's perspective through the design process. He was open to this arrangement and looked forward to bidding on the project when the design was done.

We launched the integrated design phase with a conference call with Taylor and Graham. With Graham being a two-hour drive away it wasn't practical to have a face-to-face meeting. But the email conversations that followed the introduction call proved that the conference call was just as effective in building a working relationship.

Graham is a certified passive house consultant, certified green building professional, LEED accredited professional, and an architect. He keeps himself up to date on Passive House and high-performance buildings by attending conferences, reading, and networking. Taylor is a licensed general contractor and he prefers to read articles and watch videos to learn about new materials, methods, and construction techniques. I could see their complementary styles with a common passion toward green building working out nicely. Graham would send Taylor links to Passive House articles like the "Cost Effective Passive House as European Standard" or an article on method to fasten furring strings to sheathing through foam insulation. Taylor would suggest things from his experience like having the deck height be a half inch lower than the finished floor height to ensure a smooth transition and avoid a tripping hazard. When we considered whether to raise the roof height of the 1947 addition (master bathroom and closet) to match the main house, Taylor took measurements and answered Graham's question of whether the existing structure had adequate space for insulation. Ultimately the decision was ours to raise the roofline or not. We didn't. Observing the objective discussion between two professionals informed our decision.

On a Thursday morning in March we saw Taylor's lanky frame striding toward the house. He greeted us with a friendly, "Hey, how's it going?" and a quick handshake. His presence conveyed confidence and competence. This was the day he arranged to have various subcontractors come over to examine the house so that they could bid on their portion of the work. The insulation guy, the drywall guy, the painter, the floor refinisher, the tile guy, and the Marmoleum lady showed up at different times during the day. They asked questions, took measurements, and left after letting Taylor know they'd get back with their bids soon.

A week later Taylor sent us an email. The estimate for Phase I, house remodel, was just under $300,000. We had the flexibility of repaving the driveway and rebuilding the garage in later phases of the project at an additional cost.

"Wow, this is doable!" I was excited.

"All right. Let's get to work on trimming costs," said Kurt, "Now that we know the baseline, we can finesse this."

Value engineering

Value engineering is the activity where you scrutinize the cost and ask:

Can we achieve the same result using a different method?

What would it cost if we replaced material x with material y?

Can we find a different source for this material?

Do we really need this?

In a new home (like the condo I bought in 1994) this value engineering activity had already been done for me by the real estate developer. I got to choose the different levels of finishes for an upgrade fee, but it was quite limited. The real estate developers and spec builders stay in business by being really good at minimizing cost and delivering high-perceived value.

When doing the remodel of our own house, the value engineering exercise of what to cut and what to change was not so black and white. Emotions and attachments come into play. My *ofuro* or soaking tub was one such item. I valued the experience of being able to soak up to my neck in hot water, much warmer than the limit on outdoor Jacuzzi. It wasn't energy efficient or water efficient compared to soaking in the bathtub in the hallway. But it was my splurge item.

Another item was countertop material. We knew many places at that time were having a fire sale on granite countertops. This was in 2010 when the housing industry was still struggling after the bust. Although we could have had granite countertops for much less, we selected PaperStone®. It's a product made from recycled paper held together by non-toxic resin. It comes in several different colors and we liked the dark mocha colored surface which matched the green recycled tile we'd found. Here again we made an intentional choice based on our personal value. Did we achieve much in the way of reducing cost in value engineering? Not really, but it reflected what we valued, and we felt good about making material choices that were durable, resulted in lower energy and water use, reused existing materials (even if more expensive than new materials in some cases), promoted good indoor air quality, reflected the aesthetics of 1920s period style, and had functions that met our lifestyle.

Working together as a couple

Midori gave us the opportunity to learn about each other. We'd been married for almost ten years when we started this project, but we'd never worked together professionally. We have different strengths, weaknesses, and working styles. We wondered if we would annoy each other. So far, our complementary skills have fallen into place. We gained appreciation and respect for each other as we navigated through the design phase.

Over the years I've learned to defer lighting and aesthetics to Kurt. With a lifelong passion for photography, Kurt's sense of light is second nature to him. He sees things through the lens of a discerning artist. Even if I'm confident of his aesthetic sense, I'm pleased when he asks me for my opinion. I take on the lead role in contract review, bill payment, and record keeping. When we need to make a decision on something, I run it by him first. We implicitly follow the rule of "no surprises." We had heard about people who had the worst moments of their marital life during home remodels and used this strategy to make it through the project and remain happily married to each other.

What we learned in designing for life style and budget

Design is the expression of our values. It's the ultimate exercise to clarify our personal values and make sure they are represented in the places where we'll live.

❖ Home inspection report and testing for toxic material is like getting a physical check-up and lab tests to know the current condition.

❖ Simplicity and craftsmanship of Arts and Crafts style set our theme and made the aesthetic choices clear.

❖ We appreciated that Passive House Standard is architecture agnostic—it doesn't dictate the look and feel of the building.

❖ Regulations change over time and are meant to keep occupants safe, which means a barely passing grade from performance perspective.

❖ Visualizing what we do in each room defines design elements.

❖ Integrated design informs decision making.

❖ We don't need to buy everything up front, but choosing appliances and materials up front provides a more accurate estimate.

❖ Getting a good estimate at the design phase avoids sticker shock.

6
Researching and Specifying Materials

Making the list

It was fun to look through websites, magazines, and books to get ideas and learn what to do and what not to do. At some point we had to stop looking and choose among many options. Some were easy. Some were clever. In reality the research, selection, and purchasing activities spanned more than two years as we considered wood, doors, cabinets, appliances, lighting, and more. As specific items were entered on the materials selection list and the specification document, we felt a small sense of relief and closure.

Making green and happy choices

We often asked ourselves, "How do we know we'll end up with a house that we feel good about living in?" We didn't leave it entirely to chance. First we got clear on what was important to us.

At this point we knew what activities would take place in each room. We had a good idea of what we wanted for the look and feel of the place. We wanted the house to be made of materials that were good for us and kind to the planet.

Most of all, we wanted the operational performance to be pretty darn good. For us pretty darn good meant comfortable air temperature, good air quality, quiet, minimal gadgets, low energy use, low water use, low maintenance, and a house that made our lifestyle feel seamless. We wanted all the stuff that made us happy had to be translated into a set of documents. We felt the more explicit we could be with our specific choices, the better off we'd be.

In the specification document we listed the details that were important to us. For example:

- We preferred re-use and deconstruction over demolition and disposal.
- We wanted the toilets to be plumbed from two sources—one from a filtered rainwater catchment tank and the other from the city supply.
- For the two-way, three-way, and four-way push button light switches, plugs, and Arts and Crafts cover plates, we specified oil-rubbed bronze from http://www.rejuvenation.com or equivalent (and so forth).
- What type of nails to use to frame the house? We'll let the contractor decide that. What type of towel rack to install? We wanted to choose that.

The question that came up from having such a detailed list was, "Who buys it? The contractor or the homeowner?" We made a column on our Material Selections list on Google Docs spreadsheet and labeled it "owner-furnished." We used this to keep track of what we wanted and shared it with our architect and builder throughout the design process. For items for which the contractor could get better pricing and could warranty the installation (like sheetrock and windows), we indicated the contractor would purchase.

There were over fifty items on the materials selections list that were our responsibility to buy: Murphy bed, lighting fixtures, house numbers, mailbox, sinks, plumbing fixtures, and so on. Taylor called these owner-furnished/contractor-installed (OFCI) items. For us the deciding factors to put something on the OFCI list was whether or not it was a good use of the contractor's time to research and buy the things we wanted and whether they had access to better pricing. When the dust settled the fifty or so items on our list turned out to be about $50,000.

We also thought about contingencies and identified second and third choices for some items. If the clothes washer and dryer combo we set our sights on during the design phase was not available a year later when it was time to install them, we could simply go with a fallback choice rather than scramble at the last minute. What we didn't know was when to buy them. If we tried to do a just-in-time procurement and some items weren't available when the construction crew needed them, we would be holding up construction. If we bought everything all at once, we wouldn't have a place to store everything. We figured we'd work out the timing when the construction started. Kurt is especially good at hunting for deals and making purchases happen in a timely manner, so I wasn't worried.

Navigating green

Deciding what to put on the material selections list spreadsheet was straightforward sometimes and at other times not so easy. We wanted to be good green citizens of this earth, but the sheer number of all the good things we could do felt overwhelming at times. To keep our sanity, we kept our focus on energy reduction. Passive House Standard guided us down this path. For other areas, we used our personal values and priorities to decide what to install in the house.

Making decisions based on energy efficiency is relatively straightforward. The energy efficiency and rating data of equipment or an appliance is readily available. So is data on thermal performance. Insulation materials, windows, and doors have R-values. We felt good about making quantitative, rational decisions when performance ratings were available. Choosing materials based on indoor air quality criteria was more difficult.

Sure, we knew to avoid chemicals like formaldehyde that can be toxic, allergenic, and carcinogenic. Formaldehyde and other chemicals are referred under the umbrella of volatile organic compounds (VOC). This means the chemical has a low boiling point and it evaporates at room temperature. This evaporation is commonly referred to as off-gassing.

Off-gassing construction materials may include plywood, particle board, paints, varnishes, carpets, adhesives, solvents, varnishes, upholstery fabric, vinyl flooring, sealing caulks, and more. In other words, a lot of stuff contains VOCs. Each chemical in the VOC category in different concentrations has different health effects. To make it simpler for consumers to make healthier choices, manufacturers of paint and other products label their products as zero-VOC or low-VOC.

I knew that reviewing manufacturer's Material Safety Data Sheet (MSDS) could help us make informed decisions on what to bring into the house. The MSDS themselves don't tell you whether or not to avoid a specific material. They are provided by the manufacturer to inform people working with the product what chemicals are in it and advise them of procedures for handling and working with the substance. The difficult to pronounce chemical names are all listed on the MSDS, and with some research, we could make our own decisions. I felt like I needed to understand a lot more about chemistry (a subject I did not enjoy in high school) to make sense of it.

At the time we didn't know about the research commissioned by Bill Hayward of Hayward Lumber. He and his family suffered various ailments caused by the house they moved into in 2008. Even a well-respected expert in green building like Bill can fall prey to sick buildings, even in a luxury home on the Monterey Peninsula. After his experience, he commissioned research to identify products that were both high performance and non-toxic. He hired experts to review the MSDS, product performance, and to interview manufacturers and chemists to come up with this evaluated products list. If we were to do our house project today, we would reference the evaluated product list on

Hayward Healthy Homes website (http://haywardhealthyhome.
com) as a starting point.

Even without having the Hayward Healthy Homes list, reading the chemicals listed in the safety data sheet was enlighten-
ing. If the MSDS identified certain ingredients as "proprietary" or
"trade secret," that was a red flag. Manufacturers are not obliged
to reveal what is proprietary. We didn't know what was in them
and whether they were toxic or not.

If we were to do it over again, we would still focus on energy
and refer to the evaluated products list from Hayward Healthy
Homes. Perhaps we'd choose the same materials. We would be
more vigilant about researching and verifying the manufacturer's
specification data sheet to flag and avoid "bad stuff."

Another aid in finding out if a material is "bad" is the Red
List from the International Living Future Institute. For their Living
Building Challenge program, they specify various chemicals to
avoid with the intention to create a materials economy that is
non-toxic, ecologically regenerative, transparent, and socially
equitable. The chemicals on the Red List can be found on https://
living-future.org/redlist. Asbestos, lead, formaldehyde, and volatile organic compounds mentioned in previous chapters are on the
Red List along with other chemicals with different toxicity levels
and effects. Had we known about this list we would have used it
to further scrutinize the manufacturer's data sheet.

The advice given by homeowner Cyndi struck a chord during materials research: "When you reach the point of 'I just don't
care, do whatever' is exactly when you do need to care. Be sure to
save a reserve of patience for that moment." Patience and energy
are needed at the point of decision fatigue. Though we heard this
early on and knew that it was coming, knowing about it didn't
ease the pain.

Wood products

Midori was mostly made out of wood, which probably came from
the local forests. Ninety years later, Midori needed new wood for

her new decks, replacement sheathing, framing repairs, and decorative accents. Although wood is a renewable resource, if it's not managed in a sustainable fashion, it can be depleted or cause harm to the local community and the environment it's harvested from. We felt the responsible thing to do was to make sure that the lumber used in the construction project came from a source that was managed in a sustainable fashion.

A simple way to specify lumber is to ask for wood that has Forest Stewardship Council (FSC) certification. Just as there are organic certification labels on various produce at the grocery store, FSC is the label that conveys the lumber can be used with a clear conscience. There is overhead associated with the certification, so it does cost more, and some companies that practice good sustainable forestry may choose not to get certification for their products. Although we chose to go with FSC certified wood for Midori, if we were to do it over again we might simply do a bit more research on the practices of local lumber companies such as Big Creek Lumber and forego the certification label.

Concrete

About four miles away from Midori, at the top of the single track trail in Pogonip City Park, is a piece of local history—a lime kiln. Around 150 years ago limestone was quarried in Santa Cruz and used for building materials throughout the region. Each lime kiln was fired by using about 140 cords of locally harvested wood to cook the limestone at somewhere between 1,500 and 2,400°F in a six-day process. Cooked limestone is used to make Portland cement. Very likely Midori's original porch, footers, and foundation were made using local cement from these quarries.

Making cement is an energy- and resource-intensive process. To make it greener, fly ash is used to reduce the amount of lime needed. Fly ash is ash leftover from burning coal in a power plant, and it makes the concrete more durable and stronger. Using fly ash in the cement for Midori's additional foundation around the mechanical room and the footers for the deck posts made sense, at least on the surface. We specified a minimum of 25 percent fly ash and ended up using a 35 percent fly ash mixture from Graniterock.

Through this process we learned that what looks to be green may not be. Later, when we looked at the interactive map on the EIA website, we noticed that there are hardly any coal-fired power plants in California. In fact, the nearest coal-fired plants are hundreds or thousands of miles away, which means we used more energy and created pollution to transport the fly ash. What appears to be a simple green decision to use fly ash in concrete can become more nuanced based on where one lives in relation to a coal plant (and if fly ash from that plant is used in the cement).

Fiberglass doors

Wooden doors would be right in line with Midori's Arts and Crafts style and there were many manufacturers and styles of wooden doors to choose from. Still, those choices didn't quite have the performance we were looking for. The older wooden doors had an R-value of about two. Fiberglass doors with polyurethane foam cores had R-values double or triple the older wooden doors. We valued energy efficiency and low maintenance, so Graham pointed us toward fiberglass doors.

The search for our fiberglass front door started with Therma-Tru. Then we looked at PlastPro and were able to go to a showroom in San Jose to touch and feel the door. Later we learned about ProVia, a company focused on old-world craftsmanship based in Ohio in the heart of the nation's largest Amish population. Kurt took charge of the online searches, making phone calls, and got pricing for the doors. Never having shopped for front doors before, we were surprised at how expensive they can be. In addition to having good R-value of 4.7, ProVia door fabrication included a lengthy process to stain and cure the finishes on the door at the factory. It was much more expensive than the others—almost twice as much. We thought we could buy a less expensive naked door from PlastPro at R-value of 3.7 and have the contractor stain

it after it was installed. We didn't fully appreciate the factory staining process until we moved into the house.

Our focus was on energy performance, ease of maintenance,
and cost. A fiberglass door with a polyurethane foam core provides energy-efficient insulation. In order to perform well, the
door needs to seal well too. Graham told us about the multi-
point locking system from Trilennium that secures the door into
the frame at three points. In addition to the bolt that engages
near the handle, there are two other bolts that solidly grip the
frame with a loud "ka-chunk" sound when the door handle is
pulled upwards. Visually I can see the door pressing a couple of
millimeters into the gasket when the door handle is pulled up.
In addition to helping the door keep its shape and fitting snugly
into the frame, the multi-point locking system greatly improves
the air sealing. It's also really secure. I can't imagine anyone
kicking the door down.

Of the different styles of doors from PlastPro, we chose the
Craftsman-themed Fir Grain Series model with simulated divided
lite (SDL) giving the look of muntins for the kitchen door. For the
front door we chose the Fir Grain Metropolis model. It has a dentil
shelf (small, repeating blocks) that adds to the Craftsman style.

Shoe box

Shoes-off home is great because it helps keep the floor cleaner. But
what do you do with the shoes? At our condo this practice resulted
in shoes cluttering the entrance area. Despite the neat shoe organiz-
ers in the bedroom closet, the entrance area becomes cluttered with
various footwear—running shoes, sandals, dress shoes, boots, and
flip-flops. I like the convenience of having the shoes by the door
but the visual clutter is annoying. How can we have both the convenience and a tidy look?

Creating a *getabako* in the entrance area was the simple solution to our problem. In a Japanese house the getabako is located
in the entrance area to store shoes. Once the sliding door to this
shoe cupboard closed, the visual clutter goes away. Since Arts and

Crafts style is influenced by Japanese aesthetics, having a getabako made perfect sense.

The problem was the ideal location was already spoken for. Kurt's large speakers were to be placed "just so" in the four corners of the living room for the audiophile in the house. This left no room for the getabako near the front door. What shall we do? Attempting to logically convince the other of the merits of one's pet feature until the other caves had the wrong energy. We had to think outside the box. Literally outside the box. Into the wall.

The solution evolved to become a piece of built-in furniture that recessed into the wall and protruded into the dining room. This made sense for us because the wall space was open during the remodel, and it was easy for the cabinet maker to create a custom shoe cupboard using the same type of wood as our kitchen cabinets. The front is flush with the wall so it doesn't conflict with the speaker space, and the back looks like a simple decorative stand. It turned out to be about the same price or cheaper than buying a nice piece of Craftsman furniture. Later this large floor speaker standing next to the recessed shoe box became a visual reminder of our ability to creativity solve a couple's conflicting priority problem.

Mudroom desk

Magazines, letters, bills, and junk mail seemed to enjoy having a conference on the kitchen table. We facilitate it by bringing in the stuff the mail delivery person drops off in our mailbox. Obvious junk mail receives priority handling and goes straight into the recycle bin. Other pieces of mail that need a decision require a temporary landing spot. The most convenient place is often the kitchen table. These mail pieces slowly grow into a stack that gets pushed around at mealtimes. The presence of the pile in our condo grated on our nerves.

"Feeling tidy" wasn't explicitly identified in our values exercise, but we felt it. As much as our lungs wanted to breathe clean air in the house, our eyes yearned for clutter-free space. There's only so much that can be achieved by saying, "If you promise to pick up after yourself, I will too." Forming new habits requires work. So we agreed on forming a new habit once we moved into the renovated Midori Haus by designating a place in the kitchen/mudroom (other than the kitchen counter) where mail could sit until disposed.

Our solution was a little built-in desk next to the pantry and the mudroom bench. The mail slots are at my eye level. This by the way is quite low since I'm only five feet tall. Each of the mail slots is labeled: Kurt, Chie, Household for utility bills and such, and Other for storing address labels for outgoing mail. Above the mail slots is cabinet space for storing office supplies such as printer paper, extension cords and such. There is a pull-out drawer under the mudroom desk where we can keep reference manuals for appliances.

We used the area under the desk to do more tidying and avoid the visual clutter of the networking equipment: router, modem, cables and such. Rather than installing wireless equipment, we chose to hardwire the network connections to various rooms to minimize exposure to wireless signals.

Kitchen cabinets

When it came to choosing kitchen cabinets, we did spend obligatory time at Home Depot, Lowe's, and Ikea because big box stores are good at providing value to their shoppers by offering a handful of choices within a reasonable price range. Using cabinets from the big box stores would be a savings over custom cabinets if we could make the modular standard dimensions fit into our G-shaped layout. But we found that two sinks of different sizes, a small oven, a slim dishwasher only eighteen inches wide, and a slim, tall fridge were not going to fit in the standard cabinet dimensions. Often the material used in those cabinets contained formaldehyde, a chemical we did not want.

In the end, we pursued custom cabinets after hours of gazing at the photos in *The Bungalow Kitchen* book. We especially liked the kitchen photos from a 1920 Bungalow in Seattle with Shaker-style cabinets in cherry wood. It had the nice period look that felt grounded and calming.

Selecting a custom cabinet maker wasn't really straight-forward. The referrals we got by word of mouth were for firms that did not have websites with pictures showing off their work. I imagine most of them did good work and did not need websites to bring in customers. We talked to a few, but getting prices over the phone from custom cabinet makers from remote locations when they have not visited the site felt a bit exposed. In the end we went with the custom cabinet maker Taylor recommended. Like the other cabinet makers we talked to, Richard Loughridge did not have a website, but he was only ten miles away and came to our house to take careful measurements and draw some simple sketches. It worked out beautifully.

Backsplash and tile

Choosing tile for the kitchen backsplash took a circuitous route. When Kurt's brother and his wife remodeled their house, they created a bright sun using mosaic tile as the backsplash behind the cooktop. We liked the idea of having tile artwork as part of our wall. So we looked at books on Arts and Crafts style. What appealed to me, though, was a postcard I found at the gift shop at Asilomar Conference Center in Monterey. We took the post-card to a local Arts and Crafts tile designer and commissioned her to come up with a tile design using the postcard as an inspiration. We wanted this artwork behind the large sink rather than the cooktop. The artist suggested having the theme from a backsplash feature wrap around the kitchen on all tile surfaces as a thin horizontal line.

We were excited when we got the design sketch, and we tried to visualize how this would look on the wall with the cherry cabinets and the mocha colored PaperStone® countertop. After holding up the image (colored with different color palettes) with sample pieces of cherry wood and the dark brown countertop in front of the backsplash space, we came to the sad conclusion that it wouldn't work. It would be too busy and would detract from the simplicity of the smallish kitchen.

We knew that having samples that we could see and touch was important, so we drove forty minutes to the showroom at Fireclay in San Jose. They had a wide array of samples of tile using recycled materials. These are locally produced in the town of Aromas, just twenty-five miles away from Santa Cruz. After sitting with us to go over the dimensions and colors of the kitchen cabinet and countertop, the sales lady encouraged us to check out their sample room. Thousands of tiles in different textures and colors were organized in boxes according to style and color. Walking through the rows of shelves, we picked out sample tiles of different hues and shades. After filling out a sample checkout form, we headed home with a small, heavy box filled with different styles of off-white, blue, and green tiles.

We placed the different sample tiles next to the sample of cherry wood and the mocha countertop to make our choices. We both gravitated toward a light green color called "green kelp." Seeing the different tiles against the lighting in the kitchen validated our choice. I updated the material selections spreadsheet with the kelp green color in the Debris Series of tile from Fireclay and returned the samples.

The other place where we specified tile was the shower in the master bathroom. We liked the Green Tech brown tile from Ergon, a company that makes engineered stone.

Pre-rinse spray

It was a good thing we kept the backsplash tile simple because we ended up choosing a commercial pre-rinse spray that stood twenty-four inches high. This functional and water-conserving plumbing fixture would have detracted from any decorative backsplash. The path toward this heavy duty pre-rinse spray, the type seen at the back of restaurants, started with an inspiration at a friend's kitchen. She had a sleek, spray-rinse fixture designed for residential kitchens. It was elegantly designed and looked lovely on her island sink, and she loved it. When we started pricing them out, we were surprised by how expensive they were. The big box stores carried inexpensive ones where the spray fixture built into the faucet could be pulled out to spray and retracted back in. They seemed flimsy.

Swinging the durability pendulum over from flimsy to rugged, we landed on the online pages of commercial pre-rinse spray assemblies. These products are valued for functional performance and durability in commercial kitchens. We figured that since the models and styles don't change much, replacement parts would be available for decades. The powerful sprays would be perfect for cleaning cutting boards, large pots, cast iron pans, and any large serving dishes. The dishwasher is water efficient, and having a powerful pre-rinse spray would help us conserve more water.

The main constraint we worked around when choosing a pre-rinse spray was making it fit in the space between the countertop and the bottom of the cabinet. I've seen some really tall pre-rinse spray fixtures. We needed something short. By looking over the configuration of the Fisher deck mounted pre-rinse spray diagrams, Kurt figured out that using the shortest riser and stainless steel flex line would make it fit.

Garbage disposal

We used to think that a garbage disposal was a standard appliance in the kitchen—like the refrigerator. After all, the purpose of the garbage disposal is to avoid clogging up the wastewater pipes. But where else would we put the fruit and vegetable peels and scraps from the dinner plate? Throwing them out in the trash can would make the experience of opening the trash can smelly. Better, we thought, would be a compost bin, because the non-meat food scraps could participate in the natural decaying process and return to the soil. (My tomato plants like the compost.) Diverting waste destined for the city landfill, however small, extends the life of the local landfill.

Simply trapping the solid material in the sink using a strainer and adding that to compost became the plan. It would help us save water used for flushing scraps through the disposal. Plus we would avoid using electricity for something that doesn't add value to our lives. We figured we wouldn't be helping the wastewater treatment plant by sending them a garbage disposal smoothie.

Appliances

Like most people, we spent a fair amount of time online choosing appliances and looking up energy usage, consumer reviews, functions, features, and comparison shopping between retailers. We focused on reliability, low energy usage, low water usage, and most importantly, the physical size. Since there are only two of us in the house, we don't need the largest capacity that a growing family requires. Space in the kitchen is tight. So is the space in the hallway closet where the washer and dryer will go. Essentially we were looking for appliances like me: small and compact.

The dishwasher was the easiest to pick because Miele's eighteen-inch-wide dishwasher performs well and has a good reputation. We would have loved to have a second dishwasher, but we had no space. One of the houses I visited on a home tour had two eighteen-inch-wide dishwashers. The Miele was for regular day-to-day use. The other, the cheapest one they could find, served as a drying rack. The owners abhorred the look of a drying rack cluttering their countertop space. Theirs was a pretty small kitchen, too, but their priority was on the second dishwasher. Our priority was to have a second sink. Different priorities, different solutions. Both sets of homeowners are happy with their choices.

Refrigerator: What made Kurt happy with the Miele refrigerator was the visibility of the contents. With eighteen lights showering the contents in a warm glow and clear glass offering views through the shelves, it would be difficult for a pickle jar to get lost in the dark. It's a slim fridge, only thirty inches wide, and it's tall. With the freezer configured on the bottom, the top shelf of the fridge is above my reach. This suits Kurt fine because that's where he'll store his stash of treats and food I don't like to eat.

We saw the demonstration of the induction cooktop at the Miele showroom in San Francisco. As explained in Chapter 5, we liked seeing and touching the appliance. It makes it more real than looking at pictures online. We also liked asking questions in the showroom rather than being engaged by someone from who knows where via online chat. It was important to us to see the product before we made the decision, so we visited a handful of different stores in Santa Cruz, San Jose, and San Francisco. The key point we remembered from the kitchen remodel class we took was to get clarity on the power sharing and power boost capabilities of the induction cooktop because the promotional literature can be misleading. If we were simply replacing a gas cooktop with an induction cooktop without changing the wiring in the house, the capacity of the wire would determine the size of the cooktop to be installed. Since Midori's existing wiring did not meet the current building code, we'd be changing out all the wiring. We just had to make sure the induction cooktop was on a dedicated circuit and the wiring matched the power needed by the cooktop.

Vent hood: We wanted a vent hood to remove cooking odors. We narrowed our focus to a recirculating vent hood because we were concerned about meeting our airtightness goal for Passive House. Most homes are equipped with kitchen vent hoods that are ducted and exhaust to the outside. In a Passive House the ducted vent hoods require a mechanism for controlling air flow while maintaining airtightness. We chose the ductless recirculating vent hood to avoid complexity and eliminate the external penetration. The recirculating or non-ducted vent hood sucks the air above the cooking surface through its charcoal filters and pushes the air further upwards until it escapes through narrow vents near the ceiling. Basically it's scrubbing the air, not evacuating it. The choice was really easy from a selection of one, because of the two recirculating vent hoods we saw, only the Kobe model came in the island style. We actually liked the Vent-A-Hood model better because it had a larger charcoal filter and we thought it would do a better job of controlling the cooking odor, but it only came in the wall-mounted style.

Washer and dryer: We chose the stackable set from Bosch. The front loading washer is very water efficient. The small capacity is perfectly fine for the two of us. The small and compact form factor was the most important criteria since it would need to fit into the hallway closet next to the heat recovery ventilator.

Steam oven

We liked the idea of having a convection steam oven for taste, health, energy savings, and convenience. Steam transfers heat food more quickly than air can so less energy is needed for cooking. Water also can hold more heat than air.

A smaller oven cavity saves energy too. My experience with ovens in the past was limited to free-standing ranges thirty inches wide with an oven below the stove top. The oven cavity is usually about 4.5 cubic feet. Since only a small portion of the space was used for baking cookies, cakes, or lasagna, most of the heat was wasted. Having a smaller oven would be perfect for us. We'd use less energy to heat the smaller oven cavity, and need less time to pre-heat it.

Annual energy usage for a refrigerator is easy to estimate because it runs consistently throughout the year, but the annual energy usage of an oven is much more difficult to estimate. Annual energy use for an oven is highly dependent on the usage. It makes a big difference if it's used daily to bake bread or if it's not used for baking and has been relegated as storage space. I love to bake cookies and cakes often, so my oven usage falls in the medium-heavy range of the usage scale. A smaller-cavity oven represents greater energy savings for a baker than a non-baker.

Further, a smaller size makes it easier install at the countertop level built into the cabinet. I never cared much for doing a half squat over the hot oven door. It was especially nerve wracking when I was holding a heavy water bath to make flan, my favorite custard dessert. I saw other advantages in having a steam oven. I could cook rice perfectly, so I wouldn't need a rice cooker or a vegetable steamer. A steam oven can be used for preserving food, eliminating the need to boil a large pot of water to do canning. Bottom line: it's a versatile, multi-purpose appliance just large enough for a two-person household.

Our first exposure to a steam oven was at the Miele showroom in San Francisco. The Miele convection steam oven had a nice user interface with preset functions: baking a cake, roasting a turkey, cooking rice, and others. Before committing to buying the first thing we saw, we wanted to compare another manufacturer's steam oven. A friend mentioned another German brand, Gaggenau. I hadn't heard of that brand before. Perhaps there's a reason I've not heard of it. Someone mentioned that if you have to ask the price, you can't afford a Gaggenau. Yikes! "Well, it doesn't hurt to just look," we told ourselves and headed over to Purcell Murray in Brisbane, California (not Australia).

Soft warm lighting bathed the beautiful luxurious kitchen layouts at the showroom. The elegant appliances from Bosch, Thermador, Gaggenau, and other high-end manufacturers' appliances stated their presence in an understated but commanding way. The Gaggenau steam oven sported thick glass and stainless steel, conveying easy cleaning. The control panel had two separate dials—temperature on the right, humidity on the left—and a touch screen for setting different programs. Most functions could be easily set by a turn of the dial rather than having to press through a maze of screens. We really liked that it offered more flexibility and control over cooking the different dishes than the steam oven from Miele where the preset programs controlled the temperature and humidity. I flinched when the sales lady stated the list price. It was a lot more than the already expensive Miele steam oven, and nothing about this place said, "let's bargain."

The Midori Haus purchasing department did not let that deter him. "Shop hard!" was Graham's advice, and Kurt took that to heart. A few days after our visit to the fancy showroom, he found a lightly used Gaggenau steam oven on eBay. The seller was another fancy kitchen showroom in Atlanta that was replacing their Gaggenau steam oven with a newer model. It had been used in a demonstration setting and kept in good condition in their showroom. Half price. But it still cost more than a convection oven by GE or Kenmore. The notion of being able to steam fish, veggies and add a touch of moisture to cakes was so very appealing that we bid on the eBay listing. Nobody else did.

Weeks later it arrived on a pallet and we took it over to the local appliance service center to have it tested. Three days later when the technician told us it was working fine, we breathed a sigh of relief. We had them pack it up again and we moved it into the storage shed next to Midori's detached garage where it sat for ten months.

Lighting fixtures

Lighting fixtures sat in the storage shed for a long time too. Not wanting to miss out on year-end sales, Kurt placed an order for most of the lighting fixtures from an online retailer, The Bright Spot. They arrived a little after Christmas, about nine months before we needed them. Our neighbor, well-experienced in remodels, turned us onto http://thebrightspot.com where we found a good selection of Arts and Crafts style lighting fixtures with good prices. Like with appliance shopping, we did visit specialty stores that carried lighting fixtures, but the physical selection of Arts and Crafts lighting fixtures was limited. In this case online shopping fully met our needs.

Our primary focus on choosing lighting fixtures was the aesthetics of the Arts and Crafts style. For energy efficiency we planned to use the screw-in type LED light bulbs. Achieving energy efficiency for lighting was easy as long as the lighting fixture was built to take conventional screw-in bulbs. Kitchen lighting a was a bit more difficult because the California Title 24 Code required 50 percent of total kitchen lighting wattage use high-efficiency fixtures. This meant we couldn't pick lighting fixtures that accepted the old incandescent bulbs. So we settled for a lighting fixture that took a tubular fluorescent lamp with three prongs that met the code.

Kurt chose the lighting fixtures and bulbs. I simply reviewed and agreed to his choices. This is an example of how the division of tasks fell into place based on our skills and interests. I felt at home in the role of accounts payable department and legal department as well as caterer delivering home baked treats to the construction site. But I was less confident with aesthetic choices. Kurt excelled in this area. He is also gifted in driving closure on open issues. Lighting is especially important to him because his eyes, with years of training in film photography, see colors and textures that I only vaguely grasp. Kurt really got into the Arts and Crafts aesthetics. The simple beauty of stained wood displayed in understated elegance to honor the craftsmanship that conveys attention to detail felt grounding. The simple yet elegant styling of the lighting fixtures he chose complemented the wood.

Adding built-in furniture

Built-in furniture is an enduring expression of using beautiful wood to serve a practical purpose. The original example in the house was the buffet in the dining room. After we decided to add a shoe box built-in between the living room and the dining room to solve the shoe clutter problem, we asked ourselves: Are there other opportunities to de-clutter with built-in furniture? Yes: our books, compact discs, and photography stuff. These objects show our varied interests and are important to Kurt. We wanted them to be stored neatly with the simple look of wood providing a sense of calm.

The hallway was wide enough to have a built-in bookshelf without feeling cramped. We chose the space between the living room door and Kurt's office door for the bookshelf. Kurt figured out the dimensions that would optimize storage for his collection of books and sketched it out to have the cabinet maker build it. I couldn't envision a place for a built-in bookshelf for my set of books. So I decided I would use a portable Ikea shelf until I figured it out.

We have quite a collection of CDs and some vinyl records too. In the past, our CDs lived in the dresser drawers in our bedroom. We made several reference visits in the neighborhood and were inspired by one person's vast CD collection. He filled several walls with open shelves specifically designed to store his large collection of CDs. We created a wall-mounted shelf and added doors and crown molding to give it the Craftsman Shaker-style cabinet look. The cabinet doors provide visual calm, and by installing a small latch on the doors, the contents will stay in the cabinets during an earthquake.

Earlier I mentioned we like to host slideshow parties. Kurt has slides, lots of them. So we designed built-in shelves inside the closet in Kurt's office to store the maximum number of slide boxes containing images from numerous trips and his arts photography. When the bi-fold closet door closes, even the yellow and black box containing a Kodak Carousel Transvue 140 slide tray will disappear from view.

Kurt's photography collection includes large-format photographs he printed in a darkroom. For these, we decided to use a slightly different configuration of the PAX system of wardrobe furniture from Ikea. The pull-out drawers are perfectly sized for storing large photographs, and the shelves are configurable to store additional items, again hidden from view once the sliding door is closed.

There was one more opportunity for built-in furniture—the vanity in the master bathroom. We wanted to have a vessel sink, the type that looks like a ceramic sink sitting on top of a table with the faucets protruding from the wall. Rather than looking for the perfect vanity from a catalog, we chose to have one made with the same material we chose for the kitchen cabinet and countertop. For us this turned out to be cheaper than buying something pre-made.

Murphy bed

Following the principle of choosing space wisely as described in *Not So Big House* by Sarah Susanka, we kept the footprint of the house the same and did not increase the size of the house. We thought about making use of the attic space, but that wouldn't add much value to the house and it would be a hassle to put in stairs and have the foundation and framing beefed up. But what about space for visitors? Realistically, a guest room would likely be occupied by family and friends 2 percent of the time. We are not operating a bed and breakfast, so don't need a dedicated room for guests. Office space, on the other hand, would be used almost daily.

Installing a Murphy bed was a good solution because it could transform a space to serve dual purposes. We chose a Murphy bed that looks like a classic Arts and Crafts cabinet from Wilding Wallbeds. The matching desk, night stand, and filing cabinet in the same cherry wood and Shaker style fit Midori's character perfectly. We also purchased a mattress from them designed specifically for Murphy beds. Most mattress lie flat like a pancake all the time, but a mattress that is used in a Murphy bed stands on its side most of the time. It's important that this mattress be designed for upright storage to avoid bulging or slumping at the head.

Wall layout is important to consider. If we were fitting a Murphy bed into an existing room, we'd be limited in where we could install the bed. It wouldn't work well against a window or a closet. Since we were replacing the walls, we had the opportunity to design the windows to perfectly flank the Murphy bed.

This Murphy bed and furniture ensemble presented cost savings because we didn't have to create an addition to the house for a guest room.

Toilets

A while back water districts provided incentives to replace older 6 gallons per flush toilets with 1.6 gallons per flush toilets. We went further than that to conserve water. We chose the Stealth toilet after talking to a representative of Niagara Conservation Corporation we met at the water conservation conference hosted by our utility company, Pacific Gas & Electric. It seems funny now to think back and realize that we selected this without physically looking at the product in a showroom. We saw the specs on a brochure that said 0.8 gallons per flush and watched a video on YouTube of a guy demonstrating how effectively Niagara Stealth works by flushing handful of colorful jelly tubes. The air pressure assisted flush seemed to work well and the reviews were favorable.

An alternative to this was to use a dual-flush type of toilet where there are two separate buttons—one for liquid waste and one for solid waste. Based on the combined usage, this would turn out to average about 1.2 gallons per flush. We figured that if the Niagara Stealth didn't work for us, we could replace it with the dual-flush toilet later.

If we were truly hardcore about saving water, we would have gone with composting toilets and not use any water to flush toilets. But we decided we weren't ready for that yet.

Ofuro

Every house has that one weird thing the homeowners obsess about. For me it was the experience of soaking in a tub of hot water up to my chin. A standard bathtub like the one in the hallway bathroom just doesn't cut it. It's too small and not deep enough. But the tiny space allotted for the master bathroom couldn't accommodate a large tub.

Graham suggested an outdoor hot tub. "I can relate to wanting to soak in hot water at the end of the day," he said. "I have a small Jacuzzi on my deck and I use it few times a week." An outdoor hot tub was worth an exploration, I thought. "If you insulate it well, it won't take much energy to keep it warm," Graham advised. "There are ways of keeping the water clean without chemicals too."

For me the memories of soaking in a wooden tub in our tiny apartment as a child in Japan brought up nostalgia. Traveling to various *onsen* or hot springs triggered relaxing and calming feelings as well. I wanted those feelings, but I was disappointed when we went to the local hot tub store. The outdoor hot tubs did not meet my need because of a safety feature that prevents the water from being heated above 105°F. I was looking forward to soaking in 110°F. I saw more reasons not to go for the outdoor hot tub, and putting in chemicals to keep the water clean and using energy to maintain the water temperature just below my desired temperature was not worth it.

I needed a deep, soaking tub, and I wanted to fill it with hot water heated by the sun. My inspiration came from a local Japanese woman who had remodeled her house to include the traditional

Japanese wooden tub. She had laid out her bathroom in a Japanese style with the shower on the outside. She even ordered heating elements from Japan and had her contractor install everything to her specification. We didn't have the space to create what she had so we kept looking.

Searching for places to buy tubs led us to a large warehouse in Fremont called Tubz. They have hundreds of different types of bathtubs displayed on the showroom floor. Most kitchen and bath showrooms have limited space and highlight only a handful of items they carry. Tubz has a unique advantage over boutique kitchen and bath shops because customers can get a sensory answer to the question, "How does it feel to be in the tub?" as opposed to looking through a catalog and interpreting the dimensions. I could take off my shoes and sit in one tub, then hop over into the next one and the next. After a few of them I figured my time was better spent looking for the deepest tubs and stepping into those.

After two visits there we decided on the MTI Yubune tub that lets two people sit in it comfortably. We ended up getting a good deal by paying cash on the discontinued floor model. Ordinarily this would get built into a bathroom with a custom tile enclosure built to fit the tub. Since we didn't have room in our master bath, this tub would go on the back deck right outside of the master bedroom. Eventually there would be landscaping and furniture on the deck to provide for peaceful soaking in moonlight.

Insulation and layers of clothing

Although I've used the analogy of a sweater to convey the importance of insulation, it wasn't exactly like shopping for a cardigan or blazer at Macy's for Midori to make her look pretty. It was akin to shopping for long johns or thermal underwear, because we wouldn't see the insulation when Midori's transformation was complete. Performance mattered more than looks.

The "hat" (the insulation in the attic) was simple. Blown-in cellulose insulation fit the cost-performance bill for the attic since we were keeping our nine-foot ceiling in the rooms and the generous vented attic. The distribution ducts from the heat recovery ventilator snaked over the ceiling joist before dropping into the wall cavity. We wanted these ducts in the ceiling to be buried in the cellulose to minimize heat loss in the winter and heat gain in the summer.

Midori's layers of sweater and jacket was a little more complex, but not unconventional. We wanted her to wear dense packed cellulose insulation in the wall cavity between the drywall and the sheathing. For her "windbreaker," we chose exterior sheathing made of oriented strand board (OSB) which is made of strands of wood held together by synthetic resin so the panels are suitable for load bearing applications like flooring and wall sheathing. These panels were adhered to the framing using a sealant and then nailed to the studs.

On the outside of the OSB sheathing, we chose a roofing material, TopRock DD from Roxul, a mineral fiber insulation comprised of volcanic rock and recycled slag (by-product of steel and copper industries). Since it doesn't contain any nutrients for mold to grow in, we wouldn't have to worry about it getting wet. If it did, the mineral wool would eventually dry out and would continue to perform well. Another benefit of mineral wool insulation is fire resiliency. If we used a rigid foam product for the exterior insulation, it would release chemicals if it burned in a fire. Mineral wool insulation won't burn. It's made out of rock fibers. The problem with this material is availability. It's manufactured in Canada and not readily available through the local building supply stores. (They've created a manufacturing facility in the Mississippi since we renovated Midori.)

On top of the mineral wool is the house wrap, which is like a raincoat to keep out the moisture that comes through siding. Finally, on her outer layer Midori sports Hardie Planks, cement fiber planks. These were installed in a horizontal layer fastened to the furring strips on top of the house wrap and the rigid mineral wool. This took a bit of detailed carpentry because we asked the contractor to give Midori a cute flared-out skirt in the period style. The combination of these materials provided another benefit of Midori's thick outerwear: soundproofing.

For the first ninety years of her life, Midori only wore flip-flops on her feet. We were about to outfit her with warm socks and waterproof shoes. Deciding on how to go about doing this was interesting. During the design phase, Taylor brought an insulation subcontractor over to the house for a meeting, and Graham participated via speaker on the mobile phone. We had explored methods of creating a solid air barrier under the floor joist as well as filling the cavity with some sort of insulation material. We asked about stapling a plastic sheet on the bottom of the floor joist and filling the cavity by using a long hose to blow in cellulose. Maybe, we said, it'd be better to manually tack fiberglass batts in the floor joist cavity and nail large pieces of plywood to cover up the bottom of the floor joist if we could get the plywood under the floor.

The insulation sub siting across the table didn't seem enthused. Spray foam. That's all this sub wanted to consider. He extolled the virtues: performance of R-5 to R-6 per inch, good air sealing, less labor. Alternative methods would require having someone wriggle around the crawl space for days. Graham cited projects that used spray foam that did not air seal well. That information would elicit a note of panic in those who have worked on Passive House projects. Every last bit of CFM reduction counts when the airtightness target is 0.6 ACH_{50}. But to those who are unfamiliar with Passive House, the reaction is, "What's the big deal with a few CFMs here and there? Spray foam would deliver tight enough air sealing results."

60 years carbon payback

Kurt and I wanted to avoid spray foam for another reason: to minimize greenhouse gas emissions. A few months earlier, in a lecture at the Pacific Energy Center in San Francisco, Alex Wilson (whose Environmental Building News & GreenSpec newsletter is held in high regard) shared a story of an environmentally conscious homeowner. Like us, this homeowner wanted to reduce the greenhouse gas emissions from his electricity usage and remodeled his home to make it energy efficient. He chose closed-cell spray foam to provide air sealing and insulation. It was only after the job was complete that he learned that the chemical used to mix the spray foam onsite releases a greenhouse gas much more potent in its global warming impact than carbon dioxide. He calculated the length of time it would take to repay the greenhouse gasses released into the atmosphere from using spray foam with the greenhouse gasses avoided by using less energy at his energy-efficient house. It turned out to be 60 years. Ouch!

Learning vicariously through another homeowner's experience is valuable. That homeowner did the best he knew at that point in time and gave us a gift by sharing his knowledge. We took that lesson to heart and chose not to use spray foam. We know that we all make decisions based on the information we have at that time and move on. Otherwise we could be waiting forever the perfect timing and perfect information. We'll probably make our share of mistakes along the way too. We'll be sure to share them.

What we learned in researching and specifying materials

Thinking through the daily flow of our lives clarified our need for specific built-in furniture, plumbing fixtures, and appliances. While these are installed toward the end of the construction, knowing the requirements up front at the design phase ensures installation will be smoother. Avoid regrets by doing detailed research.

❖ Keep track of owner-supplied material using a spreadsheet.

❖ Green encompasses a wide range of attributes such as conserving water, lowering carbon footprint, sustainable stewardship of renewable material, promoting good indoor air quality, reducing waste, and responsible supply chain practices.

❖ Pick a focus (we chose energy) and drive decisions around that focus to keep sanity.

❖ Refer to evaluated products list from Hayward Healthy Homes to choose materials and systems that promote good indoor air quality.

❖ Choose wood that is managed and harvested in a sustainable way: either do your own research on a lumber company's practices or look for FSC certification.

❖ Fly ash mixed in with concrete is greener if you live near a coal power plant.

❖ Multi-point locking system on doors provides physical security as well as superior air sealing.

❖ Fiberglass doors perform well, thermally speaking.

❖ A Murphy bed helps create a multi-purpose room.

❖ Whenever possible borrow sample pieces (tile, flooring, countertop) and place them together in the kitchen or the bathroom to see if it works.

❖ Fancy appliance showrooms go through periodic updates and lightly used appliances may be found online.

❖ An induction cooktop requires a dedicated circuit and existing wiring may not be adequate to deliver the power needed.

❖ Vent hoods typically exhaust kitchen air outside of the house and the heat is lost.

❖ Recirculating vent hood used in conjunction with the heat recovery ventilator can remove cooking odor, though it takes longer than a conventional vent hood.

❖ Check the local building code on whether they require lighting fixtures that specifically reject incandescent bulb.

❖ Save water by using air pressure-assisted flush toilets.

❖ Choice of material, such as walls and insulation, locks us into the performance, benefit, and consequence of using that material for the life of that material, up to thirty years or longer.

❖ Let the house wear the sweater and windbreaker (insulation and air barriers) so you don't have to wear outerwear clothing inside the house.

❖ Scrutinize foam insulation and choose based on what's important.

❖ Think outside of the box, maybe through a wall for built-in furniture.

❖ Save water and energy by not installing garbage disposals.

❖ Faucets used in commercial kitchens work in homes too.

7

Construction Agreement

Construction agreement

Construction phase is where the detailed design and specifications become reality. Before diving in, we took care to have a good construction agreement in place because it lowered our risk of overspending and made us feel better about ensuring the house transformation outcome. As we navigated the process, we learned what we needed to give the contractor to get a good bid, how to minimize our risks, how we can write our own contract, and more.

A new green building specialist

About the time we were getting ready to submit our plans to the city's building department for a permit, an unexpected email landed in my in-box.

"Uh oh, this is not good," I muttered as I scanned the email.

"What's wrong?" asked Kurt.

"Joe Fullerton is leaving the City of Santa Cruz and there's a new Green Building Specialist."

"Damn! We thought we had the inside champion to shepherd our plans to avoid hiccups. You just never know what they'll nitpick on."

We'd developed a good working relationship with Joe and he was interested in what we were doing. "He wants us to come in and meet his successor, Jennifer."

We met in the conference room in the city's building department. After the usual introductions and handshake, Joe gave Jennifer a synopsis of what we were trying to do with our house along with a brief overview of the Passive House Standard.

"We want to encourage homeowners like Kurt and Chie who are committed to building green. So we want to help them as much as we can," Joe said.

Jennifer held strong sustainability values and a bachelor's degree in construction management. Her practical experience with construction began early as she experienced home remodeling close and upfront as her parents undertook various remodel projects of their home. She seemed quite interested in our project.

We exchanged emails after that initial meeting. Jennifer pointed us to useful resources such as a salvage company and an upcoming free class from PG&E featuring the Thousand Home Challenge (THC), a program we were intrigued about. The goal of the Thousand Home Challenge is to demonstrate the potential to reduce total annual site energy consumption of existing North American homes by seventy percent or more. The Challenge has a collaborative community that shares information on different combinations and paths toward deep energy reduction. Energy efficiency, renewable resources, community-based solutions, and behavioral changes count toward reduction. The proof is in the pudding. In this case, the pudding is a year's worth of utility bills.

Submitting paperwork for the permit

On the morning of July 26, 2011, while hauling seven copies of our architectural plans up the stairs to the building department's counter on the second floor, I thought, "Huh, this took longer than I expected."

Eight months previously, when we signed the agreement for architectural and Passive House consulting services with Graham, we confidently told him, "We expect the permit process to take about four months because we're really focused on this and will make decisions quickly to move this along." We truly believed that. We felt we could move the design process much quicker than a typical homeowner full of work and family responsibilities. In retrospect, I can see that planning and design is not a straight function of time available. It's more about mindset and how we make decisions and our comfort level for making decisions based on less than perfect information.

Because we had no competing responsibilities, we spent more time digging into various aspects of the design to satisfy our thirst of learning and to be assured of performance. We were about to empty our savings with this remodel project, and that was scary. We wanted it to work. We wanted to be happy in the house we'd be living in for the rest of our lives. We wanted it to perform well. We wanted the systems and the materials to be durable and resilient. Getting the details right was critical, because we would not be able to afford a sequence of band-aid fixes, much less a major surgery of the house, a decade down the road because of some failure we didn't anticipate. This anxiety was amplified by the fact that neither of us had done anything like this before and we had no background in architecture or construction. So we were cautious and took the time to learn about building science and deliberate on material choices and systems.

While waiting for my name to be called at the counter after signing in, I worried about how much I'd have to pay for the permit. A while ago when we were considering building a brand new house, someone mentioned that a building permit averaged about $16,000. I blinked in disbelief when the inspector behind the counter asked me to write a check for $1,371.66. I was positively smiling when he told me that I'd have to pay the balance when I picked up the permit and the amount likely would be another $5,000 or $6,000.

That was great news. If the green building program really moved the process along and issued the permit quickly, I'd be even happier.

It didn't happen at the lightning speed I had imagined. We had over three hundred green points going into the process, way over the seventy points needed to get to the top of the pile for a plan check. We learned that building a working relationship with the green building specialist helped a little, but she had no influence over how the plan would be scrutinized if the work was contracted out to an outside engineering firm. Sixteen days after I submitted the plans, I got an email from CSG.

"Who the heck is CSG?" asked Kurt. There were thirty-one comments on the plan we'd submitted.

"Let's get this over to Graham and see what he says."

Graham didn't seem too surprised with the comments. Some of the comments were simple "crossing the t and dotting the i" work for Graham. Some items were a little more involved. Besides having architectural plans updated by Graham, we needed the structural engineer to update the three pages showing the details of the south-facing wall, foundation, and roof. Further clarification was needed from the mechanical engineer from Zehnder, the maker of the heat recovery ventilator system. It took a while to coordinate the correction details on our end before re-submitting the plans.

The second round of plan checks went in around the time that Graham and his wife were having their second child. His taking time off didn't delay the process, and neither did Taylor taking time off for his wedding in June. We appreciated the fact that these guys managed to keep their life going without affecting their business and our schedule.

Bidders conference

As we were nearing the end of the second round of plan checks, we started working on contractor selection. We decided to hold a bidders conference, which meant sending out the plan and specifications to three companies that were on the short list and inviting them to a meeting at the house. We would give the same information to each bidder and we would answer their questions so that everyone got to hear the same information. We decided to have

Graham present in the meeting to explain Passive House Standard and the challenges of air sealing.

We put together the "invitation to bid package" consisting of a full set of architectural drawings, detailed specifications, the materials selection list, asbestos report, lead-based paint report, house inspection report, Passive House target summary, and an invitation letter describing the process. We ran the idea of a bidders conference past Gary. He said that contractors usually do bidders conferences for commercial projects. He felt that if the economy had been better, they might not be interested in this approach for our residential project. His advice: "Why not give it a try?"

On a sunny day in October, about a year after we'd bought the house, Kurt, Graham, and I were seated around the old dining room table with Jon representing Fiorovich Group, Ron representing Talmadge Construction, and Taylor representing Santa Cruz Green Builders. We shared documents, our philosophy, our goals, and the basics of Passive House. We introduced them to Midori and her quirks and charm.

They all left after having a look around the house and we eased into the waiting period before we got the bids. Soon after the bidders conference I heard back from Jeff Talmadge, who respectfully declined to bid. He'd had a death in his family and didn't feel able to work on a challenging project at that time. We appreciated him being straightforward on this.

We needed a new third bidder. We reached out to one of the companies listed on the Green Building Awards list. We invited the contractor over to the house, handed him the same packet of documents given to the other contractors, and gave him the Midori tour. He was friendly and definitely subscribed to sustainability values. He asked a few questions and went away to prepare his bid.

Contractor feedback

We knew the ballpark figure based on Taylor's earlier estimate, so we weren't worried about having sticker shock when the bids came in. What surprised and intrigued us were the questions from the contractors as they prepared their bids.

Each contractor had his own take and preferences. For example, Jon wanted to know about the interior doors. Reusing the existing interior doors would be more expensive than getting new doors that were pre-hung. He wanted to know if we were attached to reusing the interior doors that were just so-so? Hmm. We definitely wanted to reuse the crystal door knobs with the aged patina, but the door? Maybe not.

Jon also asked us if we were OK with the formaldehyde in the mineral wool. What? We did not pay attention to the material safety data sheet (MSDS) of the mineral wool. We took another look and saw that it was a small amount of formaldehyde. The mineral wool would be installed on the outside of the air barrier and would be sandwiched between the OSB sheathing and the cement fiberboard siding. It wasn't like being in a nail salon and breathing it in a higher concentration in an enclosed area. We also heard that the amount of formaldehyde in mineral wool is minimal and mostly dissipates after the product is formed. So we decided to accept having a trace amount of formaldehyde on the exterior insulation.

Taylor was a bit more serious during this period than his usual easy-going self. Although Taylor was quite familiar with the scope of the work, he too had additional questions. For example, painting can be done in different degrees of work intensity that affects the smoothness of the finish. The more time they spend sanding, the more even and smooth the result. Apparently there is no standard for this, and different painters take pride in the detail of their work. These little differences on various construction details made it more challenging to evaluate the bids in an apples-to-apples comparison. But it also presented an opportunity to learn more about the alternatives out there to modify the specs.

Each time a new question came up, we reflected on our personal values and priorities for this project.

Minimize risk with fixed bid

While waiting for the bids to come in, we began the construction contract conversation with Gary. As an attorney who specializes in construction law, Gary's primary focus is keeping people out of courts by having a good contract in place with educated home-owners and contractors. He has authored the book, *The Contractor's Legal Kit: The Complete User Friendly Legal Guide for Home Builders and Remodelers*, and offers legal templates online. When we gave him the name of the contractors we invited to bid, Gary told us that two of the three contractors we had invited to bid were his clients and that it was not ethical for him to take sides or serve as the arbitrator in the case of a conflict. We appreciated his honesty, and he mentioned that both contractors were good and had solid track records.

Still, we needed to protect ourselves. Gary advised getting fixed bids to minimize our risk. "The more details you have upfront the better job the contractor can do to give a fixed bid," he said. "Once the fixed bid is signed, the contractor is on the hook for the delivery of the job regardless of the changes in market condition. It protects you."

He said that contractors often want homeowners to sign a time and materials or a cost-plus contract, which shifts the risk from the contractor to the homeowner. In a time and materials contract the contractor can charge the market price for the material at the time of construction, but that could be different than what it was at the time of the bid. Also they can charge more labor time if they find some aspect that takes longer than expected. To us, that sounded like signing a deal that has an open wallet. Fixed bid was definitely the way to go.

Watch out for mechanic's lien

Another contract element Gary told us to watch out for is a mechanic's lien. We'd heard a horror story about this a couple of months earlier. A homeowner in Palo Alto had a mechanic's lien placed on his house by a subcontractor hired by the general contractor. The homeowner had paid the general contractor, so he was shocked to see the mechanic's lien. It turned out that the general contractor had money problems because another project he was working on had gone belly up and he was short of cash. He was not paying his subs. The homeowner ended up paying the sub for the money owed and fired the general contractor. The lesson here was that it can happen to anybody. It wasn't the case where the homeowner hired an unethical contractor who put in a low-ball bid. The home-owners were bright, well-intentioned individuals wanting to do the right things for themselves and the environment and hired the best contractor for the job. The contractor had passion for sustain-able design and wanted to showcase this house in his portfolio. But cascading events originating from a business situation that did not involve the homeowner led to the mechanic's lien fiasco.

Gary said one way to protect ourselves from this situation would be to have the general contractor have the subs sign a lien release at the end of their portion of the job as a way to insure our payment to the general made it to the pocket of the sub. Another way to protect ourselves, Gary noted, would be to write joint checks, that is, write the names of both the general contractor and the subcontractor on the check for what the general owes the sub. The general then endorses the check and gives it to the sub. It's a way for you to pay the sub through the general.

Milestone-based payment schedule

According to Gary, contractors normally want to break down the total job into ten equal payments. We didn't like the idea of paying for work that had not been done. Gary said to check that the pay-ment schedule in the construction agreement reflected milestones of the construction (and not dates) and pay only for the work that had been performed.

Events and milestones can be broken down by foundation, framing, roofing, walls, windows and doors, insulation, etc. "It's best to ask your contractor to specify the milestones and amounts so that he has a say in the sequence and the amount," Gary said.

"Great, I like that approach," I said.

Gary said he'd send us a template of the fixed-bid contract so we could start filling in the details.

"Just don't tell the contractors you're working with an attor-ney because they'll clam up if you do."

Bids came in

Three weeks after the bidders conference the bids from the contractors came in. Our instruction to the bidders was to provide a fixed bid that was broken down into three phases: (1) remodel of the house; (2) repaving the shared driveway; and (3) redo the detached garage that was utterly falling apart. The property line falls in the middle of the cracked driveway that is seven feet wide. Our neighbor very much wanted to have this repaved and split the cost with us. Besides making the driveway look nice, we wanted to avoid water pooling in the garage after a rain storm. We wanted to raise the edge of the garage foundation where it met the driveway by a couple of inches and slope the driveway down toward the street. As additional protection, we wanted to install a drain at the garage end of the driveway and connect it to a pipe to route water out onto the street.

The third contractor's bid was a simple one-page document with a number that was twenty-five percent more than the others. When we asked him for details he simply said, "When I look at a project I know what it would cost at the gut level. I don't have details I can give you." To us that meant he either was not interested in this job or he was not a details kind of guy and shied away from counting the leaves in the forest. But we do count the leaves in the forest and would very much like to work with someone who can navigate and communicate the big picture as well as the details. Jon and Taylor both did this with ease and we scrutinized the details in their bids.

Jon's and Taylor's bids were similar in the level of detail yet with a few differences. If we saw something in Taylor's bid but not in Jon's, we called them and asked clarifying questions. They were both very knowledgeable and their pre-sales skills are excellent. We'd already done reference checks early on and they both came in solid. They were on even footing as far as chemistry was concerned, they both were committed to green building practices, and were both willing to learn and apply new things. We could easily work with either one of them. The deciding factors boiled down to who would have a better chance of delivering air sealing to achieve 0.6 ACH_{50} and cost.

Deciding factor

Kurt and I brainstormed to come up with a plan. We decided to bring in Terry Nordbye as the air sealing consultant to increase the odds of hitting the air sealing number. We felt both Taylor and Jon could work effectively with Terry, but that Taylor might have an advantage because he would be doing the electrical and plumbing himself whereas Jon would be using a subcontractor.

To hit the air sealing target of 0.6 ACH_{50}, we decided to create incentives—bonuses, including a small bonus for passing each interim blower door test. We decided a big incentive would be to make the last payment contingent on hitting the final blower door test at 0.6 ACH_{50} or better.

For us, Taylor had an advantage on the air sealing probability. And even after all the clarifying and scrubbing the numbers on various line items, Taylor's bid was lower than Jon's.

"OK, Santa Cruz Green Builders it is," Kurt said, and he called Taylor to give him the news.

Constraints covered in the contract

Scope (or quality), time (or schedule), and cost (or budget) are the three legs in the project management triangle. Change in cost, schedule, or scope affect each other. One way to understand this principle is to imagine cooking something. Suppose I'm baking a pie for a party and I browse through the recipes. The first recipe has a tantalizing photo with exotic ingredients. I don't have some of the ingredients and I don't want to make a trip to the specialty food store. The items in my pantry determine the constraint (or the limiting factor) called scope (or quality). The second recipe calls for simple ingredients, but it needs overnight preparation and there is not time for that. In this case time (or schedule) is the constraint. I finally choose a third recipe and start lining up the ingredients on the counter. When I look in the fridge, I see I'm out of eggs. I zip over to the grocery store to buy eggs, but remember that I reorganized my wallet the night before and don't have any credit cards with me. I barely have enough cash to buy eggs. So I switch from a dozen organic eggs to half a dozen conventional eggs. The cash in the wallet represents the cost constraint, which now has affected quality (or scope). By the time I get home, there is really no time to make and bake a pie, so I switch to making something completely different that has a shorter baking time. Here the time or schedule constraint affected scope. Changes in schedule, cost, and scope all affect each other. The obvious solution to this hypothetical scenario is to go to the bakery and buy a pie or cake. In our case there was no suitable pie or cake (home) at the bakery (real estate market) available.

Our dream green home journey began with a focus on the quality (or scope) leg of the project management triangle. Since there wasn't a house on the market that met our criteria, we chose to transform an old house. To make the transformation successful, we paid special attention to the construction agreement to minimize risk and ensure the desired outcome. Since many things can change during the course of construction, we would protect the scope (or quality) by having detailed documents such as material selections list and Passive House criteria along with the architectural plans referenced in the construction agreement.

We would constrain the cost by having a fixed bid rather than a time and materials bid. We'd also ensure that payment would match the work done by specifying a milestone-based payment schedule. The change-order forms would be used to avoid surprises. If unexpected things came up, we would discuss them and formalize the extra work scope and cost that wasn't in the original agreement. We budgeted about 15 percent of the fixed bid amount for change orders and didn't tell our contractor that we had this extra buffer. We kept it in our back pocket.

Some of my friends who remodeled their homes paid close attention to scheduling details. They had to figure out temporary rental arrangements while construction took place. If the construction schedule slips, there is the cascading implication of additional rent and timing of moving out and back in. To protect themselves, some homeowners explicitly include penalty clauses to insure on-time completion. We didn't have that constraint. We continued to live in the condo. Delays in the construction schedule didn't result in a hardship for us, so we chose not to include language in our construction agreement for schedule penalty. We figured that by having a milestone-based payment schedule, the contractor would want to finish each milestone to get paid.

Construction agreement and deposit

Everyone in the Passive House community told us to order the windows early. So we researched and selected our windows early on. By the time we signed the construction agreement with Taylor we were ready to order windows. The second check we wrote to Taylor was the materials deposit for the windows. The deposit that accompanied the construction agreement was for $1,000 to get the project started. In California it's illegal for the contractor to ask for more than 10 percent of the total home improvement contract or $1,000, whichever is less.

As for the other items on our owner-supplied materials list Taylor simply told us, "I'll tell you when to order things."

Lessons learned: construction agreement

Choosing the right contractor for the job is important. We wanted someone who we could trust, who would do a good job cost effectively, and who we could get along with.

❖ Always get bids from three different contractors.

❖ Use fixed bids to shift risk from homeowner to contractor.

❖ Write our own construction agreement with the help of an attorney to protect what is most important to us.

❖ Make the payment schedule in the contract match the milestones in the project.

❖ Take precautions against mechanic's liens.

8
Stripping Away the Old

Learning from deconstruction

Construction finally began. The first phase involved removing different layers of the house, and as we did we got a glimpse of the history of Santa Cruz through the materials used in the house. As the house was stripped down to foundation, floor, framing, and roof, we asked ourselves: can someone else use the things we remove from the house? What can the building tell us? How do we communicate and align the team to focus on Passive House Standard?

Salvage sale

Originally we wanted to use the deconstruction service from Whole House Salvage in San Mateo. This deconstruction service is the equivalent of having a yard sale. Instead of looking at clothing and pots and pans on the front lawn, people come into a house (after signing a wavier at the door) to see if they would like to buy the flooring, appliances, sinks, countertops, cabinets, windows, and other items. Buyers get a good price if they're willing to uninstall their finds and haul them away. It's a treasure trove for hardcore do-it-yourselfers who relish bargain hunting, especially when a recently remodeled house changes hands and the new owner wants to redo it in his or her style. We really liked the Whole House Salvage business model that facilitated re-use of material. We chose not to do this because our house didn't have many interesting and eye-catching items to attract a big crowd to the deconstruction sale.

Removing old furnishings

I chose to sell things myself. Perhaps posting ads for old furniture and appliances on Craigslist gave buyers the impression of a gullible old person. I've sold many things on Craigslist and this was the only time I found myself in an unusual email conversation. Hanna was relocating from another state and was interested in buying the old O'Keefe & Merrit gas stove in Midori's kitchen. It's a lovely piece from the 1950s with a built-in clock and a cooking chart, each framed in dull chrome freckled with rust. A hint of cherry red paint still lingered on the clock's sans serif numbers. A cute set of matching salt and pepper shakers completed the vintage feel. During my getting-to-know-Midori days, I made a few satisfactory meals and also experienced my very first apple butter canning with this stove. Since we decided not to have any gas appliances inside the house, the stove had to find a new home. Beautifully restored vintage gas stoves could fetch $400, but this was not in pristine condition. It was sturdy and functional. So I listed it for $150 using the best photos I could take with my phone.

Hanna claimed the stove that was the perfect kitchen appliance she was looking for. She asked me to remove the listing from Craigslist because she'd be sending the check to me via FedEx. OK, I did. Soon she sent a company check via FedEx that was in excess of the amount of the sale price. In an email she asked me to cash the check and give the extra $200 to the handyman who would pick up the stove to pay for his fee. Humph, strange arrangement. Before cashing it, I spoke with the bank teller and asked if they could tell me if the check was good or not. He told me that banks have no way of checking the validity of the check at the time you deposit them. That's why they sometimes put a hold on deposits. I would have incurred bank fees, lost the stove, and $200 if I actually proceeded with this transaction with Hanna because the check would have bounced after a week, long after the handyman was gone. On Craigslist I found the warning that spelled out the details of the scam that perfectly matched this scenario. So heeding the advice on the warning page, I reported the incident on the Internet Crime Complaint Center and ceased communication with Hanna. I'm glad to have avoided the Internet scam drama, but I still had a deadline to deal with.

It was my responsibility to find new homes for the vintage appliances and furnishings we acquired with Midori. By this time, it was more important to quickly get rid of things rather than get the best price. Back to Craigslist. This time I held a cash only fire sale of table, chairs, stove, refrigerator, TV, dressers, twin bed, and more. It's amazing how many people willingly jump and haul your stuff away if you offer to sell it for $5. I donated some of the items that did not sell to a local charity, and volunteers came to take them away.

We did not sell everything that came with the house. We kept the hand-cranked Silvertone phonograph as well as old coat hangers from different cleaners. These were not the type of wire hangers used today, but nice, wood coat hangers with the name of the business and four-digit telephone number after the telephone exchange name imprinted on the wood—Marcus Parisian Cleaner on Fourteenth Street in San Francisco, telephone number UNderhill 4242, or the Capitol Cleaning & Dyeing Plant on Brady Street, phone MArket 8338.

The fire sale (minus bits of history I wanted to keep) put us back on schedule, and we submitted the third round of plan check corrections to the city planning department after Halloween. This was the last and final round. While we waited for the permit to be issued, Taylor patiently volleyed documents back and forth with us to finalize the construction agreement. After several revisions, it was signed on Wednesday, November 30, 2011. Taylor was more than ready to go. When we first met with him almost a year earlier, we painted an optimistic picture of starting the construction in May because we thought the design and permit would have been done within four months. He probably knew better but he didn't say anything to us. He simply continued to fill his calendar with various jobs in his focused, pragmatic way.

With the signed construction agreement in place, things moved quickly. Up went a temporary, locked construction fence and in came a blue and white plastic porta-potty unit on the northwest corner of the house next to the electrical panel. The connection point for the power line from the street moved from the corner of the house to the temporary spot.

I didn't realize that the porta-potty served two purposes. Besides the obvious purpose of providing a place for workers to relieve themselves during their work shift, it also serves as the connection point for electricity. The construction crew needs electricity to run their power tools and the house would have no power during construction because the electrical wiring was to be replaced.

With all that in place, the first part of deconstruction started with the careful removal and storage of interior doors and trims. Freed from all past furnishings, Midori was ready to be stripped down.

Asbestos removal

Before the walls came down, Midori got a visit from men in white suits to remove the asbestos-containing popcorn ceiling. Removal of asbestos requires a special license to ensure that it's done properly. All the windows were taped and sealed. Protruding from the front door was a refrigerator-sized vacuum unit that sucked out the air inside the house and contained the asbestos debris in the filters.

It was on this day that I made the trip to the building department of City of Santa Cruz to pay my final permit fees of $4,672.77 and pick up the stamped plans and the lime green job card.

This card would be posted in a visible area at the construction site to show that the work was permitted. In some cities like San Francisco, the job card is a computer printed form with detailed information. In the City of Santa Cruz, it's a simple form with three fill-in-the-blank spaces. The person at the permit counter picked up a fat black marker and wrote "Permit number B11-0279 issued on 12-13-11" and our address. That was it. We were required to keep a copy of the set of plans with the building department's stamp on site during the construction. This is what the building inspectors would refer to when they would come out for various inspections during the course of the construction project. Getting the permit from the City of Santa Cruz took us 4.5 months from the initial submission date through three rounds of plan checks with CSG. We paid a total of $6,044.43 to the city.

When I got back to the house with our brand new permit, Taylor's truck was parked in front of the house next to the asbestos removal company's truck. I dared not go inside such a space. I dialed Taylor's cell phone and he popped out from the side door wearing a mask and goggles. "Here's the approved plan and the permit," I said as I handed him the bundle. He seemed pleased that the permit was in place and, hands-on contractor that he is, disappeared back into house.

Revealing layers of history

A few days after the visit from the men in moon suits, Taylor was supervising his crew as they carefully removed the windows, doors, and the bead board. We planned to reuse the bead boards that were part of the mudroom wall and convert them into part of the half wall of the kitchen counter bar. Until then the deconstructed bead boards would be stored in the garage along with the vintage phonograph, the lovely antique furnishing we acquired with the house.

"Your house is getting naked," said Taylor.

Indeed she was. As I took a closer look at Midori's torn clothing, I saw layers of history. In the front, redwood planks emerged once Taylor's crew had peeled off the fake brick siding. Interesting. I suppose the real estate agent who lived in the house in the 1950s preferred the look of the bungalow style that was popular in Chicago rather than the original lap siding look. I could see a piece of black plastic-looking sheet for a rain screen beneath the redwood siding. That made me wonder if they used plastic materials in the 1920s. A little research revealed that yes, the first commercially used synthetic plastic Bakelite was invented in 1907.

Under the rain screen was skip sheathing—planks installed diagonally to provide shear strength for the wall. Nice wood. The planks shielded from the weather under the front porch were in good shape. Under that was air space (no insulation material in the cavity) 3.5 inches thick, basically the size of the wall cavity created by the 2x4 stud.

Why the heck is the piece of lumber used for framing called 2x4 if it's not exactly two inches by four inches? It turns out the two-by-four (2x4) lumber dimension is accurate when it's originally cut, soon after the tree has been felled. Then it shrinks as the moisture evaporates out of the wood in the drying process, so the two-by-four lumber actually measures around 1.5 inches by 3.5 inches in thickness. Beyond the air space was lath and plaster, the interior wall. Apparently the brick siding facade lasted longer on the least weather beaten north side of the house because the other three sides were covered with stucco and painted powder blue.

Lath and plaster

I'd heard of the term lath and plaster before but never fully understood it until I saw it from the backside. It kind of looked like a side view of multi-layered cream cheese sandwich. Lath or thin strips of softwood (perhaps pine, fir, or cedar) the color of toasted bread were fastened to the framing of the building with a small amount of space between the strips. Wet plaster would then have been applied quickly to the lath, then smoothed over to give it the look of a clean wall. Plaster can be made of lime, gypsum, or Portland cement. It cracks if the span of the lath is too long. Long ago people working with lath and plaster determined that plaster doesn't crack as easily if the span is sixteen inches or less. I've heard that the tradition of "sixteen on center" (spacing framing studs sixteen inches apart) came about because of this. Today with the use of drywall, plaster cracking is not an issue so "twenty-four on center" is the advanced framing technique preached by green building professionals to minimize the use of wood.

Bricks behind the kitchen wall

The undressing of Midori also revealed the contents of the mystery space in the center of the house. Graham was wondering about the mystery space when he took measurements of the house to draw the as-built diagram. The sum of the internal room measurement didn't add up to the external wall-to-wall measurement. The missing space was somewhere near the kitchen. I was so curious to discover what this mystery space was.

We found out when they removed the large tank of the hot water heater (seismically strapped to the kitchen wall). When we opened a cute, thin door originally used to store a fold-down ironing board, we saw a wall of brick. Bricks were stacked from the ground in the crawl space up through the attic in a thick column measuring 2 feet by 3 feet. A hidden chimney. Perhaps there had once been a brick oven or a hearth for cooking in the original kitchen. Antique gas stoves from the 1920s are available for sale at antique stores today, so it's possible that Midori was plumbed with gas and the original kitchen sported a Wedgwood or Magic Chef gas stove. I'll never know. Certainly they did not have electric cooktops in those days. But that thought made me wonder if the city was even electrified in 1922. It was.

Electrification of Santa Cruz 100 years ago

Fred Swanton and Dr. H.H. Clark formed their Santa Cruz Electric Light and Power Company in 1890. Electrification made a splash in Santa Cruz in June 1907 when the second casino at the Santa Cruz Beach Boardwalk opened with a blaze of lights at night. It earned the title of "Atlantic City of the Pacific." In 1918 electric light replaced the oil burner at the Lighthouse where the ray of light could be seen for 14 miles. So we imagine our street, barely a mile from downtown, would have had electric service when Midori was created in 1922.

In the early 1900s the knob-and-tube wiring was the prevalent low-cost installation method to wire a house for electricity. Ceramic knobs fastened to the building frame kept the copper wire in place, and the ceramic tubes protected the copper wires passing through the holes drilled in the joists or studs. Suspended in air, the knob-and-tube wiring dissipated heat easily. That was fine when houses were built without insulation, but as insulation became the norm the knob-and-tube wiring became a liability. So in 1987 the National Electrical Safety Code prohibited the placement of insulation in contact with this type of wiring. The presence of knob-and-tube wiring in our crawl space and ceiling was evidence that Midori's electrical wiring was at least 25 years old, if not older.

1920s Santa Cruz

As the layers came off the house, we wondered what was going on in Santa Cruz about the time Midori was born. The Santa Cruz Library answered the question. A couple years after Midori was built, Santa Cruz hosted the Miss California pageant, where nineteen-year-old Faye Lanphier was chosen as Miss California in 1924 and was later crowned Miss America in Atlantic City. Santa Cruz hosted the pageant for many years, but it eventually relocated.

Not so the local farmers markets which have showcased the abundance of local produce for decades. Photographs in Margaret Koch's book, *Santa Cruz County, Parade of the Past*, showed farmers pulling up their horse-drawn wagons and buggies in the Farmers Free Market on Front Street every Saturday morning. Today the city of Santa Cruz continues to have a vibrant farmers market scene. I can choose to go to one of the three weekly farmers market to buy fresh organic produce: Saturdays at the west side, Sundays on the east side, and the larger eclectic one on Wednesdays downtown.

In the 1920s different architectural styles were popular in Santa Cruz. These include the Gothic Revival style of 1860s, Italianate style of 1870s, Stick and Eastlake styles of 1880s, Romanesque and Queen Anne styles of 1890s, and Mission Revival of 1900s, which emphasized traditions and styles from the East Coast. In the 1920s Midori's style, the California Bungalow, stressed a return to simple handcrafted workmanship as well as the integrity and beauty of materials in their native state. After the bungalow style, when population grew rapidly after World War I, quantity rather than quality became the new criteria for building. We felt fortunate as we learned about Midori's architectural heritage, for we value the simplicity and natural look of wood.

Kick-off meeting

Santa Cruz Green Builders were about to experience attention to detail, specifically in the area of air sealing, that is beyond anything they'd ever experienced before. We wanted them to succeed. So we held a kick-off meeting with the team to explain the importance of Passive House concepts and do a bit of team building. I remembered Gary saying, "Contractors don't want to spend the time attending classes," when we were brainstorming on ways to improve the odds of meeting the air sealing target. What the crew needed was not classroom instruction full of theories. They needed a pep talk. With pizza and beer. And my signature oatmeal-orange-chocolate chip cookies.

We invited three experts for the meet-and-greet pep talk with Taylor's crew. Graham Irwin, architect and Passive House consultant, carpooled with Terry Nordbye, a general contractor and air sealing consultant. Patrick Splitt, a solar thermal designer who lived few blocks away, was there too. Half a dozen guys from Taylor's crew who had spent some time working on the deconstruction phase gathered around respectfully. They wondered why this was important enough to pull them off the job.

We, and our experts, explained the Passive House concept, the importance of air sealing, characteristics of high-performance homes, etc. Graham emphasized how important this project would be in setting an example, not just for Santa Cruz but also for California. "You guys are making history," he said. "You guys will be famous after this is built. You'll be rock stars in the construction industry."

That got them charged up, and so did our trip to Upper Crust Pizza & Pasta. Sharing a meal is a good way know everyone better. Over lunch we found out that one of the crew members lived just half a block away from our house. We knew we succeeded in hiring local talent when we learned Taylor lived just two miles away. Having an enthusiastic crew member just a stone's throw away was a bonus.

Reuse and recycle

While we didn't hold a salvage sale with Whole House Salvage, a few items from the house got second life. Some of our interior doors ended up at Restore, which is an arm of the nonprofit Habitat for Humanity. It has a retail facility that is like a thrift shop for home construction. Some other items found a second life via the power of "free." In this college town, furniture taped with a piece of paper marked "free" miraculously finds a new home in record time.

The local dump has a fancy name—Santa Cruz Resource Recovery Site. They live up to their name. Wood, metal, paper, plastic, glass, and concrete that can be reused can be dropped off at designated spots within this facility. From there they can be recycled. The stuff we don't want to dump into the sewer, such as medication, paint, and chemicals, are handled in the hazardous material tent where the workers dispose of these items in a manner that won't contaminate groundwater. Taylor ordered large, dump truck-sized bins to be placed in the driveway during reconstruction. His crew did a nice job of sorting the debris from deconstruction. After it was hauled off to the Resource Recovery Site, we learned that 82.6 percent of it was recycled. Only 18 percent of Midori's old self went into the landfill.

Unforeseen repairs

The original house had three bedrooms and one bathroom. Midori's nearly perfect square shape was great for energy efficiency. Her shape changed in 1947 when the owners made a small addition to create a second bathroom and a small kitchenette, turning the southwest corner bedroom into a self-contained rental. As the house was stripped down to her skeleton, we saw that construction on the addition was not on par with the rest of the house. It had the most water and termite damage and the foundation was less robust than the main house. Taylor found one of the floor joists to be simply hanging. Unattached to the post and pier or the perimeter foundation, it did not provide any structural support at all. The floor was severely termite eaten. The toilet had been installed improperly, with the fixture screwed into the foam that filled gap between the wood floor and the waste pipe. No wonder it felt unstable when I sat on it.

There was another area with a lot of rot from water damage—the window near the original fireplace. That fireplace had been damaged during the 1989 earthquake and was boarded up. The disturbance from the earthquake probably created gaps by the window, allowing rainwater to trickle down into the sheathing.

The fixed-bid contract included $1,750 for repairs and unforeseen items. Problems found during deconstruction quickly consumed that contingency fund. Another problem we found during this phase was that the ceiling joists were inadequate to hold the extra weight of the planned attic insulation, so we decided to beef those up. The first change order we signed in December 2011 included about $5,000 of various repairs and strengthening of Midori's bones. We felt good about it, though, because it was a fraction of the money we had allocated for change orders, and we were making changes to improve durability.

At least we didn't have a mold problem like our friends did. When our friends in Oakland opened up the walls in their house during their remodel, they found the wall cavity next to the bathroom covered in mold. This happened because the bathroom exhaust fan was installed improperly. Instead of ducting the exhaust to the outside, it remained inside the house. Years of moist air from showers and baths simply got dumped into the wall cavity to feed the mold. Yuck.

Lessons learned: stripping away the old

It felt good that our old materials could be reused and recycled. It's rewarding to avoid sending stuff to the landfill. It also feels good to be able to do what's right for the house without having to agonize over surprises.

❖ Salvage sales can be effective if there are enough interesting items.

❖ Watch out for scammers when selling old furnishings on Craigslist.

❖ Stripping away the layers of the house can reveal hidden problems.

❖ Set aside funds to address hidden problems beyond what's specified as an allowance in the contract.

9
Relationship with Rainwater

Rainwater issues

After Midori was stripped down to her bones, the crew worked on the outside before any work was done on the inside of the house. The infrastructure installed outside below the ground is not sexy, but it is important for health and durability. We studied each aspect of our relationship with rainwater on our property. As each issue came up, we chose the best approach for ensuring our safety and health, protecting the house, and making good use of rainwater.

Soil and drainage

During our first winter with Midori, there was flooding around the garage: a few inches of water pooled on the cracked concrete driveway, and the grassy area around the shed became marshy after heavy rain. Our neighbors told us that the water table is high in our area. Compounding that is a layer of heavy clay which doesn't drain well beneath the topsoil. The report from the surveyor informed us that that the water pooling in the garage area is more than just the rain falling on our property. The negatively sloped, seventy-foot-long driveway created a flow of rainwater from the sidewalk all the way back to the garage. We intended to address that after the house was done by repaving the driveway and fixing up the garage that currently hosts rot, mold, termites, and rats. Meanwhile, anything we stored in the garage would have to be elevated to prevent water damage. Half a dozen pallets did the trick.

When we talked to our neighbors about water and flooding, we were surprised to find that everyone had a sump pump on their property. They felt that was the best solution to poor soil drainage for their house. We didn't want to install a sump pump on our property and discharge rainwater into the storm drain. For our green approach, we believed that letting the ground soak up the rainwater and recharge the aquifer was better.

Still, we were curious about why everyone in the neighborhood had a sump pump. Placed under the house, a sump pump moves excess water from under the foundation to the side of the street to run down into the storm drain. Besides the chunk of clay under the topsoil that prevents water from draining by gravity, there is complex water movement underground. We are on a flat patch of land at an elevation of 80 feet. The elevation goes up to over 800 feet just three miles away in a stair step fashion. This means there is a constant flow of rainwater and spring water moving from higher ground toward sea level. We can't see the movement of water in the network of veins and channels underground, but we can imagine them having an effect on the water table below our house.

We got a glimpse of what was happening underground by having a monitoring hole dug up. Instead of having an expensive soils test done, we hired a contractor who specialized in installing septic systems in rural areas. They used a hand auger to dig a two-inch-wide hole. When they extracted the auger after drilling down eleven feet, they found different types of soil. Characteristics of the soil at different depths were noted by inspecting the soil attached to the auger's teeth. We needed to know how far down the clay went before we would know if we had a chance of letting the rainwater soak into the ground naturally. For the water to reach the sand layer eight feet below surface, it needed to get through seven feet of clay soil. No wonder the water did not drain easily.

The septic contractor placed a plastic pipe into the holes he dug up—one in the front yard and another in the backyard. We noted the water table by sticking a tape measure into the hole. In March 2011, toward the end of a very rainy year with thirty-three inches of rain, the water table was high. Our tape measure showed the underground water level was just thirty-six inches below the surface. In December 2011, heading into a rather dry year with only eighteen inches of rain, the water level was eighty-five inches below the surface. We concluded that we did need a sump pump to keep water away from the foundation during wet years when the water table was high. Another indicator: the home inspection report showed that the wooden posts in the crawlspace showed signs of high water in the past. We certainly wanted to avoid having Midori's feet rot away or a host a colony of mold. So we need to keep our perimeter foundation, posts, and piers dry.

Prioritizing water issues

We were initially worried about different problems associated with too much water and felt frustrated. So we asked ourselves, "What problem are we trying to solve?" It turned out there were several, so we prioritized them. We just needed to solve the problem one drop at a time.

Our first priority was to ensure the health of the house and occupants. This meant durability, structural integrity, and avoiding moisture problems that lead to mold and rot. The second priority was to minimize negative impacts on the environment from stormwater runoff from our property. The third priority was based on our conservation mindset: make use of the rainwater falling on our roof to reduce the amount of water we would buy from the city water department.

The first priority of ensuring the health of the house had three strategies: reduce moisture in the crawlspace by covering the ground with plastic; remove any standing water under the plastic by installing a sump pump under the house; and divert water away from the perimeter of the house with a French drain.

The second priority was to minimize the negative impact on the environment from stormwater runoff from our property. The solution to this was to lay a thick layer of mulch on the ground at the end of construction.

The third priority of harvesting rainwater required changes to the infrastructure on our property, specifically connecting the gutters on the roof to pipes that convey rainwater from the roof to the rainwater tank.

Minimizing moisture in the crawlspace

Like most homes of this vintage, Midori had a crawlspace between the floor and the ground. The crawlspace was vented. We're fortunate that this space was large enough to move about by crawling rather than slithering. I would have fainted if I'd found something else slithering around with me as I was crawling around down there taking measurements and photos. The ground was cool and hard, but I knew it would be quite damp after a rainstorm.

I wondered why dampness in the crawlspace was bad. After all, we don't visit that space often much less live there. When we took a building science class from our local utility company, we learned that "stack effect" makes the damp air in the crawlspace a bad thing, especially in the winter. Since heat rises, when the house is heated in cold weather, there is a slow movement of air from floor to ceiling. Warmer air near the ceiling tries to escape through cracks and gaps in the ceiling or in the walls. When it does make its escape, the space vacated by warm air pulls up the air below. The replacement air comes through the cracks in the floor, bringing moist, moldy air from the crawlspace.

At the West Coast Green trade show we talked to a company that specialized in addressing this crawlspace problem by encapsulating the crawlspace. Their method was to apply several layers of plastic sheeting over the ground, including a patented liner that had pencil eraser-sized dimples to let water and moisture move below the liner. Their customers experienced dry crawlspaces and benefitted from energy savings since the crawlspace temperature was a bit warmer. We liked the idea but not enough to pay almost $9,000 for their customized solution. Instead, we had Taylor install 20 Mil black plastic sheet in our crawlspace and tape up the seams. This actually benefitted them later because their crew spent a couple of days on their backs in the crawlspace to install insulation under the floor.

Before Taylor's crew laid the plastic sheet on the ground, they installed a sump pump about twenty-four inches below grade near the center of the house. It would kick on if it detected water pooling there. The water from the sump pump would feed into the drainage pipe taking water out to the street to flow into the storm drain.

Keeping water away from the foundation with a French drain

A French drain is the simple solution to keep water away from the foundation. Perforated pipes would convey excess water in the ground toward a designated spot specified in our plans. Despite the name, it doesn't come from France. A French drain, according to Wikipedia, is named after Henry Flagg French of Massachusetts, a lawyer and assistant secretary of the United States Treasury in the nineteenth century. French described and popularized the method in his book, *Farm Drainage*.

At this point in our construction project, the crew dug a shallow ditch about 12 inches wide and 18 inches deep along the perimeter of the house. They lined the ditch with landscape filter fabric and filled it with three-quarter inch drain rock to hold perforated ABS pipes. The pipes were placed in the trench with just enough slope to gravity-feed the water to the lowest point in the southwest corner. Now when it rains, the water that trickles into the pipe drains out to the street. The drainage rocks and the landscape cloth prevent the pipes from being clogged with dirt.

Three S's before storm drain

My routine to see the progress of the construction was to ride my bike from our condo over to the construction site to talk to the crew and take photos. Sometimes I'd tuck a tub of cookies or lemon bars into the bike bag for the crew. The rainy season in Santa Cruz is January. Walking around the construction site in that month was a challenge. After it rained, the ground would be wet for days because water would just sit on top of the clay soil. Walking about the yard took effort not only because I needed to watch out for the trenches, but also because the clay stuck to everything, especially shoes. I could easily gain three pounds of mud from walking around the construction site.

Taylor's crew experienced heavy boots daily. As a temporary solution, he got some straw bales and sprinkled straw over the clay to create a path. Our long-term solution wasn't much different. We planned to cover the ground with wood chips at the end of construction. Since our clay soil doesn't drain easily, we could slow down the rate of infiltration by letting the wood chips soak up the rain.

During heavy storms there would be more rainwater seeping through the topsoil and it would need to be pumped out to the street. We wanted to avoid that because there are negative side effects of sending the rainwater down the storm drain: polluting the ocean and causing erosion. We worried that our stormwater would go directly to the ocean, picking up whatever pollutants it encountered along with way to the ocean such as metal dust particles from cars braking, dog poo, bird poo, pesticides on the lawn, trash on the sidewalk, and more. We also worried about erosion at the point the stormwater was discharged. If the stormwater pipe emptied out at a place like a river bank with lots of earth, then the heavy volume of water from the rain could cause erosion. Erosion near the road could cause the road to crumble and create hazard and expense. Even though these problems didn't occur within our property boundaries, we still felt a responsibility to solve our part of the problem.

Just as we were feeling bad about using a sump pump, we found a map of the city's storm drain system on the Santa Cruz

County website. By navigating through this geographic information system, we learned that rainwater discharged from our property is routed to Neary Lagoon, a wetland with bioremediation features. This is a city park that has a boardwalk that meanders over a freshwater marsh filled with fish that feed off the bottom. So not only is the stormwater captured and given a new life as a water feature in a public park, tall reeds and other vegetation in the marsh filter pollutants. So the consequence of sending rainwater to the storm drain was not too bad after all.

We still chose to do our part to retain the rainwater on our site by mulching 4,000 square feet of unattractive grass on our property because spreading wood chips or mulching has dual benefits. During the wet season, it absorbs water and prevents excess stormwater runoff. During the dry season, it keeps the ground under the mulch moist much longer, reducing the need to irrigate plants in the yard. During our search for the best way to deal with stormwater, our mantra became "slow it, spread it, and sink it." These are the three S's before resorting to storm drain usage.

Rainwater harvesting

Another way to avoid sending rainwater into the storm drain is to harvest and use it onsite. One approach would be to route the drain pipes attached to the gutter on the roof to the rainwater tank. Most people use rainwater collected from their roofs to irrigate their garden. While that was the original intent, we were inspired by a system we saw at the San Francisco Zen Center in Marin County. They were constructing a dormitory built to the Passive House Standard. When they held a mid-construction tour for the public, we saw that they were using the rainwater to flush the toilets in the dormitory. When the tour guide explained how the system worked, a light bulb went off in my head. We are in the habit of flushing clean drinking water down the toilet every day. About one fifth to one fourth of indoor water use at home goes down the toilet. That's clean drinking water. This practice is bewildering to people who live in countries lacking clean, reliable sources of drinking water. We flush this precious resource down the toilet every day without even thinking about.

We liked the idea of using a natural resource falling on the property to address the largest portion of indoor water use—toilet flushing. So while we didn't have this specified in our plans, we asked Taylor to put in the rainwater pipe and an electrical conduit while he had the yard all dug up. It would be much more expensive and complex to do it at a later phase. This was part of change order Number Two. The extra digging, pipes for conveying rainwater, electrical conduit for pump, and digging up a deep rain garden with drain tunnels cost less than $2,000. Installation of the rainwater system would be a future project.

Lessons learned: relationship with rainwater

Part of having a durable house is having the relationship with rainwater appropriate for the soil. Rainwater presents different problems. Rather than trying to fit a green solution to the problem, focus on the problems and prioritize them.

❖ Knowing the soil type and the water table helps in creating the appropriate strategy for managing rainwater.

❖ Remember the three S's for managing rainwater on site: slow it, spread it, sink it.

❖ Seal the crawlspace to reduce moisture and mold problems.

❖ A moist crawlspace can introduce mold into the living space and cause health problems.

❖ Install a French drain to keep water away from the foundation.

❖ Do all the digging in the yard all at once to put in pipes, even for future projects.

10
Setting Bones (Framing)

Choosing and treating lumber

Midori had good bones but needed to have some broken ones repaired. Some places needed beefing up to accommodate changes in window positions and sizes. We chose and treated lumber with our green sensibilities and considered forest stewardship as well as improving durability by treating the wood.

Trees are important

Midori's bones came from wood harvested from local forests almost one hundred years ago. A glance at a map of Santa Cruz shows the city is still bordered by the Pacific on one side and dense forests on the other. A logging industry grew up here, and by the mid-1800s there were more than two dozen lumber mills in the area. Early logging firms preferred to cut only larger trees. This avoided clear-cutting of the forest for the most part. The forest floor received more light when the large trees were removed, which made the smaller trees grow. After the turn of the century, the economy turned from resources to tourism and logging tapered off but did not disappear.

Today we enjoy hiking, biking, and running in these forests. The trees provide us with oxygen and they absorb the carbon dioxide we create. Forests regulate water flows, absorb greenhouse gasses, and provide habitats for animals and plant species. We want the trees and the forests to continue to provide us with these benefits we take for granted. So when we purchase wood from companies that practice forest stewardship, we are voting with our dollars to show that treating the forest as a valuable, sustainable resource is important to us.

What is stewardship anyway? When I was in college majoring in economics, I took a class called Natural Resource Economics as an elective, mostly out of curiosity, but also because I thought I would learn something about stewardship and ways to make decisions on natural resource management. Economics may conjure up images of numbers, graphs, and data, but I found it fascinating. When economics is boiled down to a discipline, it is a study of human behavior on how choices and decisions are made. The choices presented in economics classes were often in the form of a trade-off between capital and labor to achieve a goal to maximize production or profit. In our project to renovate Midori, we were trying to maximize our happiness by making choices based on our personal values within the constraint of our budget. With natural resources like fisheries or forestry, the key to maximizing profit over the long run is to harvest at a rate equal to or slower than the growth rate of the fish or trees. If everything is harvested all at once (like clear cutting of forests) there will be a boom followed by a bust and it's not sustainable.

How would we go about choosing a company or product that practiced good stewardship of the forest? It would be rather exhausting to learn about the practices of every lumber company to see if they were managing their forest responsibly in a sustainable, healthy way. Happily, we learned that just as we've come to rely on the organic certification label on food we buy, we can simply look for the Forest Stewardship Council (FSC) certification for the lumber. As with many certification programs, there is extra cost associated with it and that is included in the price of the lumber. Is it worth it? For us the answer was yes.

Local lumber

Midori's original bones and skin came from local trees. We liked the idea of using local wood. The wood used for the deck, framing new window openings, and replacing the rotten pieces came from Big Creek Lumber Company. This local, family-owned company was founded in 1946 and has a history of innovative forestry practices and careful land stewardship. A friend of mine took a tour of the Big Creek Lumber Company during college and learned that redwoods grow slowly when crowded but when thinned, the remaining trees "release" and grow faster. So redwood trees are ideal for sustainable harvesting. Plus it's pretty cool that the current president of this company is a woman. She's a third generation member of this family business, which focuses on forestry, manufacturing, and has a wholesale division.

Preventing termites

I've been told that termites don't like redwood and would rather eat other types of wood in the vicinity. We found that to be true. During deconstruction we saw some redwood rotted by water damage, but hardly any termite damage. The heavily termite-damaged master bathroom floor seemed to be made out of a different type of wood. The original framing was made of redwood, so termites would likely continue avoiding it. We used new wood for framing differently sized window openings, repairing damaged wood, and strengthening the ceiling joists. The new wood needed protection.

With the framing open and accessible during construction, we could protect our wood at little extra cost. In our plans we specified a product called Bora Care, which can greatly reduce termite damage by having it applied to all the exposed wood during construction. The product is a clear liquid that comes in a plastic container. Blue dye was added to the spray pump to give a visible indication of where Bora Care was applied. The active ingredient, borate salt, is a natural mineral salt. When the termites, ants, or beetles eat this borate salt, they lose the ability to extract nutrients, so it is the ultimate diet drug for termites. No matter how much they eat, they can't nourish themselves and they starve to death. In addition to keeping the bugs at bay, Bora Care will kill and prevent algae and wood decay fungi. Insects find it toxic, however, mammals, birds, fish, and reptiles can excrete excess boron so it has little effect on them. The borate salt stays in the wood and provides long-term protection.

It's a good thing we applied Bora Care because we did see evidence of termites during construction. "Look, there's a termite crawling around here," said Taylor as he pointed to a translucent worm-thing the size of a rice grain. It was squirming on the termite-eaten floor of the master bathroom. Up until this point I only knew about flying termites since they were more prevalent in the area where I grew up. Ground termites live in the soil. They are adept at civil engineering and tunnel through the dirt. Evidence of ground termites are these dirt tunnels, often along the foundation wall. Seeing evidence of live termites, we decided to tent the house and have it fumigated at the end of the construction before moving in to eliminate stragglers. Durability was one of our intended outcomes. Mitigating termite damage would ensure strong bones for Midori for years to come.

Lessons learned: setting bones (framing)

Trees serve a valuable role in our ecosystem. When we buy lumber, we can choose to buy it from companies that are practicing good forest stewardship and sustainability. When wood is used in the house, we can ensure the wood has a long life by making it unattractive to termites.

❖ Buy lumber from companies that are managing the forest responsibly and sustainably.

❖ Find out whether or not the lumber is harvested sustainably by either researching the practices of the local lumber company or looking for the Forest Stewardship Council (FSC) certification.

❖ Treat wood with Bora Care to prevent future termite damage.

11
Choosing Eyes (Windows)

Passive House windows

Windows are important for so many reasons. They provide light, air, view, style, and thermal comfort. They are also the weakest part of the house and the most expensive. We had a steep learning curve about windows that met Passive House criteria. Beyond the obvious—shape, style, and color—we needed to think about selecting framing material, understanding visible transmittance, coating glass to control heat (low-e coating), choosing the placement on the wall (innie or outie), and achieving the Arts and Crafts muntin look using simulated divided lite bars.

Eyes for Midori

Choosing eyes for Midori was another area where Kurt's photography experience and physics background played a role in research. We wanted her eyes to be aesthetically pleasing with the look and feel of the Arts and Crafts style. We wanted the rooms to be lit just so during the day from the sun, and we wanted the rooms to be comfortable during the day and at night. It was important to us to pick the type of windows that would minimize the transfer of heat, whether to keep the house cool on a hot day or keep the house warm on a cold night. We wanted the operable window to leak the least amount of air when it was closed, if not airtight. Whatever we choose, it was important that it performed well and lasted a long time since the windows were the most expensive component of this remodel project. We paid close attention to the details as we climbed the learning curve of windows suitable for Passive House. When Kurt did the windows research for Midori in 2011, the selection of non-imported high-performance windows was limited.

In 2010 we attended a lecture in San Francisco by Dr. Wolfgang Feist, founder of the Passivhaus Institut in Germany. He said that cost reduction for high-performance windows is not a technological problem but a market function: as demand increases cost decreases. Here in the U.S. the demand for Passive House has not reached a point where there are many window manufacturers producing Passive House windows competitively. When Passive House Standard came about in Germany, there were just a few manufacturers that produced high-performance windows that were suited to the standard. Over the last two decades, many mid-sized window companies sprang up to create better performing windows. It's now at a point where Germany has more than fifty companies manufacturing high-performance windows and the pricing is competitive. Besides windows, there are many different products certified as Passive House components, such as ventilation systems, entry doors, and others which are listed in the online database maintained by Passivhaus Institut.

Passive House windows

We noticed that most of the windows we saw during Passive House tours in the Bay Area during 2010 and 2011 were imported from Europe or Canada. Using those as a starting point, Kurt contacted several companies to get information about the windows to compare the cost performance. "These guys just don't respond. They need lessons in customer service!" Kurt exclaimed as he was ignored by the window manufacturers. In a way, that was understandable. They focused on providing larger volume orders in countries where they had a distributor network. A small order like ours would be a pain for them to manage and deliver.

Until we learned about Passive House, we thought we just needed to get double-paned windows with low-e coating to have good performance. Well, the devil is in the details and windows have a lot of them. Windows are the weakest point in the house. Unlike walls that can be well-insulated and quite thick, windows are much thinner and have moving parts. It's challenging to make operable windows air tight. The double-hung windows typical of 1922 vintage bungalows are too leaky for Passive House. Windows need to be thermally broken, meaning there should not be a direct path of material that can easily conduct heat in and out of the building. Glass on windows must have appropriate coating to temper the heat movement. Low-emissivity coating or low-e coating comes in different flavors too. Getting all of these details right took research and patience. Windows are the key to making Passive House work. We had to get it right.

Cascadia's performance matrix was an eye opener. This matrix listed the performance criteria of different window frame types such as wood, aluminum, fiberglass, and vinyl. We wanted wood that was true to the Arts and Crafts style, had good strength, low environmental impact, low condensation potential, and good energy performance. But wood is more expensive, less resistant to water, and not as durable as some of the other material. Aluminum is strong and durable, but it has a high environmental impact and its energy performance is poor. Vinyl contains nasty chemicals and while it's cheaper than other window frames, the performance is not consistent. The obvious choice according to the performance matrix chart was fiberglass, which is what the fiberglass manufacturer wants you to arrive at. Window frames made out of spun fibers of glass and resin are durable, have good energy performance, relatively low environmental impact, and a cost on par or lower than wood. Plus the materials are close cousins. Fiberglass is made out of glass. As the window expands and shrinks with the weather, the glass and the frame expand and shrink at the same rate. If the frame and the glass expanded and contracted at different rates, the sealant between them would degrade faster. Convinced that fiberglass was the way to go, Kurt narrowed down the choices to two manufacturers and got quotes. In 2011 the fiberglass windows we came across were made by Serious Materials in California and Cascadia Windows in Canada. Serious Windows was the only U.S. manufacturer located in the San Francisco Bay Area.

Glass or Mylar?

Of the Passive Houses we visited during our design phase in 2011, only one used American-made windows from Serious Materials. (Since then Alpen acquired the brand from Serious Materials.) All the other windows were foreign made. Wanting to source locally where possible, we drove to Sunnyvale to have a look at the cross section of the Serious Windows. The business we visited was not a retail outlet. From the curb it looked like any of the commercial boxes that house high-tech engineers and corporate types in the office zones of Sunnyvale, Santa Clara, and San Jose.

Why would a corporate establishment receive homeowner visitors in their conference room? I didn't know, but Kurt's gift of gab resulted in us having an appointment at their corporate headquarters to have someone show us a cross section of the window. The smallish conference room we sat in felt sterile and the fluorescent lighting cast a cold light. The marketing lady managed to take time from her busy schedule and received us warmly. She showed us the cross section of the window and answered our questions.

We knew that Serious Windows had a weight advantage. Three pieces of glass can make triple-pane windows quite heavy. But with a Mylar film in the middle layer, Serious Window is able to provide the performance of triple pane windows without the extra weight and cost of the glass.

What's in the glass?

I had an opportunity to ask my favorite walking encyclopedia some questions about glass while driving back from our window shopping appointment. I knew that years ago glass used in windows contained lead, but not anymore. I also have observed that retail shelf glass at a store appears green when you look at it from the side. But I didn't know why.

"Hey, Kurt, I'm curious," I said as we headed toward the freeway.

"Curious about what?"

We love conversations that start this way.

"Well, I know that lead was taken out of glass because it's dangerous. But why did they use it in the first place?"

"You know that glass is made out of sand, right?"

"Yeah." I looked out the side window. Not grainy at all.

"Those tiny quartz pieces, sand, melt at a very high temperature. Introducing lead into the sand makes it melt at a lower temperature."

"Oh, OK. They used lead in glass for manufacturing efficiency."

"Right. Not only was it efficient, it was also good for light. Lead will let light through the glass without affecting the colors."

"Really?"

"Yep. When you look through the old windows at our 1922 house, you'll see the colors in a natural state. Lead is pretty nice for letting true colors through."

"Hmm." I tapped the window beside me. "So, what do they use in glass now?"

"Mostly soda-lime. It has a greenish tint. It looks green because the materials block the wavelength of red light. You may notice when you look through windows that people look a bit greener—and less bright."

I put on my sunglasses. We were in Sunnyvale, aptly named. Nothing today was less bright, but I played along. "Why less bright?"

"Because with every air-to-glass contact, you lose approximately 5 percent of light."

"Really?" He really is a walking encyclopedia. "How do you know that?"

"I know it from studying physics."

I rolled down my window halfway to look at the edge of the glass. "So if there is 5 percent degradation of light for each air-to-glass contact, then double pane windows lose 20 percent of brightness and triple pane windows lose 30 percent?"

"Yes, approximately."

"Those demo windows we saw had a gray tinge. When we get triple-paned windows with additional low-e coating on the glass, the house will be darker, right?" I looked at my arm, half bathed in direct sunlight and half bathed in the light coming through the partially opened window. Sure enough there was grayish green veil on my arm where glass-filtered light landed. I wondered if we would lose part of the "happy feeling" we got at the house from the single-pane lead windows letting in bright natural light.

Measuring light transmission

Later at home Kurt used his photography gadgets to demonstrate how the light could lose brightness through layers of glass. He's an old school analog photographer with a collection of cameras made in the 1930s, and our freezer space is generously allocated to film that's no longer made. Over the years I've acquired an appreciation for looking at interesting textures on weathered, hand-cranked cement mixers, ageing fire hydrants, and quaint farm equipment at dawn or dusk, patiently waiting for him to capture the right lighting.

The light meter Kurt uses to confirm the light intensity before he sets the f-stops and exposure on his camera is also analog and quaint. He made me appreciate it in a new way for this lesson about light. He held the light meter under the fluorescent light in the kitchen of our condo, and it indicated 64. That's the baseline. Then he grabbed three glass slide mounts and stacked them so that there was a little bit of air between each piece of glass to simulate a triple pane window. He then took a new reading under the three pieces of glass, and the reading dipped to about 45, which is 30 percent less than 64. Fascinating. The home kitchen science experiment proved Kurt's earlier statement to be true. There is 5 percent degradation in light intensity with each glass-to-air contact.

This meant the amount of light coming into the house through the windows would be 30 percent less than through the original leaky, single-pane, inefficient windows with the pretty leaded glass. I felt a little sad about losing the light quality, but it was a trade-off I was willing to make for energy savings and thermal comfort. I didn't know if I'd be able to notice the decrease in light indoors when the house was done. I imagined the 30 percent loss of light would be welcome, however, in the south-facing rooms with large windows and French doors.

Low-emissivity coating

Something else comes through the window besides visible light—heat. A cat will nap on a sunny windowsill during the winter when it's cold outside because it's warm and comfy in the sunlight. But a cat would not approach the toasty window during a heat wave in the summer. It's too hot.

We humans have figured out clever ways of controlling the amount of heat coming through the window so that cats can nap happily near the window. When I was growing up in Hawaii, it was cool to have a car with tinted windows. It was the equivalent of giving the car a pair of cool sunglasses. Toward end of college, I had saved enough to buy a tiny, mint green Honda Accord hatchback. Soon after I got the car, I asked a friend to tint my windows. He cut sticky pieces of film to size and pasted them onto the glass from the inside. The car felt cooler while I drove around in the tropical weather, and I felt cool driving around in a car that had the coloring of mint-chocolate chip ice cream.

Emissivity refers to the effectiveness of the material's surface to radiate energy. Low-emissivity coatings (low-e for short) on the windows are used to control the amount of energy radiated by the glass. The low-e coating applied to window glass looks nothing like the dark window tints I had on my car in Hawaii. Low-e coating is virtually transparent. It is an effective gatekeeper of light waves that would please Goldilocks. It doesn't let in too much of the short wavelength light because ultraviolet (UV) light can damage or fade the furnishings in the house. But it does let in the medium wavelength light (visible light) so we can see our way around the house and enjoy the view out the window. Low-e coating blocks the long wavelength light because that is infrared (IR) light, which is heat, and we don't want to overheat the house.

On a triple pane window, the outermost surface, which comes in contact with the wind and the rain, is surface number one. The flip side of that piece of glass is surface two. Moving in, the middle glass will be surfaces three and four. The innermost glass is numbered surfaces five and six. Surface six is what the cat will press up against when taking a nap on the windowsill. Not all of the glass surfaces would get the low-e coating. The low-e coating would be applied to Midori's windows (eyes) on the number two and number five glass surfaces of each window.

The rationale for this plan is that the low-e coating on surface two will keep the heat from the sun on the outside, and this will keep Midori comfortable when the outside temperature is hot. The low-e coating on surface five will keep the heat inside the house from escaping to the outside when it's cold outside. The space between the glasses is filled with argon gas, a noble gas with low reactivity to other chemicals and which provides more resistance to heat transfer than air.

Trade off: performance vs. tax credit

Tuning high-performance windows to the regional climate and the compass orientation of the building is a critical part of the Passivhaus design. In our house plan, the glazing area was 17 percent of the total wall area, which was about 2 percent more than the original house. South-facing rooms, master bedroom, and my office increased the glazing area considerably to the point where structural engineering calculations were required for the permit. The window openings in the other rooms got slightly larger or smaller. Only the dining room remained the same.

For a while the U.S. government incentivized homeowners to install windows with low-e coating by giving tax credits to homeowners who installed windows that met the EnergyStar standard. The low-e coating for this standard was the favored approach to keep the heat out of the house to reduce air conditioning use. Tax credit was available to homeowners who installed windows that kept heat out of the house. This type of incentive is great for homes with heavy air conditioning use. In Santa Cruz hardly any homes have air conditioning because the climate is mild. In fact, we need more heating than cooling during the year. With Midori we chose to optimize the low-e coating for the daily and seasonal path of the sun. Some of our windows are coated to bring in heat and other windows are coated to keep the heat out. This meant we didn't get a tax credit. We chose energy performance specific to our local climate over federal tax credit for the windows because one-time tax savings of few hundred dollars didn't seem like good trade-off for greater energy savings that yielded better return over the long term.

We wanted Midori to use the warmth from the sun to heat the interior space during the winter when the sun angle is low. The south-facing windows needed to let in the heat during the winter, so those would need a high solar heat gain type of coating. This wouldn't be an overheating problem in summer because the windows would be shaded during the summer by a shade cloth or vines growing over the arbor. We chose to have coating that would keep the heat out applied to the windows on the east and west walls for dealing with the heat from daily sunrise and sunset. We chose the same type of coating for the windows on the north wall even though it wouldn't have any direct sun on it.

Cascadia windows

Getting the other fiberglass window makers to respond to our inquiries took an effort. Eventually a Passive House consultant in San Francisco managed to connect Kurt with a Cascadia distributor who was based out of Oregon. We saw an example of a Cascadia window used in a Passive House project at the San Francisco Zen Center's new dormitory. The Cascadia windows in a commercial brown color looked good.

Meanwhile Taylor was trying to get us to source the product through Tom Nedelsky at Santa Cruz Millwork. We met Tom at the local Home and Garden Show and we talked to him about our project. He seemed sincerely interested. Following up with a meeting in his shop, we saw a cross section of a triple-pane thermally broken window from a German firm, Bildau & Bussmann. We briefly considered them but decided not to pursue because the windows were made out of wood and we wanted fiberglass. Tom was intrigued with the Passive House Standard and was interested in getting our business. He went over and beyond the customer service of all the window distributors we dealt with. In a matter of weeks he became a Cascadia distributor and suddenly, getting Cascadia information became much easier. We did choose Cascadia windows because it represented good cost performance and we felt good about having local support.

It turns out, Tom lives just two blocks away from our house and has a short one-mile bike ride to his shop. He makes custom doors and windows as well as represents several manufacturers. It's somewhat comforting to work with a small local company that has been around for a long time, and with someone who shared similar sustainability values and beliefs. Tom made sure we had the order for Cascadia windows just right before placing the order. He insisted on having them provide shop drawings and came onsite with the shop drawings to measure each and every one of the rough openings for the windows and checked each against the shop drawings. Measure twice cut once. Isn't that the adage used by carpenters? It's even more true with custom windows.

The large windows on the north side of the house were fixed windows, meaning there is no mechanism to operate (open or close) the windows. The window opening was the same size as Midori's original window, so the framing didn't change. Taylor reinforced the framing because the Cascadia windows with three panes of glass are much heavier than the original single-pane windows. Each pane of glass is four millimeters thick (about one-fifth of an inch) and they are spaced a half-inch apart.

Two of our windows are tilt-turn casement windows. When I first saw them it seemed like magic. An ordinary inswing window opens by turning the handle and pulling it inward. It's not much different than operating a door. The magical part of a tilt-turn casement window is the tilting feature. To tilt the window, we first return the window to the closed position and then gently pull on the handlebar pointed upwards so the window leans inward. The tilted position of the window leaves an opening of about six inches at the top, just enough to let some breeze through without worrying about the window slamming shut.

Most of the smaller windows are awning windows where there is a hinge on the top of the window and you operate it by pushing out on the bottom. It looks like an awning when it's fully opened.

Muntins

We asked to have unique grid patterns on the windows to make them look like old-fashioned muntins. A muntin is a strip of wood or metal separating and holding small panes of glass in a window. Because it was impossible or cost-prohibitive to manufacture large sheets of glass prior to the twentieth century, larger dimensioned windows were assembled from many smaller panes of glass joined together with muntins. (The word is a mash-up of Middle English, Middle French, and Dutch.)

Like other homes of this vintage, Midori had wood windows but surprisingly lacked muntins. She was definitely missing the grid patterns of different sizes that gave other Arts and Crafts homes their character and charm. So we decided to give her window dressings. To gather ideas for the patterns, we walked around neighborhoods with bungalows and noted the muntin patterns. Different muntin patterns made the patchwork of glass look appealing while creating larger windows. Most of the houses on our street have grid-pattern muntins where the top third of the window has two rows of rectangles. Some have the prairie-style patterns where single muntin is placed parallel and close to each of the four sides of frame. A couple of blocks away are homes with original windows featuring diamond-shaped muntin patterns.

For Midori's new windows, simulated divided lights (SDL) were used to create the look of muntins. Inch-wide fiberglass strips were adhered to the glass surface on both outside (side one) and the inside (side six) of the glass. We also had spacer bars of the same size installed between the middle glass pane and the outer glass pane that traced the pattern of SDL adhered on the outer glass.

Trade-off: moving gas line vs. inoperable windows

The dining room was the only room in the house with only inoperable windows, although we really wanted to be able to open and close the windows above the built-in buffet.

Initially we specified awning type windows for the dining room, like the windows in the living room. Then we learned the city's building code doesn't allow operable windows within six feet of a gas meter. Our gas meter is right under these windows. It has a vent, and the natural gas leaks ever so slightly. I can actually smell it when I get near it. But we really wanted windows we could open. We thought about keeping one window operable and making two fixed, but that would look unattractive. Moving the gas line and the meter was expensive. Even if we did move it, where could it go without affecting another operable window? This was an indoor air quality and safety concern, and there just wasn't a way to get what we preferred, so we accepted having all fixed windows in the dining room.

Innie or outie?

We've heard of stories where a late window delivery causes the entire project to fall behind schedule. In our case the windows arrived early on a damp March morning when the scent of heavy clay mud lingered after the rain. The delivery truck backed into the driveway. We watched the most expensive purchase of our project unveil itself piece by piece as the delivery man, Tom, and Taylor gripped and guided the larger windows using big suction cups attached to a handle. Even the territory sales manager from Cascadia came down from Seattle to witness their windows being delivered to the first Passive House project in Santa Cruz. Taylor was two weeks away from installing the windows. He gave specific instructions to place them in various rooms in the house so that they were properly staged for installation.

The exterior wall was nine inches thick and the windows were only 2.5 inches thick at the glass. Now we had a new question: Where should the window be placed? Did we want an innie or outie? In other words, did we want to place the windows on the inside, flush against the interior walls, or did we want them flush against the exterior cladding? Or maybe simply have them sit in the middle? My gut reaction was to have windows installed flush against the exterior wall so that the six inches of the interior wall would be covered by a sill and make a perfect place for a cat to take a nap. Not that we had cats, but the image seemed comfy and cozy. Before we gave our final answer to this question, we checked in with Graham. He confirmed that in our mild climate, the thermal performance due to placement of the windows is not critical and the exterior mounted look would simplify the flashing details by eliminating the exterior window "niche."

Lessons learned: choosing eyes (windows)

Windows provide important functions such as fresh air, lighting, style, view, and thermal comfort. Windows are the most expensive component and there are lots of details to consider when choosing windows.

❖ When we shopped for windows, we found the insulated fiberglass windows to be better for durability, performance, and cost.

- ❖ There are different options for low-emissivity coating on windows, and we chose the coating that will provide heat gain for the south side of the house but minimize heat gain for the north, east, and west sides of the house while maximizing visible transmittance everywhere.

- ❖ We got the look and feel of muntins, which are typical for bungalow style, by using simulated divided lights (SDL).

- ❖ When faced with a trade-off situation, we looked at the alternatives and made our decision based on what was most important to us. We chose energy performance over tax credit, and we chose aesthetics and cost over ability to open windows.

- ❖ In our mild climate it doesn't matter where we install the window (innie, outie, or middle) in the depth of the wall, so we chose the installation style that visually pleased us.

12
Rethinking and Replacing Systems

Thinking behind the walls

At this point in the construction, we could see the infrastructure that's usually hidden behind the walls. We reconfirmed and sometimes changed the placement of the light switches and plugs by walking around and imagining how we interacted with the room. Seeing the actual pipes, ducts, and wiring validated our rethinking of the systems explored in the design phase.

Rethinking and connecting the dots

The basic needs of the occupants in the house had not changed since Midori was created in 1922. We still needed fresh air inside the house, water and energy delivered to the house, waste hauled away. Simply replacing the innards of Midori (the digestive, nervous, respiratory, and circulatory systems) with the equivalent of what she had before would be a disservice to her and to us. We had an opportunity to rethink what would make sense with today's technology and whole-house systems.

The Passive House Standard guided us through our rethinking with a focus on energy efficiency to make good use of every kilowatt hour of electricity and therm of gas consumed. Given the strict energy budget target, we had to think about how different choices that appeared unrelated (hot water pipe diameter, underfloor insulation, and method of heating water) deeply affected the energy use and our comfort.

Building codes are, in fact, a guide, and they are in place to ensure the health and safety of the occupants. They set the standard of what's minimally required. As imperfect as we may perceive them to be, it saves time from having to research and put in place things that could harm us—lead-based paint, asbestos, carbon monoxide, poor structural integrity so that the building could collapse, and more. California's energy efficiency code for buildings, Title 24 Section 6, aims to conserve electricity and natural gas so the state does not have to build more power plants. As Midori's construction was going on in 2012, the California Energy Commission announced it had saved Californians $74 billion in reduced electricity bills since 1977. We wanted to do more than what these regulations were prescribing, and the Passive House Standard guided us in addressing energy. For other areas such as water and air quality, we connected the dots.

Connecting the dots between the water that comes out of the tap and its point of origin is an interesting exercise. So is connecting the dots between wastewater leaving the home and going to the wastewater treatment plant and eventually going out into the environment. Just as Passive House standard opened our eyes to the importance of source energy, learning about where our water comes from and where it goes gave us a perspective of how our daily lives can affect the overall freshwater cycle in our community. Connecting the dots between what's going on in the neighborhood and the air we breathe inside the house is another way to guide thinking of how to replace a house's systems.

Rethink plumbing

The plumbing system is like the digestive system of the body. There is one point of entry for the clean water to come into the house from the water meter on the sidewalk. The water gets distributed throughout the property through a network of supply pipes. All of the wastewater from the kitchen, laundry, and bathrooms is removed from the house via gently sloped wastewater pipes to feed into the sewer lines.

We knew Midori needed new pipes because the house inspection report advised to have the copper and galvanized plumbing removed and replaced. Midori still had her original ceramic wastewater pipes connecting the wastewater from the house to the city's sewer line.

The location of the pipes did not change much. The bathrooms were in the same place even though the faucets and showers were moved. The kitchen sinks and the clothes washer were located close to each other in the middle of the house so it all tied in nicely. The layout of the water distribution network was simple.

The big questions were: what to replace it with and how best to conserve water.

Point of view and our values

Perspectives matter in rethinking the plumbing system. We live in California where the annual rainfall varies much more than other states and we experience droughts that makes us hyper-aware and sensitive to water conservation. Water conservation values, however, don't always translate from one place to another. Diaper use is one example. I've heard someone say that if you live in a place that has more water than landfill, it's preferable to use cloth diapers and wash them, but if you are in a place where water is scarce and landfill is plentiful, perhaps disposable diapers are more appropriate. It's a judgment call, and sometimes even knowing the entire life cycle of a product is less important than knowing as much as possible about the place we live so that decisions made can be place-specific. Midori gave us an opportunity to learn about our place—where our water comes from, where the waste-water goes, how electricity is produced, how construction waste is handled, the characteristics of our climate, and what the local government wants the residents to do based on rebates and incentives.

We lived in a coastal area of California during a drought. We wanted to receive the gifts of natural resources falling on our property. To make good use of sun and rain, we had to build the infrastructure to receive them. Values of maximum energy efficiency and locally sourced, non-toxic materials were high on our list. The specific choices we made in our project were based on our personal values and the characteristics of our location (climate, geology, infrastructure, watersheds). These choices may not translate or apply to other people's specific projects, so research is critical to make good choices.

Local water

Just as there is a network of pipes distributing water throughout the house, the State of California has a network of pipes and canals to deliver water from one region to another. For example, San Francisco receives 85 percent of its water from the Hetch Hetchy watershed in the Sierra Nevada Mountains about 200 miles away. Unlike many cities in California that are connected to various water highways in the state, Santa Cruz relies on its own watershed.

"The watershed" refers to a basin shaped by the natural geography of the region that holds water in the area. It can consist of lakes, rivers, underground aquifers, and any other pockets where water can accumulate. The watershed relies on local rainfall, so when we start getting less rain than usual, our supply of drinking water goes down.

Not surprisingly, residents of Santa Cruz pay attention to water usage. Daily water usage per household in the city of Santa Cruz is 92 gallons a day compared to the California average of 160 gallons per household. Even if we had the ocean right next to us, we can't drink the water from the sea without doing energy-intensive processing to remove salt. In fact the debate of whether to build a desalination plant in Santa Cruz was hotly contested by local residents. The Charter of City of Santa Cruz was amended to require voter approval for desalination projects (Measure P) following the 2012 election with over 72 percent vote. We tend to be vigilant about and dedicated to water conservation in our city.

Water is relatively scarce where Midori is located and we needed to pay attention to her water efficiency features. In addition to having water efficient toilets, faucets, showerheads, clothes washer, and dishwasher, we made changes to her water distribution system.

Pipe diameter matters

If I took a ten-minute shower and the shower head had a flow rate of 2.5 gallons per minute (GPM), then 25 gallons of water would go down the drain during my shower. If I replaced the 2.5 GPM shower head with a low-flow shower head, say 1.5 GPM, then the ten-minute shower now would use only 15 gallons, a savings of 10 gallons per shower. If I shortened my shower to five minutes, then I would use only 7.5 gallons. That's a good start, but more water can be saved by rethinking the plumbing infrastructure.

When I took the hot water heater course taught by Gary Klein, I sat next to a guy who lived in a house much larger and slightly older than Midori. When Gary asked, "So what do you do between the time you turn on your hot water and get in the shower?" the guy next to me said, "Well, I turn on the hot water and go downstairs to make coffee and do a few other things, then I go back to the bathroom to see if the water is warm." He's not intentionally wasting water, and if he changed his 2.5 GPM shower head to a 1.5 GPM shower head, it would almost double his wait time. He'd save water during his shower, but he'd still waste as much water as he did before during warm-up because the amount of cooled-off water in his hot water pipe would remain the same.

The lesson here is that the distance between the water heater and the shower combined with the diameter of the pipe determines how many gallons of cooled-off water need to run through the pipe before it's comfortable to step into the shower. The fatter the pipe, the more water. The longer the pipe, the more water.

Collecting warm-up water and using it in the garden, as many Californians do, is great for conserving water, but it still wastes the energy that was used to heat the water in the first place. Using a smaller diameter pipe and having an efficient layout of the hot water distribution pipes in the house saves both water and energy.

We had a great opportunity to save both water and energy by re-plumbing Midori's hot water pipes. The distance between the water heater and the shower was determined by the layout of the rooms. Fortunately, the run length of the pipes was fairly short— the mechanical room holding the water heater is right next to the master bathroom, and the guest bathroom is just on the other side of the master bedroom. We chose small-diameter pipes for Midori's distribution pipes, only three-eighths inches. The pipe holds only one cup of water for about every ten linear feet. This means the shower in the guest bathroom may have up to one-quarter gallon of water to flush out before getting hot water. The beauty of this is that once the new pipe infrastructure is in place, the low usage will continue for the life of the pipes.

Dual plumbing for rainwater

Another way to reduce potable water or drinking water usage in the house is to find an alternate source for non-potable water. We need potable water for drinking, cooking, and bathing, but it is only a tiny portion of the water used inside the house. Statistics from East Bay Municipal Water District showing the breakdown of indoor water use convinced us that we have an opportunity to save water. On average, according to EBMUD, 20 percent of indoor household water goes down the toilet, and another 19 per-cent is used in the clothes washer. It seems silly to have the utility go through the trouble of extracting, purifying, and piping clean drinking water to our homes just so we can flush one-fifth of our household water down the toilet.

Inspired by what we saw at the San Francisco Zen Center in Marin, we asked Taylor to plumb the house so that the clothes washer and toilets can take water from two different water sources—one from city water (drinking water) and one from rainwater. At the San Francisco Zen Center, they captured and collected rainwater in a large tank. Normally when people do rainwater harvesting, they use the rainwater for irrigating their landscape. But at the Zen Center, they had the rainwater filtered and treated and used it to flush the toilets. I thought that if we can use the sunlight falling on our roof to heat hot water, why can't we use the rainwater falling on our roof to flush our toilets? It made sense.

So we tracked down the experts who designed and installed the Zen Center's system to see if we could install a similar but less complex system. It was a no go. Partly because it was expensive, but mostly because the administrative hurdles seemed onerous. We were told that besides getting the approval from the building department and the water department of the city, we would need to go to the health department at the county to get their approval as well. Stories we heard at the time indicated the caution and regulations would make our system expensive. Two years later, the California State Plumbing code change of 2013 explicitly stated the requirements for non-potable indoor use of rainwater (toilet flushing and laundry). But we were designing and deciding in 2011.

We talked to some folks who had installed rainwater systems for toilet flushing without getting a permit, but we decided not to go that route. It's my nature to do things by the book. We knew we would be sharing information. I started blogging about Midori to share updates with our friends and family. Had we gone with a non-permitted system for rainwater, writing a blog post about it would be like inviting a building inspector to ticket us. We also intended to have house tours to share our learning. We wanted to inspire others to think differently about their living space and also continue the paying forward nature of those who generously shared information with us. It wouldn't be a good example if we were red-tagged.

We decided, however, to have dual plumbing installed while we had Midori's walls open. This would avoid doing expensive surgery down the road to open her up again to put it in later. For each of the toilets and the washing machine, there was an extra stub-out capped and connected to the purple line that terminated in the backyard where the rainwater tank would be installed. The rainwater pipes were purple to clearly distinguish them from the potable water lines.

Reusing water

Another way to conserve water is to reuse our lightly-used water. This is called gray water. We had a three-way valve installed next to the clothes washer drain outlet so that we could choose to direct the spent laundry water either to the landscape to water the fruit trees or to the sewer if the laundry water contained anything that wasn't appropriate for the landscape. Local building codes differ, but in California the laundry-to-landscape feature can be installed without a permit as long as some simple guidelines are followed.

We didn't have Taylor install the irrigation plumbing in the yard to direct the laundry water to the plants because we didn't know where we'd be planting the fruit trees. The existing fruit trees on the property, two apple and two orange trees, seemed to be doing just fine without irrigation. The new fruit trees to be planted would need some care and maintenance until they were established. So the laundry water could serve that purpose. When we do start using the laundry-to-landscape feature, we need to remember to stop using Borax as an additive to the detergent in our laundry as it is harmful to plants.

We have another source of gray water. Remember my ofuro? Taylor plumbed the soaking tub on the deck so that the wastewater wouldn't drain to the sewer. He connected the drain to the hose bib next to the deck so that we could connect the garden hose and freely water the plants within the hose's reach.

We could have maximized water re-use by having a full-blown gray water system by routing wastewater from the sinks and the showers to the landscape and recycling the heat from these waters with an innovative product from an Australian company called Nexus eWater. Australia is driest continent on earth, and inhabitants managed to reduce water use down to forty-three gallons per person per day during their drought. They can teach us a lot about water conservation. While it would have been cool to take the wastewater from the sinks, showers, and water appliances and reuse both the water and the water's heat, we didn't quite have the appetite to do this. Not yet, anyway. Why? Because we're a bit shy about being on the bleeding edge and did not want to be the first installation in the U.S. It would have meant jumping through hoops to satisfy concerns of building officials to get the permit. Perhaps decades down the road when we need to consider updating our plumbing system, we'll consider this.

PEX piping

The guy in my water heater class who went downstairs to make coffee while he waited for hot water in his shower had the "trunk-and-branch" type of plumbing layout, which is typical of residential plumbing. Trunk-and-branch is like a tree with the large diameter mainline (trunk) supplying water to smaller diameter branch lines supplying rooms with twigs connected to the toilet, shower, and sink fixtures. It has some drawbacks. A person taking a shower is likely to scream if someone flushes the toilet next to the shower because that would temporarily reduce the amount of cold water going to the shower. The layout of trunk-and-branch line is simpler and uses less plumbing than the "home run" or "manifold" layout.

We chose the home run distribution layout not just to eliminate those cold-water screams, but also because it allows for smaller diameter pipes, which reduce heat loss and wait time. Yes, we needed more materials than the trunk-and-branch method, but we didn't use copper pipes for distribution. Copper is expensive compared to cross-linked polyethylene tubes (PEX) both in materials cost and labor cost. Copper pipes are rigid and need special fittings to make the bends and turns. Soldering a 90-degree turn or a T-junction on copper pipes takes much longer and greater attention to detail is needed to make sure it doesn't leak. Flexible PEX tubes can make an easy, sweeping turn to enable water to travel smoothly by avoiding harsh right angle turns that cause friction. Just as with copper pipes, PEX comes in different sizes. We chose three-eighths inch PEX tubes for our distribution pipes, which are attached to the manifold in the wall of the mechanical room. Fortunately the plan checkers didn't comment on the pipe diameter when we submitted the plans for the permit. The cold water lines outside the house connected to the hose bibs and were slightly larger three-quarter inch PEX tube.

Taylor is wonderfully talented and, as stated before, he does the plumbing and electrical work himself. I watched him install the PEX lines under the house in the crawlspace to see how they connect. He inserted a metal expander tool into the end of PEX tube with the connection joint and temporarily expanded it. Then he removed part of the tool and quickly inserted the mating end of the PEX line before the connection closed up snugly between the two. It was fast and seemed much simpler than joining copper pipes.

Rethink ventilation

If the plumbing system is like the digestive system of the body, then the ventilation system in the house is like the respiratory system. Midori never had a proper respiratory system. She had an exhaust fan in the kitchen and a furnace that blew hot air from the register on the floor. She breathed deeply when people in the house opened the windows, but mostly she breathed randomly through various cracks and crevices because her shell was so leaky. The plan was to create an envelope around her body like a beer cooler or a thermos, and it would be practically airtight. She'd need a good respiratory system to breathe, a heat recovery ventilator (HRV) to bring in filtered fresh air, exhaust stale air, and continuously recover heat in the process.

When I first learned about the HRV ventilation system, it made me examine and think about the condo we lived in and the shortcomings of the conventional system. When the kitchen vent hood exhausted warm, moist air (full of cooking smells and combustion byproducts), both the undesirable air and the heat left the house in a hurry. How much air? Depending on the model and speed setting on the vent hood, the air volume sucked out of the kitchen could be as little as 150 cubic feet per minute (CFM) or as much as 900 CFM. I often think of these cubic-feet-per-minute numbers by visualizing twelve-inch-thick queen-size mattresses (60 in. x 80 in.). If a powerful kitchen vent hood ran at 900 CFM, then the air volume equivalent to eighteen queen size mattresses would be removed each minute. The house would be gasping to bring fresh air into the house. If all the windows and doors were closed, the house would pull in air through the fireplace flue (path of least resistance), dragging soot and dust back into the house, or in through cracks in the floor, bringing in moldy air from the crawlspace. Yuck. Plus in the winter, cold air would replace the warmed air going out of the house, making the heater work that much harder. This is called backdrafting.

When we learned about backdrafting, we did a test where Kurt stood by the wall heater and I turned on the kitchen vent hood. Sure enough he felt air flow on his hand. This backdraft experiment right in our living space at the condo started a routine of cracking open a window before turning on the bathroom fan or the kitchen vent hood. With a properly air-sealed Passive House with the HRV, we wouldn't have to worry about backdrafting and air coming in from random and unhealthy places.

Heat recovery ventilator (HRV)

Among the hundreds of models of HRVs from various manufacturers, we chose the ComfoAir 350 model of HRV from Zehnder. We went with the sure thing rather than comparison shop. The ComfoAir 305 from Zehnder is a certified Passive House Component, which means it passed the testing criteria set by Passivhaus Institut and performs well. It was interesting to note that the various Passive House residences we visited in the Bay Area all used Zehnder HRV and the owners seemed happy with it.

Midori breathes differently than humans do. While we can breathe in and out through either our nose or mouth, she breathes in through her nose and breathes out through her mouth. We placed her "nose" on the east side of the house pretty much by process of elimination. The south side of the house would have been too hot. The north side faced the street, so not only would the vent be visible from the front, there would be car exhaust. Midori's west side was the driveway and was in the general direction of a very busy street with lots of car exhaust. The east side of the house was quiet and had trees flanking the fence of a friendly neighbor. So we chose the side with the trees, which provide oxygen and clean air. From a profile view, the small awning placed over the air intake opening really does resemble a small nose. We put a bug screen over her nose, for obvious reasons!

The Zender HRV treats incoming (supply) and outgoing (exhaust) air differently and has different pipes for these air sources. The HRV fan pulls in fresh air from outside the house through a ComfoPipe. This seven-inch-diameter tube is buried in insulation in the attic. It runs from the east side of the house to the center of the house where the HRV body is located. Within the HRV body there are two removable filters. We chose the finer pollen filter (F7 or MERV 13) to further keep the air inside the house clean.

What's brilliant about the HRV ventilation unit is that it recycles heat. Once within the cavity of the HRV body, the air passes through a heat-exchange core. Instead of carrying off heat with the moisture and cooking odors, the core of the HRV has a chamber that enables the exhaust air to give off heat to the incoming fresh air. This core is a practical and clever design that allows air-to-air heat exchange between incoming fresh air and exhausting stale air without mixing the air. Fresh air stays clean during the heat exchange. Imagine it is 45°F outside and a nice and toasty 75°F in the kitchen from baking cookies. In the heat-exchange core, the 75°F exhausting air gives off its heat to the incoming fresh air that is thirty degrees cooler. The fresh air distributed through the house is a bit cooler than the toasty kitchen air, but it's a lot warmer than the outside air. The energy used to raise the air temperature is a tiny amount of electricity to run the fan in the HRV body, the equivalent of energy needed for one LED light bulb (10W) to two incandescent light bulbs (198W), depending on the fan speed setting. It's simple, elegant, and efficient.

Midori is outfitted with more flexible ComfoTubes that are only three inches in diameter to distribute air to different rooms. These ducts are perfectly sized to fit into the conventional wall cavity framed with 2x4 lumber. The ComfoTubes are ridged on the outside, but the inside is smooth to let the air flow easily. When I first saw the ComfoTubes laid out, it looked like an upside down squid with tentacles reaching out to different rooms above via the attic.

Thoughtful deliberation went into the placement of each room's supply air register. Should it go on the ceiling? On the floor? High or low on the wall? For most of the rooms we chose low on the wall, slightly higher than the electrical outlet. It looked better low than high, and heat rises. For the master closet and the dining room, they are up on the ceiling. In the living room there are two registers, one on the ceiling and one on the wall. At each of these designated spots in the room, the ComfoTube is connected to a diffuser, a box about the size of a child's shoebox, that is connected to the transfer grill. We briefly considered getting a decorative grill in the style of old houses, but decided it would be better to let the grill blend in with the wall rather than draw attention to it. So we selected a white rectangular grid with pencil hole perforations arranged in rows and columns. The volume of air delivered to each of the rooms feels like a soft whisper rather than the blaring white noise delivered by conventional forced-air heating systems. Fresh air is supplied to the bedrooms, kitchen, living room, and the dining room.

Stale air is routed through the exhaust ducts back into the HRV before it is expelled outside of the house. Stale air is extracted from the bathrooms, kitchen, and laundry cubby. Air in these rooms tends to be warmer, moist, and smellier than in the other rooms. Air is extracted out of these rooms through a round return diffuser cover attached to the diffuser box in the ceiling. Air travels through the ComfoTube back into the body of HRV to serve as the heat source for incoming air. After the stale air exchanges heat in the HRV core, it heads straight up through the roof in another seven-inch-wide ComfoPipe, and enters the atmosphere through her "mouth" at the roof. From the outside, the vent sticking out of the rooftop looks like any other bathroom conventional vent in the neighborhood.

We decided the best place for the HRV control panel, which is almost the size of a business card, was on the kitchen wall next to the steam oven. The control panel allowed us to make simple changes such as adjust the air flow rate or change the temperature set point for performing the summer bypass. Increasing the air-flow will be part of our new cooking routine.

In the bathrooms Taylor installed a manual spring-loaded timer switch next to the light switch. Turning the dial on the timer past ten minutes would trigger the HRV to operate on setting three, the highest flow rate, for the duration of the timer plus an additional thirty minutes. The HRV returns to the prior setting when this timer function has been fulfilled. The main difference between the conventional bathroom exhaust fan and the HRV system is the duration. While conventional bathroom exhaust fans are turned on and off by the user, the HRV is removing the air from the bathroom all the time. Continuously, 24-7. So even if we don't turn on the timer before taking a shower, the air is being exhausted. The timer is used to increase the exhaust rate temporarily.

The summer bypass is a feature that evacuates the stale warmer air from inside the house without sending it through the heat-exchange core. This is useful during the summer when cool night air is used to provide slight interior cooling with no extra energy burden. The temperature set point to trigger this bypass is manually set, higher in the winter and lower in the summer.

A lot of thought went into the HRV for our passive house, and for many good reasons. The first one is comfort. This device solved the problem of providing constant fresh air in a fairly sealed environment. We get to breathe fresh, filtered air all the time, and the temperature of the house stays consistent over a long period of time. Second, we save energy with the HRV because it reuses the heat in the house and reduces the additional energy needed for heating. This means conventional heating such as a furnace is no longer needed. A much smaller heat source will do. Third, it's quiet.

Conventional bathroom and kitchen exhaust fans move a lot of air quickly with a loud whirl or whoosh. We find that annoying. Since the HRV will be installed right in the middle of the house in the hallway closet, loud noise was a concern. That concern was dispelled when we saw the Zehnder HRVs at Passive Houses in the Bay Area and noticed how quiet they were. As with the sound of a refrigerator or a quiet dishwasher, you can hear the HRV operating if you stand right next to the HRV body and listen, but there is no sound coming out of the supply air registers in the bedrooms or the exhaust registers in the bathrooms.

Perhaps the most important benefit of the HRV is health. Knowing where and how the air in the living space comes from provides peace of mind. Remember Bill Hayward and his family experiencing prolonged illness caused by mold and other impurities wafting up into the living space through random cracks in the house? He is now a big proponent of HRV installed in a tightly sealed house. It empowers the occupants to bring in fresh air from controlled known source rather than random unknown places.

Rethink heating

"Please show location of furnace."

That was a comment written on the plan check document as we were going through permitting. Graham politely replied, "The building will be heated with a hydronic coil connected to the hot water heater and the heat recovery ventilator. It is notated on Sheet M1.0 on the Mechanical Plan."

When Graham ran the calculation using the PHPP software, it showed that to keep our house comfortable, even on the coldest nights in the winter, we'd need less energy than what a hair dryer consumes. It seems like a ridiculously low amount of energy, but we had faith in Passive House. One Sky Homes conducted a test in a newly constructed Passive House twice the square footage of Midori just thirty miles away in San Jose. Their experiment proved that an ordinary 1600-watt hair dryer can keep a Passive House comfortable on a cold night. The story is on YouTube, searchable with keywords "hair dryer home energy use."

If we hadn't encountered Passive House and had simply done a remodel built to code, we would have needed a conventional heating system to keep the house comfortable. I imagine the HVAC contractor would have selected an oversized system based on his experience and rule of thumb. Or perhaps he may have gone the extra mile and performed the Manual J and Manual D calculations specified by the Air Conditioning Contractors of America (ACCA). Either way, the thinking for a traditional heating and cooling system for a conventional house is, "Given the house in a specific location, determine the type of system needed to keep the occupants comfortable." The amount of energy used for the system is an afterthought.

The Passive House approach is different. The amount of energy used by the system is an important design criteria. The thinking is, "Given the specific location and the maximum energy limit, determine how the house will need to be built for occupant comfort." Just as people in Chicago wear thicker winter clothes than in Santa Cruz, the houses too wear thicker clothing in colder climates.

Yet even with the mild climate of Santa Cruz, Midori will still be wearing thicker clothing than her neighbors—clothing made like a thermos, airtight and well-insulated to keep the inside temperature constant for a longer period of time. So even in the summer when we experience 95°F heat during the day, she just needs a sunshade and seal up like a thermos to preserve the relatively cool inside temperature within our comfort range. We're fortunate to live in a climate where the cool ocean water lowers the temperature to between fifty and fifty-six degrees at night so that we can simply open the windows at night to cool the house down. Most houses in Santa Cruz don't need air conditioning, but all houses in Santa Cruz need heating. With average low temperatures in the low forties, Midori needed heating to keep us comfortable. We weren't going to use a hair dryer like in the video test, so where would the heat come from?

It comes from various low-energy sources such as the occupants' body heat, lighting, waste heat flowing from the refrigerator, cooking in the kitchen, showers, computers, and all the other normal activities of living in a house. When there is not enough heat from the normal activities, the house needs a boost, the equivalent of that hair dryer operating on a medium setting or a portable space heater used in garages that put out the same amount of heat as a hair dryer. A conventional furnace, even the smallest one, puts out too much heat. Radiant floors, where hot water circulates through the tubing under the floor, will overheat the house.

It was a challenge to find a low-energy solution in a market full of over-sized heating devices used to heat conventional homes. Graham guided us toward a heat exchanger coupled with the HRV. This would boost the air temperature just a little bit when needed. Even better, I thought, if the source of the energy for hot water heating could be the sun. (Details are described in the next chapter.)

Rethink wiring

The wiring of the house is like the nervous system of the body. It carries signals for action. Midori's nervous system is a lot more complex today than it was ninety years ago. Lights don't just turn on and off, they also dim. Speakers convert signals conveyed through the wires to project music into the room. Computers, electronics, televisions, and other devices all connect with wires, different types of wires. Then there are telephone landlines, plugs in the walls, appliances, gadgets. Hair dryers!

We did not reuse any of Midori's old wiring. The old knob-and-tube wiring had to go because it was a fire hazard. There was no benefit to reusing the telephone and internet wiring. We wanted to put in new sets of wires to serve our lifestyle. Just as we did with the plumbing and ventilation, we thought through our lifestyle and needs to define and install a new nervous system (wiring) for Midori.

Before rewiring the house, we had to think about the flows of our daily lives and how we would live in the house. At this point in construction, the architectural drawings indicated the location of the plugs, light switches, and large appliances. Rather than simply installing what was on the plan, Taylor checked in with us to reconfirm the locations. The blue plastic electrical boxes hidden behind the wall were secured in place with a screw on the wall stud. Most of them were single but a few places near the exterior doors had larger boxes to hold double or triple switches. Boxes on the ceiling joists were placed "just so" to mark the placement of the ceiling fixture. Just as we've made intentional placement of the window openings with the Murphy bed in mind, wall sconces were set with the bed in the master bedroom. It's one thing to see the placement on paper. It became more real when we walked around the house in the middle of construction to imagine where we may want an electrical outlet.

One electrical outlet I wanted to keep was on the floor of the dining room. This was one of the original outlet positions Midori had and we liked it. We reconfirmed its usefulness when we had a slide show party and we didn't need to use an extension cord to power the projector. Plus this floor outlet would be great for plugging in a table-top induction cooktop to enjoy a hotpot meal like *yosenabe* or *mizutaki* at the dining room table.

One of the chemicals listed on the Red List is polyvinyl chloride (PVC). PVC is used as a conductor insulator in some wires used for residential construction. After we heard that it's good to avoid PVC, we looked into sourcing non-PVC insulated wires. It was very expensive, and navigating the fire code on these alternate materials was more than what we could stomach in 2011. We rationalized by saying, "Well, the PVC is a problem if there is a fire igniting the wire. That's not a regular occurrence and any off-gassing from PVC in the wire insulation would be absorbed by the sheetrock."

New wiring

We added some new wiring in addition to the wires for lighting and plugs. We asked Taylor to run the wires for stereo speakers under the floor in the four corners of the living room where floor speakers the size of medium-sized filing cabinets were marked out with blue tape. An audiophile who preferred the sound quality from an analog amplifier, Kurt had his speakers connected to his old-school turntable and CD player. This was the only wiring we would install for entertainment.

Many new homes have built-in wiring for speakers in every room, and places for televisions, home theater systems, and a host of electronic entertainment equipment. During the design phase Graham said, "You might not watch television, but you may want to consider resale value and the appeal to future homeowners." We considered that for three seconds. With a quick confirmation glance into my eyes, Kurt said, "We don't plan to sell the house for a long time," and I added, "The new homeowner can do what they want in a few decades." I was being pragmatic. Whatever we put in now would likely be obsolete by the time we sold this house.

We didn't value having an entertainment center in the house but we did value avoiding additional wiring down the road. The infrastructure that goes behind the wall, specifically wiring and plumbing, is difficult and expensive to change once the house is finished. Unlike moving the lamp around in a room, changing the location of an outlet on a wall is quite a hassle, especially since we are concerned about airtightness. This required us to think about the placement of furniture and where we would be sitting to do computer work. We hope we won't have to redo any of them.

Rather than depend on the convenience of a Wi-Fi signal to connect to the Internet anywhere in the house, we specified locations in the house for Ethernet connections. We valued minimizing exposure to wireless signals, so we had CAT5 cables wired to the desk area in Kurt's office, Chie's office, the mudroom desk, and the living room.

We know we have sophisticated sensors like our skin to validate the comfort of Passive House, but the geekier side of us wanted to capture data about the house: how much energy we used and the temperature and humidity range throughout the year. At the point when wires were installed behind the wall, we didn't know what system we would use to capture data about the house. Lacking specification from the data collection system, we simply had Taylor wire a CAT5 cable in a star configuration that came together at the mudroom desk. We figured that should be sufficient for the yet-to-be-determined data logger. We specified location of the sensors to take measurements in each room plus two outside the house.

Another sensor placement we had to figure out was for exterior lighting. We wanted the exterior lighting to be motion activated at night. We walked around of the porch and the deck area to imagine the optimal place for the sensors so that they would blend in with the exterior and still be effective.

Lessons learned: rethinking and replacing systems

We are mimicking the human body as we transform Midori. The plumbing system is like the digestive system. The ventilation system is like the respiratory and circulatory systems. Wiring is like the nervous system.

❖ Our focus on using water and energy wisely shaped our choices on plumbing infrastructure.

❖ It's much easier to install dual plumbing lines for future projects like rainwater supply for toilets and the clothes washer while the walls are open.

❖ Smaller diameter PEX distribution lines for hot water saves energy and water while reducing the wait time for hot water.

❖ With a heat-recovery ventilator in a tight house, we can save energy and breathe cleaner air that comes from a controlled source.

❖ Passive House is a whole-house approach to designing the performance of the house upfront rather than having the mechanical systems as an afterthought.

❖ Think about placement of furniture, home computer network, and sensors for wiring layout.

❖ It's good to plan for *our* future, not some imagined resale in twenty years, when making infrastructure decisions.

13
Solar Thermal Analysis Paralysis Stopped Construction

Painful analysis paralysis

Stopping construction while we figured out what to do about our hot water system was painful. We didn't have a mechanical engineer or a solar thermal designer involved in the design phase, and that came back to bite us. We needed to frame the problem, investigate solutions, and then make decisions before we could get underway again. The first question to solve was: What problems did we need to solve with our hot water system? Simple? No.

Plan for solar thermal

Tick tock tick tock. The sound of the clock marking the passage of time. For me the tick-tock was the sound of anxiety I heard late at night when I couldn't fall asleep. It reminded me that we didn't yet have a plan for the heart of the house.

The system to provide hot water and heat for the house needed to be efficient and small because the calculation in the Passive House Planning Package (PHPP) showed less than a hair dryer's worth of energy was needed to heat the house to 68°F on the coldest day of the year. A conventional furnace was way oversized for the task, akin to using a backhoe instead of a garden trowel to dig a shallow hole to plant tomato seedlings. We needed to find the equivalent of a garden trowel to heat the house. We had ideas but they weren't on pieces of paper approved by the building department.

The architectural plan drawn up by Graham and approved by the City of Santa Cruz Building Department noted, "Design and Plan of Solar Thermal System By Others." Once upon a time the architect did all of the design and drawings of the house including structural engineering and mechanical systems like heating, ventilation, air conditioning, and any other system that was part of the house. But that was a long time ago. As mechanical systems got more complex, it became customary for architects to rely on engineers to do specialized work. For example, in the set of plans we submitted, a local structural engineer did the calculation for the shear to make sure that the south wall that had lots of windows and glass doors was sturdy enough.

In our project it was up to us to select a mechanical engineer to draw up the plans and find a qualified installer to build a solar thermal system. Solar thermal plumbing was not in Taylor's bailiwick. This is one area where our version of integrated design fell short. We had the builder, architect, and Passive House consultant at the table upfront but no mechanical engineer. But as enthusiastic, intrepid homeowners wanting to do the right thing on our terms, we were undaunted when the construction progressed without having the solar thermal system and the mechanical design in place. We felt we could find the right people to design the perfect solar thermal system for us and have the plans drawn up by the time construction project got to that point. But four months after construction started, I was listening to the sound of the clock as I tried to fall asleep—tick tock tick tock.

Working around the decision delay

"Have you guys selected the plumber for the solar thermal system yet?" asked Taylor. "We need to get the rough plumbing done for the next building inspection. We can't go on with insulation and other stuff until the rough plumbing is in place."

We needed to make a decision so that he could move forward. I tried not to sound whiney. "No, not yet."

"Right. We can do a few other things that are not dependent on plumbing, but soon we'll run out of things we can do."

It's moments like this that I really appreciated Taylor's level headedness and communication style. He has the ability to convey facts without attaching an emotional charge. We knew that Taylor, like many contractors, worked on other projects in tandem with ours, so our job stalling would not be a huge stress on his cash flow. At least that's what I hoped. Construction had been progressing on schedule, on budget. Still, it must have been difficult for him to have a piece of the puzzle out of his control and to have to watch our analysis paralysis from the sideline.

We had five separate concerns to resolve: First was meeting the energy use target for Passive House Standard that met our hot water draw profile. The second was avoiding a problem we'd observed at another Passive House. Third was the cost expectation. Fourth was the health concern of avoiding Legionnaires disease. And fifth was laying the groundwork to make Midori a positive energy house in the future.

Exploring heat pump water heaters

Taylor had built houses with solar thermal systems. His opinion was that solar thermal systems (water heated by the sun is stored and used) are overly complex and expensive compared to using a heat pump water heater coupled with a photovoltaic system (water is heated by an air-to-water heat exchanger that is powered by electricity generated from the sun). He told us that solar thermal systems cost about $18,000 while a heat pump water heater coupled with PV would be closer to $11,000. Whoa—$7,000 difference between the two approaches!

Kurt felt we had to use solar thermal because although the end result of PV or solar thermal was hot water, the resiliency and carbon footprint of each system was different. As long as the sun is shining the solar thermal system will continue to operate if there is blackout. PV systems tied to the electricity grid, on the other hand, will shut down if there is a blackout because of the safety mechanisms to prevent power surges. A solar thermal system stores heat energy in a larger tank, allowing it to weather storms and cloud cover better than a PV system connected to a smaller tank. We had previously learned that for every kilowatt-hour of electricity consumed at home, almost three times as much energy was consumed at the power plant to make electricity. Patiently, Kurt explained to me that the reverse wasn't true. "Every kilowatt hour we produce on a PV panel on our roof does not always save the power plant three kilowatt of input energy," he said. If there is over production of electricity in the middle of the day where the rooftop PV systems are generating more electricity that can be consumed at that time, the excess energy cannot be shifted for later use. It is burnt up because there is no storage on the grid.

While the utility's infrastructure is playing catch up with the proliferation of rooftop PV systems, those living in an area where there is high adoption of PV systems are contributing to a headache for the utility. On bright sunny days the power plants need to produce very little in the middle of the day and quickly ramp up in the evening when people use electricity for cooking, entertainment, laundry, and other household tasks. This shape of the curve representing the utility's electricity production is called "duck curve" in California and "nessie curve" in Hawaii.

That changed my thinking. I asked him, "What if we had a battery at the house to store the electricity generated by the PV so that electricity demand for heating hot water never has to be pulled from the grid?"

"That's actually expensive, like the battery in your hybrid car."

"Uh huh. Its capacity to hold charge degrades in ten years or so too."

"The battery to store electricity from PV would need to be even larger."

I did the math. The PV system coupled with the heat pump water heater could cost as much as the solar thermal system.

We had more to think about. The solar thermal system is a lot more efficient than a PV system for heating water. About 70 percent of the sun's heat energy is directly heating the water. The hot water is stored in the tank at the house. With the PV system, only about 20 percent of the sun's energy is converted to electricity. Then later the electricity is converted to heat energy. Each time energy is converted from one form to another it loses efficiency, so it's simpler and more direct to heat the water with a solar thermal system.

Another plus for solar thermal was that it would help us when we applied for the Passive House certification.

Laying the groundwork towards plus-energy house was another consideration. Passive House building would get us to 80 percent reduction in source energy use. Kurt said that we'd want to install PV later to get to net zero energy for the house. When we eventually replaced one or both of our vehicles, we would use the sun's energy to power the vehicles. That's our future goal of being a plus-energy house.

"That's precisely why we need solar thermal," he concluded.

"How so?"

"Well, let's look at it from the amount of roof space we have." For a given amount of roof space, much more energy could be harvested using solar thermal. Using PV to power the heat pump water heater requires double the amount of roof space. This would limit our ability to generate electricity for charging electric vehicles in the future. With solar thermal, space heating and domestic hot water heating, the two largest uses of home energy, are met directly by the sun and sets Midori on course for going above and beyond a net zero energy house.

Solar thermal system

How hard is it to make hot water? Apply some heat to water and there it is. But if we want the hot water at a temperature approved by Goldilocks (not too hot, not too cold, but just right) on the ready for showers and baths without wasting water or energy, then it's not as simple as it seems on the surface. We liked the idea of letting the sun heat the water. Being able receive the sun's gift of heat takes having the right components in place to move the water, store the water, and prevent the water from boiling or freezing. The class on solar thermal system at PG&E's education center gave us a high-level overview of the components and how they fit together.

Starting at the roof there is the solar collector that absorbs the heat from the sun through its dark colored tubes and transfers heat to the heat-exchange fluid that's circulating through the tubes. When the heat-exchange fluid moves through the storage tank, it gives off heat to the water in the tank. At night when the heat is not applied to the water in the storage tank, it can gradually cool off, just like how coffee in my mug gets cold if I let it sit on my desk for a couple of hours. This is called standby loss. Just as the thermos keeps the coffee hot much longer than a mug, the solar thermal storage tank has insulation around it to keep the water hot much longer. During the summer the little bit of cooling off doesn't matter much because the longer daylight heats the water much hotter during the day than it needs to be, and by the time the sun comes up the next day, it's still plenty hot. In the winter, standby loss matters because the ambient air temperature is much lower and there are fewer hours of sunlight heating the water. If there are several days of rain, the storage tank receives no heat from the sun. This is when the backup water heater kicks on to bring the hot water in the tank up to temperature.

When we started shopping for the different parts of the solar thermal system to outfit Midori, we discovered different types of solar collectors, storage tanks, heat transfer fluids, and backup water heaters. We just needed to find the energy efficient, cost-effective combination to meet our draw profile needs.

Draw profile

Domestic hot water draw profile represents the home's character-istic of hot water usage throughout the day. A household that takes morning showers would have a different hot water draw profile than a household that takes baths at night. We knew that even if our shower and laundry patterns would remain the same, our hot water draw profile would be different with Midori.

In addition to providing hot water for showers, baths, and appliances, we needed hot water to heat the house. Because Midori would be a Passive House, her energy needs would be very low. I suppose we could have just stuck a hair dryer in a vent and turned it on to the medium setting whenever we needed heat in the house, but that would have been noisy. Our plan was to use water heated by the sun to keep us warm using a radiator type of appliance (water-to-air heat-exchange coil) that would be coupled with a heat recovery ventilator. It's based on a simple idea: when the thermostat in the house dips below a set point (say, 68°F), it triggers the pump to start circulating the stored hot water through the radiator appliance to boost the temperature of the supply air feeding each of the rooms. Because the radiator appliance is not rated for potable water, we chose to keep it separate from the domestic hot water.

We also needed hot water to fill the ofuro soaking tub. With the tub capacity being 155 gallons, a typical hot water tank of forty or fifty gallons would be too small to meet our need. The other uses of hot water were the basics: showers, sink faucets for hand washing and dish washing, clothes washer, and dishwasher. Having water-efficient appliances and only two people living in the house set this basic need pretty low. This meant Midori's "draw profile," the characteristic of hot water usage throughout the day, consisted of two polar opposites—the relatively low daily use on one end and periodic high use when the soaking tub was filled.

Midori also had the overarching need for as little purchased energy (electricity or gas) as possible. Plus it would be really good if this could be done inexpensively.

Designing out the slug

Midori was already plumbed for natural gas. Had we bought a house that didn't have a natural gas connection in place, we would have thought twice about installing a natural gas line. But it was already there and we were going to plumb an outdoor barbecue unit with natural gas. Plus heating water with natural gas is less expensive than heating it with electricity. Then there is the source energy factor of 1.1 compared to about 3 for electricity. Our preference was for natural gas.

Next question. Do we go with a tankless water heater or the traditional tank water heater? At first we thought having a tankless water heater fed by a large solar thermal storage tank would be best. The tankless water heater or on-demand water heater is an appliance with high-powered burners that quickly heat the incoming cold water to produce hot water. The tankless water heater only kicks on when the water flowing through the tank is not hot enough. The water from our storage tank would be pre-heated and the tankless water heater would hardly need to turn on.

That seemed simple enough, but the devil is in the details. The challenge we found was matching the optimum operating efficiency of the appliance to our usage characteristics—we had low-flow fixtures for showers and faucets that behaved like a gentle flow of a creek rather than a raging river. Unless we were taking a shower or running a load of laundry using hot water, the amount of water trickling through the water heater would be very little and it would need very little energy to heat it. But the appliance was not designed to do that. It was designed to make a heavy flow of cold water "instantaneously" hot, meaning it has the capacity to consume huge amounts of electricity or gas to produce a lot of heat. If our low-flow shower head drew luke-warm water from the solar water heater on a cold night, it would only need a fraction of the tankless water heater's capacity to bring it up to temperature. Even if the tankless water heater had a feature to modulate down the heat throw, the lowest setting would still be too much, wasting energy. Plus, at the lowest output setting, the appliance efficiency is poorest. Just like with the furnace, we were challenged with finding an appliance that would produce a small amount of heat. Compounding this, with the tankless water heater, there was a problem with a thing called the "slug."

We'd seen a study from researchers at Lawrence Berkeley Labs who studied several deep energy retrofit houses. Deep energy retrofit refers to whole building analysis and construction to achieve significant reduction (thirty percent or more) in home energy use. They found that the combination of a tankless water heater with preheated water using solar thermal was not as efficient as predicted. A house in the study had a solar thermal system with a tankless water heater as the backup heating source. The distance between the storage tank and the tankless water heater was minimal, but a length of copper pipe was still exposed. Even if that pipe segment were insulated, it would get cold after a while. The bit of water sandwiched between the two appliances in the exposed pipe is the cold water slug. When the tankless water heater sensed the cold slug come through, it would fire off the heater even if there was hot water behind the slug coming from the pre-heated water in the storage tank. That meant their tankless water heater was firing off unnecessarily, wasting energy.

The usage pattern made it even worse. Hand washing and other similar uses drew water for a brief moment. These short draws of hot water fired off the tankless water heater and pulled in hot water from the solar storage tank into the pipe to be cooled off again. In other words, lots of brief hand washing diminished the value of solar-heated water because of the configuration of the system.

We wanted to avoid this slug problem. This meant designing a system that incorporated the usage pattern in addition to evaluating the product's efficiency and performance.

Designing the system

It's one thing to be aware of concepts and ideas and another thing to make them a reality. There were different paths to make our desired hot water system a reality. For the talented intrepid do-it-yourselfers, the path could be do the research, buy the parts, and install it themselves. For those with money and no time, the path could be figure out who is the best person to solve and manage the problem and hire them to achieve the desired outcome. We found ourselves in the middle of this spectrum. So we took a hybrid approach where we did a bunch of research ourselves with the intent of hiring experts to design and install the system that met our draw profile and criteria. The journey began like this.

We asked Patrick Splitt, a local mechanical engineer who lives a few blocks away from us, to design Midori's solar thermal system. He'd been active in the Passive House California community and seemed keen on designing a solar thermal system that would meet our design criteria: use the hot water heated by the sun to do space heating using a hydronic-air heat exchanger, use a backup heating method to eliminate the slug, provide enough hot water for the 155-gallon ofuro, all the while paying attention to low energy usage so that we would meet the Passive House standard.

When he presented his design to us, we found it to be clever and elegant. At the heart of the system was an indirect tank from Triangle Tube. This is a tank within a tank that serves the needs of domestic hot water, solar thermal storage, and space heating all in one unit. The inner tank holds 105 gallons of domestic hot water for showers, dishwasher, clothes washer, and the ofuro. It's heated by hot water in the outer tank through the metal wall of the inner tank conducting heat. The outer tank consists of sixty-six gallons of service water, which jackets the inner tank. This service water in the outer jacket is heated through the heat-exchange coil conveying heated glycol from the solar thermal panel. If a few days of rain prevented the sun from heating the outer jacket water, the aquastat sensor in the inner tank would be triggered. It signals the pump to turn on to route the service water to the boiler. The gas boiler is like a tankless water heater, but the difference is that instead of routing the heated water into the house, it sends the hot water back into the outer jacket of the tank. The outer jacket heats the water in the inner tank until it comes back up to temperature and the pump turns off. This design eliminates the slug.

The service water also performs an important function of space heating. It travels through the closed loop of a radiator appliance we refer to as the Paul Coil to give off its heat to the air distributed through the house. When the temperature inside the house dips below a set point, say 68°F, the thermostat sends a signal to the space heating pump to start circulating the jacket water through the Paul Coil (placed next to the heat recovery ventilator). Before the supply air is distributed through the house, it heats up by passing through the Paul Coil. It keeps the house nice and warm using mostly the sun's energy and a tiny bit of electricity.

The system design using the indirect tank eliminated the concern of Legionnaires Disease because the water used for the Paul Coil is isolated from the domestic hot water.

We briefly delved into thinking of ways to conserve water by having the ofuro water kept warm to be reused several times. But in the end we decided that we'll use the ofuro for a soak or two and then the cooled-off water can simply be used in the garden for watering fruit trees and ornamental plants.

A clever aspect of the hot water system design is avoiding the complex timing schedule for the solar thermal pump. The heat-exchange fluid that moves heat from the panels on the roof to the storage tank is controlled by a pump that is powered by a pizza box-sized PV on top of the mechanical room. This ensures that the heat-exchange fluid only goes up to the solar panels on the roof when the sun is shining, optimizing the harvesting of heat energy from the sun. To prevent overheating, a controller turns off the solar thermal pump when the temperature of the heat-exchange fluid goes above a defined set point.

Elegant and expensive

After talking to different experts, we learned that plumbers are risk adverse. They like to work with familiar products and methods that have worked well for them. It makes sense from a business standpoint because they have to warranty their work and fix things if there are product failures or leaks. This means that new products or methods create uncertainty and headaches. Consequently, they are not familiar with every type of hot water heater and are much less familiar with solar thermal systems. The plumbers we contacted were either unfamiliar with the indirect tank or unwilling to try something different. Patrick, our mechanical engineer, recommended we call Duane, the plumber who had installed his designs for solar thermal systems in other homes. So we did. Indeed he was familiar with Patrick's work and was willing to bid.

"Holy crap!" I yelled as I opened Duane's email. The bid was $27,000, almost $10,000 more than we were hoping to spend.

"Maybe we need to rethink the design," Kurt muttered.

"Or maybe widen our search. Maybe both."

When we talked to Taylor about our dilemma, he conceded that Patrick was known to design expensive, elegant systems. Taylor said he would refer us to two subs, a solar contractor and a plumbing contractor, who could deliver quality work on our solar thermal system. "But you have to promise me that you'll follow through on their recommendation and not jerk them around." Taylor was trying to pull us out of our analysis paralysis.

Seeking three competitive bids

We met with both solar thermal and plumbing subs at the house. After getting into the design and discussing our needs, more ideas and approaches emerged. The price of a more complex design started creeping up, approaching Duane's bid of Patrick's design. Kurt contacted a company in Fremont that specialized in tankless water heaters. Their quote was again near the figure in Duane's bid.

I was starting to appreciate Taylor's comment about solar thermal system being quite complex with lots of moving parts. Still we weren't ready to go the PV plus heat pump water heater alternative in 2012. If we were doing this today we would seriously consider using the heat pump water heater that uses CO_2 as a refrigerant (heat transfer vehicle) that has really good coefficient of performance (COP) ranging from 4–8. COP is a measure used to describe how many units of energy are produced based on one unit of input energy. A COP of 4 means for every 1 unit of energy input into the device 4 units of energy are produced. This means it more than makes up for the loss of source energy factor of 3 for electricity.

We also had been having conversations with Graham. Solar thermal system was not his expertise, but he was very resourceful and tried to be helpful by sending us links to alternative products and recommendations. Graham had a strong preference for a drain-back type of system using water as the heat-exchange fluid that collected heat from the solar panel. We also talked about ways of reheating the ofuro. But each time we tried to save more energy and water, new questions came up. At some point we had to say enough.

Accepting the cost

Tick tock tick tock. Construction had stopped for three months now. We need to make a decision so that the exterior job would be finished before the rainy season.

"Hey Kurt, you know what?"

"What?"

"Maybe what's making this expensive is our criteria of having the system do multiple things. A solar thermal system that only serves the purpose of domestic hot water would be much smaller and simpler."

"Yeah. And our draw profile throws the curve too. If we didn't have the 155-gallon ofuro, we could get by with a much smaller tank."

"Right. But I want that."

"I know, I know. I wasn't asking you to give that up. And I want it as energy efficient as possible. We need to eliminate the slug."

"So maybe we need to come to terms with paying a lot more than we expected." I sighed and continued, "You know, the $18,000 figure got stuck in our head when we asked Taylor what a typical solar thermal system would cost. But that was probably based on a design that only provides domestic hot water."

"Hmm. Interesting. You think we would have made the decision quicker if we didn't have that set of expectations?"

"No. You still would have wanted to hunt for the best deal."

Kurt smiled, "Yeah, I wouldn't have taken the first thing that was proposed."

"OK, so shall we give Duane a call and get the ball rolling?"

"Yeah, we pushed the time end of the project triangle long enough."

So we called Duane and Taylor and got moving again. We wrote Taylor's two solar thermal plumber subs a nice note and sent them a small payment as a consulting fee for their time. This olive branch was our way to ensure Taylor's good relationship with his subs.

Released from the suspension and tension of indecision, we felt happier than we had been in months as we made phone calls and wrote emails to get others in motion for the next phase. In retrospect we may have accepted the cost of the system sooner if we considered the 30 percent federal tax credit which brought the cost of our system down to about $20,000. If we ever do this again, we'll make it a point to check in with our accountant.

Lessons learned: solar thermal analysis paralysis stopped construction

The hot water system was at the core of multiple problems we were addressing. The solution depended on how we framed which problems to solve. We wanted to minimize source energy and enjoy soaking in the large tub.

❖ Involve a mechanical engineer or solar thermal designer in the design phase.

❖ It is possible to significantly reduce source energy by using a solar thermal system for water heating and space heating.

❖ Plumbers are risk adverse and will stick to products and methods they're experienced and comfortable with.

❖ When expert opinions diverge it's up to us, homeowners, to make a decision based on our values.

❖ Clearly define the desired outcome and criteria to keep focus on the solution.

❖ Consider the net cost of the system after tax credits (and rebates, if available).

14
Toward the Finish Line

The final stretch

Finishes refer to the details that are done to enhance the service and aesthetic quality of the building. The choices we made in the design phase about the various layers and details of Midori's skin, clothing, and makeup helped Midori come alive. Although we specified a lot of details upfront, we still faced micro decisions along the way. We felt exhausted. In the final stretch of our marathon, we experienced pleasant surprises as well as regrets.

Interim blower door test

We left for vacation after making the decision on solar thermal plumbing, but the work continued. Once the rough plumbing (the portion that goes behind the wall) was inspected by the city's building inspector, Taylor moved quickly to get the air barriers in place. Sheetrock for the ceiling and rigid foam board under the floor went in place to create an airtight space in the house. When we got back from vacation, we rode our bikes from our condo to the house to check on the construction progress. We had a surprise waiting for us—a blower door in the front door! Was Terry Nordbye here?

Terry is a general contractor and a certified Passive House tradesman from Point Reyes in Marin County. He has built a couple of Passive Houses successfully and loves the challenge of making Passive House structures airtight. In other words he is an air sealing fiend. So much so that he started to do air sealing consulting in addition to his general contractor work. We're one of his early clients in this specialized work that goes way beyond caulking and weather stripping.

He emerged from behind the blower door and looked happy to see us. "We have good news! The blower door test came in at 0.6 ACH_{50}. Taylor did an amazing job."

"Oh. My. God. That's fabulous!" I beamed back at Terry and Taylor, who'd poked his head out of the house to say "hi" to us too.

While we were on vacation, Taylor completed the rough plumbing, sheet rocked the walls and ceiling, and insulated and sealed underneath the floor. With all of the air barriers sealed up, he contacted Terry to come down with the blower door to do an interim blower door test. Originally we had scoped out two interim blower door tests. The first one was meant to happen when the external walls were up yet before the windows were installed. But the windows came early, and the air barrier for the floor could only be installed when the plumbing was in place, so that test was scrubbed. This test would give the contractor the opportunity to seal up cracks and crevices that would not be accessible after the sheetrock was in place. Some of the framing was still visible and accessible.

With Midori, Taylor had hit the level of airtightness that some contractors only dream of. They had started the test around 10:00 a.m. They found some obvious holes, fixed them, and spent quite a while looking for smaller leakages and sealing them up.

"How did you find those leaks?" I asked with curiosity, "Did you use those smoke pipe gadgets to detect the air movement?"

"No, we just used our hands and ears," replied Taylor. "Terry boosted the fan speed really high, way past 50 Pascals. At that level we can hear the leaks whistling and can feel it on our hands."

Sealing Midori's underside was worth it, even though the crew had to crawl around in a cramped, dark space with insects for company. I was sure glad they did the job well enough to achieve the level of airtightness we needed.

Underfloor insulation

All that work under the house was to outfit Midori with her warm, comfy, airtight "shoes." I imagined them lying on their backs with a masks and goggles, first stuffing fiberglass batt insulation in the floor joist cavity then later having to precisely cut and nail the 1.5-inch-thick expanded polystyrene (EPS) foam board to the floor joists. They would have inched through the entire 1,574 square feet of the crawlspace to seal up the seams. They used Siga tape, Terry's preferred method of air sealing. They also used caulk, mastic, or foam, to seal up any possible cracks so that air from the crawlspace would be isolated from the living space. They'd never done anything like this before and Taylor must have done a heck of cheerleading job to get his crew to do this tedious work in such a cramped space.

At times like this, I was glad we'd been delivering a steady stream of treats from lemon bars and cookies to watermelon or beer on hot days.

Type of foam matters

Before we left for vacation, Kurt noticed that the foam boards that had been delivered were pink—extruded polystyrene (XPS). That's not what we ordered. Extruded polystyrene has a higher R value per inch (about five), but these sheets are made with hydrofluorocarbon, a greenhouse gas that is 1,430 times more potent that carbon dioxide. Instead, we chose expanded polystyrene (EPS). It has a slightly lower R value per inch (a little less than four), but it does not contain potent greenhouse gas generating chemicals. It's also less expensive than XPS.

We listed EPS in our specification document precisely to avoid high global warming potential material. While it would have been easy to say, "Oh, well, let's just use this anyway," Kurt called this out and had the material exchanged for EPS. It was a small thing but it mattered to us, and sticking with what we specified was a good way to not compromise on the green values that were the foundation of our house.

Layers of clothing

We saw Midori's clothing layers installed over a period of several months. Had we avoided analysis paralysis on the solar thermal decision, she would have been dressed much more quickly. Oriented strand board (OSB) sheathing, structurally engineered board made of compressed wood, went up early on before the windows were installed. Sheetrock on the ceiling and the rigid foam board under the floor provided the air barrier after the rough plumbing inspection was done. Once he confirmed the airtightness level with the blower door test, Taylor brought in the insulation subcontractor.

The interior wall cavities formed by OSB sheathing nailed to the 2x4 stud were filled with wet spray cellulose on a warm August day. The pinkish-gray recycled material stayed in place in the wall cavity floor to ceiling. This was left open to dry for a couple of days. While the wall insulation was drying, the insulation contractors prepared for the cellulose installation. They routed a long hose from their truck up into the attic through the attic door thirteen feet above the ground. They sprayed enough cellulose in the attic to completely bury the ventilation ducts. A tape measure marker indicated fourteen inches of depth. A year later we added ten more inches for a total of twenty-four inches of attic insulation.

Taylor's crew installed the exterior insulation—sheets of 3.25-inch-thick Roxul rigid mineral wool. Once the mineral wool sheets were fastened to the exterior wall, the windows no longer protruded. They looked flush against the outer wall.

The intent was to dress Midori in warm layers. Taylor's crew wrapped the mineral wool in Tyvek house wrap. Then they attached thin pieces of wood called furring strips over the Tyvek to create a space between the house wrap and the Hardie Plank cement fiber siding. When Midori was fully dressed, her walls measured over nine inches thick.

Fiberglass batt insulation between the rooms was not originally specified, but Taylor asked us if we wanted to put insulation in the wall cavity between the rooms. He had extra insulation material and thought it would help with noise attenuation. Midori is well-insulated and air-sealed tightly so we will hear very little of the outside noise in the house. This means we'll notice interior noise a lot more, and with the wooden floors, sounds made inside the house will reverberate even more. Great for playing my flute but not ideal for having conference calls in different rooms. So we had insulation added in the stud cavity between the interior rooms.

We've heard that in commercial buildings, the opposing sheetrocks of a given interior wall are of different thicknesses: say one-half inch thickness on one side and five-eighths inch thickness on the other side. The difference in the thickness prevents the sound from reverberating. We learned that interesting tidbit after we'd already purchased the sheetrock, so we didn't get to try it out.

Interior walls

Midori's original walls were made of lath and plaster. We went a different direction and chose to use sheetrock for her interior walls. Gypsum board is another name for sheetrock or drywall. Lydia Corser from greenspace told us about CertainTeed gypsum board called AirRenew from Saint-Gobain. Lydia keeps herself up to date on various green products used in residential construction and pays special attention to materials affecting indoor air quality. She told us CertainTeed gypsum board absorbed and trapped volatile organic chemicals (VOC) within the gypsum board and improved the indoor air quality. Lydia also recommended Murco drywall mud applied over the gypsum board. So we specified both materials.

We know that furniture, carpet, and other things homeowners bring in the house can contain nasty chemicals like fire retardants that release into the air (off-gas) for a long time. These items are relatively easy to replace. The wall, on the other hand (drywall, or sheetrock, or gypsum board), would be a pain to rip out and replace later. We chose safer materials since we didn't expect to replace the walls in our lifetime.

Fashionably distressed floor

During the design phase, we wondered what to do with the floors. The living room and the dining room had white oak, and they seemed to be in decent shape except for some termite damage in the corner of the living room. The difference between the original white oak and the repaired white oak was hardly noticeable.

We weren't certain about the rest of the house. It had hardwood floors, but we had no idea what they'd look like after all these years of being covered up by linoleum sheet in one bedroom, carpet in the other bedroom, and vinyl tiles in the other rooms. We saw a dark dried up layer of mastic covering the hallway, kitchen, and master bedroom floors when the tiles were removed during deconstruction. This was covered up with construction paper for many months and we wondered what type of wood was used for Midori's original floor.

We found out it was fir. Taylor wanted to try refinishing the floor and said if we didn't like it, we could still replace it. We finally got a glimpse of the refinished original floor in November.

"Have a look at the floor guys," Taylor said when it was safe to go into the house after the flooring work was done. We took our shoes off and gingerly stepped onto the newly sanded and polished floor.

It looked incredible. I stepped into the kitchen from the dining room, very surprised. Most homes have a transition strip covering the gap between the flooring in the rooms. Here there was none. Planks of white oak lay side by side against the fir planks without any discernable seam between them. It looked elegant.

"The wood they used ninety years ago had much tighter grains than the ones used today," said Taylor, "You can't get wood like this anymore. You'll see some repair spots with new wood. Take a look and tell me if you want other pieces replaced." Kurt readily pointed out a few places in the mudroom that had dark spots.

"Fashionably distressed" is the best way to describe the floor. Underneath the shiny finish, there were traces of imperfections and nail holes that had been patched. Some people pay extra to buy distressed wood to have this type of look. We got this with the house without having to pay a premium for it. It's a nice bonus we didn't know about.

Bathroom floors

We restored the original floor in all the rooms except the bathrooms. We used Marmoleum in those so we won't have to worry about splashing water and damaging the hardwood floor. Marmoleum is a brand name of a linoleum flooring product. It's made with linseed oil, which is a natural, renewable, non-petroleum product that is true to the 1920s styling of homes. Instead of tiles laid out in a pattern with grout in between, linoleum sheets come in wide rolls, and the bathroom could be covered in one sheet. This made it nice because the lack of seams would make it much easier to sweep and clean the bathrooms.

For the master bathroom, we'd chosen the 2498 Willow Green color of Marmoleum. We matched the color in the shower with Green Tech brown tile from Ergon. The muted colors felt calming, and I liked it a lot. The 2707 Marble White color of the hallway bathroom I liked less. It looked fine a year earlier when we took the samples from Lydia's store and placed them on the bathroom floor to imagine what it would look like in there. When it was laid out in the very white theme of the bathroom, the gray-blue marble color scheme made the floor look dirty. I know over time we won't even notice it, so we didn't try to change it. Some style and taste differences aren't major and we could live with them.

Refrigerator regret

We continued to take the free classes from our utility, Pacific Gas & Electric (PG&E), even after the design was done and construction was in full swing. When we took a class on lighting and appliances, we regretted our refrigerator choice.

The Federal Trade Commission makes it easier for consumers to comparison shop for refrigerators with their bright yellow energy guide labels showing estimated yearly operating cost and the estimated yearly electricity use. The lower the number the better. If the appliance has the Energy Star label, then we know that it met the efficiency criteria set by the Energy Star program. This criteria changes over time to be more stringent as appliance manufacturers produce more energy-efficient products. This is good.

We were surprised that Energy Star certification uses different standards for different types of fridges. Comparing the electricity usage of a compact fridge that fits under a desk with a large fridge with an ice and water dispenser won't make sense. We learned that side-by-side refrigerators, the ones that have two doors in the front with a thin vertical freezer, require a lot more energy to operate than the models with the freezer on the top or bottom. This type of fridge, even with the Energy Star label, uses more electricity than a freezer-on-top refrigerator without the Energy Star label. Prior to taking the class, we had the impression that a refrigerator with the freezer on the bottom would be more efficient because the cold air naturally falls as the heat rises. But it turned out that the common freezer-on-top refrigerators are the most efficient configuration.

Refrigeration technology came into the home kitchen about the time Midori was born. In the 1920s, it was popular to serve Jell-O at parties. It was a hip party food because refrigeration was new and cool. Especially the fancy dishes with multi-colored layers with various fruits encased in the translucent pink, yellow, and orange gelatin. Surprisingly, early home refrigerators had a respectable performance even by today's standards. So what happened in the last ninety years with the fridge? The energy efficiency didn't improve, but the convenience features did.

In the PG&E class we learned that the most efficient refrigerator was not the one we'd picked out for our kitchen. It was made by Sun Frost in Northern California. It's a preferred brand by those outfitting their RV campers and boats. With a very efficient thermal design, it's perfect for Passive House. When we saw that the Sun Frost model RF19 unit uses only 372 kWh per year compared to 442 kWh per year of the Miele model we chose, we had buyer's remorse.

"We should see if we can order this and cancel the tall skinny Miele we ordered," said Kurt.

"Well, the order for the appliance is the easy part," I said thinking out loud. "Richard made the cabinet frame already and he'd have to scrap that and make a new one. What's the dimension?"

"Darn it! It's thirty-four inches wide. We got the one that's only thirty inches wide."

"Let's measure this out at the house and see if it's feasible."

It turned out that the extra four inches for the fridge wasn't feasible. The house was already framed with countertop space that wrapped around the kitchen in a "G" shape and the pocket doors that came up to the side of the fridge were already framed in. The cost savings of buying a cheaper more energy-efficient fridge was not worth the cost of re-doing the framing and the cabinets. Plus, it would cause a delay. Most importantly, it would make the opening into the cooking space much smaller, from thirty inches to twenty-six inches. Had we known about this fridge during the design phase a year earlier, we may have been able to work it into the plan. We spun ourselves around for a couple of days on this newfound information and decided we would just have to be OK with not having the most energy-efficient refrigerator.

Decision fatigue

Some of the items on the owner-supplied materials list, like the lighting fixtures Kurt bought at the end-of-year sale, were already in the storage shed. Some of the items on the list still needed to be purchased. Then there was a steady stream of little things that needed our attention. Even though we specified a lot of stuff upfront, we still had more to research, decide, and purchase: the hooks for hanging coats at the mudroom bench, drawer pulls in the kitchen, pull handles on the cabinet, toilet paper hangers, towel hangers, color of stain for the deck, specific type of light-bulbs, mulch for landscaping, and more.

Individually these are not difficult decisions. Especially compared to the complexity and consequence of the solar thermal system. Around ten months into the construction phase, it started to feel like mile twenty of a marathon. I noticed a cumulative effect of decision fatigue where giving the answer of, "Sure, whatever is easy," or "OK, I agree," felt much more attractive than having to research, validate the choices, and find the best deal. Such was the case with the water filter under the kitchen sinks. Had we not been in the state of cumulative decision fatigue, we would have been all too happy and enthusiastic to do online research and compare the different water filters and shop for the best price. When Taylor asked if we had a water filter picked out and we said, "No," he said, "OK, I'm going to Pro Build (local hardware store) to pick up a water filter." We just acquiesced.

Paint

We chose our exterior colors early on. Midori is now covered in a dark chocolate color all over. The accent color on the exterior trims around windows and doors is the color of a green onion. Taylor recommended we give Midori a belly band in the green accent color. This was a good call. It gave a nice transition between the lap siding at the base and shingles at the top. Adding a 1x12 piece of lumber on the outside around the ceiling line gave her a nice look of a high-waisted skirt with a wide accent belt.

Remember the three layers of glass experiment with the light meter? With three layers of glass in the windows, I thought the light coming through the windows would seem a dimmer than the light through the single-pane leaded windows. But we didn't notice the house feeling dark or dim. The sunlight that came through the windows still felt glowingly soft and warm. Perhaps the color of the interior walls had something to do with it.

We chose "Angel Kiss," a very light yellow, after spending few hours looking through websites of Craftsman-style houses and bringing the swatches from the paint store into the rooms. This hue, about the color of lemon juice in a jar, felt warm in an understated sense. It worked well in the living room and dining room with the medium-dark wood trim around the windows and doors. The light lemony color is a bit more noticeable in the other rooms because the interior trims around the doors and windows are painted in bright white "Swiss Coffee" that Taylor suggested. We used EnviroCoat line of interior paint from Kelly-Moore Paints, which was labeled zero-VOC at that time, but is now labeled low-VOC.

There is one thing I wish I did differently about painting. I wish I had stuck to the zero-VOC criteria for the primer in the interior. As the painters geared up for the painting job, they mentioned that they had low-VOC primer but not the zero-VOC. Is it OK if they used low VOC primer? In the moment of decision fatigue, I said yes. Kurt wasn't happy about that. He would have pushed back and asked them to find a zero-VOC primer. In the big picture, though, it wasn't a big issue. If the AirRenew drywall did its job then trace amount of VOC from the primer would have been absorbed and trapped within the drywall. The low-VOC primer did not bother him, but he may have a lingering sense of compromise.

Selecting and testing LED

After we put on Midori's makeup (paint), it was time to install the lighting fixtures we selected and purchased almost a year earlier. Our plan was to light Midori with light emitting diode (LED) lights. I like the warm and happy feeling of sunlight coming into the dining room in the afternoon, and the color of sunlight is the gold standard of lighting. I wanted to know if the LED lights would create the warm and happy feeling at night, and how the light coming from the various lighting fixtures would work with the wall colors. It turns out it all depended on the bulbs.

When Thomas Edison worked with incandescent light bulbs over a hundred years ago, he used carbon filaments. Later tungsten was used, and it gave an orange-infused glow. In 1901 fluorescent lighting came about. The fluorescent light first appeared in those long tubes we most readily associate with offices and schools. Later, compact fluorescent lights (CFLs) were fashioned to be thin, curly, and squat so that they could be screwed into the standard lighting fixture to save energy. Even though they're energy efficient, I was never a fan of those sterile and cold lights.

On the surface it seemed easy to select the best light bulb by choosing the color temperature closest to sunlight (2700 K) with the best color rendering index (closest to 100), the longest life using the least amount of energy with the cheapest price. We quickly learned that this is the starting point and not the final destination. Just as our skin is a sophisticated thermal sensor, our eyes sense light in a way that cannot be reduced to numbers. We did our research in 2012 when LED technology was changing rapidly. It continues to change. While our product selections may no longer be useful, the selection process remains relevant.

The lighting fixtures we selected take traditional screw-in light bulbs and match the Arts and Crafts period style. Being able to dim the lights was important to us, and we were concerned about LED bulbs not dimming well. Thus it was important to test bulbs before buying in quantity. We started our testing journey at a local lighting store to check out their lineup of LEDs. Grabbing a handful of different types, we placed them in the sockets of the test board on the counter in the store. One by one we screwed in the bulb to the test socket and slowly ran the full range of the brightness control to see how they dim.

Results varied. Some had hardly any range; they would start dimming ever so slightly and then go completely dark abruptly. Others would start buzzing at the low end. We continued our test by visiting lighting specialty shops in Santa Clara, Menlo Park, and San Francisco and repeated this test with other LED light bulbs.

Lighting is really important to Kurt, and I would have been happy to have him choose the best and be done with it. But he also wanted to make sure I didn't complain about it later, so I was the obligatory participant the lighting selection process. But there was too much distraction at the lighting stores for me to tell the difference between the bulbs.

"Let's bring some back home and test them. We can come back and return the bulbs we don't like and buy the ones we do like," suggested Kurt.

"Brilliant! Let's grab one of each and get out of here."

Before we did our test with Midori's lighting fixtures, we did a curiosity test. We wanted to see if the energy usage advertised on the box matched the measurement on a portable meter. We plugged a device called Kill-A-Watt into the electrical socket in the wall and plugged a small lamp into it. The device shows how much electricity is flowing from the wall to the lamp. All of the LED bulbs performed as advertised on the box. We were surprised with the CFL bulbs. They all displayed the characteristics of overshooting as they warmed up before settling at the advertised label.

We did the lighting fixture test at night. The chandelier lighting fixtures in the living room and the dining room both had their bulbs pointed up to bounce light off the ceiling, which we had painted in the ever-so-slightly yellowish tone. The glass fixtures also had a slight orange-brown tint, making the light feel even warmer. In these, the bulbs from LEDwiser worked great because they dimmed well and the light casted out in a wide angle. The bulb that worked best for the pendant lights hanging above the kitchen bar was from Philips. This light provided warmer-feeling light because the bulb itself had a yellow tint and the light was focused straight down and didn't spread out as much. It dimmed well also. The LEDwiser bulbs worked well in the ceiling-mounted lighting fixtures in the other rooms. We chose the LED bulbs from Green Creative for the sconces flanking the bed because its color output looked best in the strapped-stone diffuser. We chose MR16 LED lights from Soraa for the track lighting in the living room to illuminate artwork on the wall because it renders optimal light for artwork display.

We would have never been able to come up with these light bulb choices by simply comparing the specifications. We had to use our eyes for each room and fixture.

Lighting affects the moods of the occupants of the house. LEDs last a long time—over ten years if the electronics hold up. While this meant we wouldn't have to replace a light bulb for a decade, it also meant we'd be stuck with our choice for a decade. In 2012 when we were shopping for LED lights, it was expensive and definitely not a throw-away decision, so we had to make sure we chose something we really liked.

Stain is a pain

We felt the gap between good intentions and execution as the different finishes were applied. By the time our noses and lungs detected the mixture of stuff in the air of our airtight house, we felt distressed. The constant flow of air through the ventilation system helped, but we weren't ready for the strong smell coming off the stains applied to wood. We knew about avoiding volatile organic compounds (VOC). We underestimated where they might show up and the impact.

Early in the design phase we paid close attention to the material safety data sheet of the cabinets and ruled out ones using composite wood materials. Even if I said OK to the low-VOC paint primer at a moment of weakness, we knew avoiding paint with VOC was important and chose zero VOC type of paint. But wood and fiberglass stain? I just assumed they came in the same options as paint. That wasn't the case. When we chose the fiberglass doors from PlastPro, we were more concerned about thermal performance and cost. The much more expensive fiberglass door would have been stained and off-gassed at the factory. We thought it would be no big deal to have it stained on site and didn't look into the MSDS for the stain recommended by the door manufacturer.

It was January afternoon, almost a year after we gathered around for the kick-off meeting, when we had a sinking feeling in our stomach. Pepe, the painter, said there was no Zero VOC or even low VOC stain for the fiberglass door. We stared at the fiberglass door in the kitchen. It had been months since the unfinished front door and the mudroom door were installed; they appeared naked in their pale, pinkish-beige skin. We thought that if the doors were stained early, they would be scratched up during the course of construction. Pepe said the manufacturer recommended a gel stain. We asked about water-based stains. Pepe said the front door might be OK because no direct sun would hit it, but the kitchen door would get afternoon sun and that would fade the stain. Then Taylor told us Zero VOC didn't necessarily mean no smell. Other ingredients besides VOC also smelled. Great.

We double checked with Tom, the windows and doors guy, about the PlastPro door stain options in hopes of finding a better answer, but he repeated what Pepe and Taylor had said.

In the end we grudgingly said OK to the acrylic stain and picked out a color. It was so stinky that it took a full month of wiping down surfaces and clearing the air before we felt comfortable enough to move in. It wasn't just the door. The stain applied to the wood finishes was stinky too. The baseboards, base shoes, window trims, and repurposed bead board were beautifully refinished—and stinky. Even the lacquer stain on the Murphy bed cabinet was off-gassing. When I placed the order, I was more concerned about whether it would fit into the space properly and have the right look. I failed to ask about the finish applied to cherry wood furniture, and I did not ask for the MSDS. Now I know that protecting indoor air quality is a matter of vigilance practiced throughout design and construction phase.

If we were to do this over again, I would compare the cost of having a local cabinet maker create a Murphy bed ensemble using sustainable wood and a non-toxic stain. If the same Murphy bed was a much better deal and I chose that, I would have it delivered much earlier and let it off-gas outside on the deck or in the shed. Same with the door. If we were to do this over again, we would have the door stained off-site and off-gas for a month or two before installing it.

Things happen

When we were agonizing over the off-gassings from various stains, we could have asked to have the doors removed and stained and off-gassed elsewhere. This would have meant leaving the house exposed to robbery and mischief. We didn't have any personal belongs moved in yet, but all of the cabinets, appliances, and plumbing fixtures were installed at this point. If someone wanted to enter the house at night and cause damage to them or steal things, it would have been all too easy if the doors were wide open.

Someone did break in during the middle of the night. The crew left the awning windows open to air out the smell. A burglar came in through the window by the master bedroom shower and stole Taylor's tools.

Even though we were so close to the finish line, things still happened. The best we could do was roll with it. On the day when we were at a salvage yard in Berkeley, Taylor sent us a message. They were re-installing the sink in the hallway bathroom. The pedestal slipped and broke into pieces. Amazingly, we were at the right place to look for a replacement. We found something comparable, took a photo, and sent it to Taylor to see if it was the right fit. It was. The sink and the pedestal from two unrelated places worked together beautifully. Thank goodness for salvage yards.

That was a fortunate find. We didn't find what we went to the salvage yard to look for, though. The interior doors we reused all had old fashioned locks with skeleton keys, and we wanted to get extra keys for decorative accents by the door. Having a functional lock on the individual rooms seemed practical. The skeleton keys look very simple, but we rifled through several drawers of keys and we found none among the hundreds we compared to the reference skeleton key we brought along.

Many people find useful things at salvage yards. Some even manage to build an entire house very inexpensively this way. Before launching into our project with Midori, I took a weekend class at the local community college called, "How to build your dream house for a song." It was the ultimate testament to a low-budget do-it-yourself home building project where the instructor shared his experience of finding cheap land at tax auctions, renting equipment, finding construction materials at salvage sales and hiring handyman for semi-skilled work. Early on I knew that we did not have the appetite for do-it-yourself work and risk the sanity of our marriage. Kurt and I expressed our differences during this project to transform Midori, but our experience seemed nowhere near the stress level described by other people during their remodel projects. Now that we were starting to see the light at the end of the tunnel, I felt fortunate to have had this experience with Kurt.

What we learned moving toward the finish line

Mistakes and regrets happen toward the end of the project when we are tired. Have patience and learn from others' experience. When things happen, roll with it.

❖ When decision fatigue sets in, it's easy to say "OK, whatever you say," but that's exactly when we need to pay attention.

❖ Different thickness of drywall can help attenuate sound.

❖ Refrigerators with freezers on the top are the most energy efficient.

❖ Custom refrigerators like Sun Frost are not sold through normal retail channels.

❖ Choose LED bulbs wisely and test them in the different lighting fixtures.

❖ Old floors with tight grains are beautiful. What's under the ugly carpet and linoleum could be a treasure.

❖ Pay attention to stain, paint, and furniture finishes early in the design phase and evaluate the MSDS to avoid harmful chemicals.

❖ If zero VOC alternatives are not available, consider painting or staining items off site and letting them off-gas elsewhere before bringing them inside the house.

15
The Final Test

Butterflies before finals

Passive House Certification requires passing an airtightness test at 0.6 ACH_{50} or better. The final test can be very intense. Going in we felt well prepared, but the feeling of butterflies in our stomach was similar to the moment before college finals. We experienced a couple of tense moments during our final blower door test as we were setting up the test, looking for the leak, and confirming air volume.

Airtightness target

Midori needed to pass a test administered by a third party to be certified as a Passive House. The airtightness criteria was stringent. Our target all along had been 0.6 ACH_{50}. This description from Steven Winter Associates http://blog.swinter.com/infiltration-blower-door-testing/ helps put that target number in context:

The metrics and math can get a little technical so let's put them in context. Here's a rough scale to compare your blower door test number to other standards:

10–20 ACH50—Older homes, like living in a "barn"

7–10 ACH50—Average new home with some air sealing but no verification and little attention to detail

7 ACH50—OK infiltration level and the 2009 IECC energy code requirement

3–5 ACH50—Good and achievable target for most new homes. The ENERGY STAR reference home is 5 ACH_{50} for climate zone 4 which covers DC, MD, VA and part of PA. The majority of PA is 4 ACH_{50} for the ENERGY STAR reference home.

3 ACH50 and lower—Tight home with great air sealing, and required by the 2012 energy code adopted in MD and coming to other jurisdictions soon.

0.6 ACH50—Super tight home and the Passive House standard.

Based on this description, we were trying to take Midori from one end of the scale (living in a barn with 22 ACH_{50}) to the opposite end of the scale (0.6 ACH_{50} the Passive House Standard). It would be easier for a contractor to hit this target if he were building a new home from scratch where he could control all aspects of the construction from the beginning to the end. A remodel is much more difficult because he needs to work around the existing inaccessible spots in the building. We were reusing the original foundation, floor, and framing. The concrete porch and the built-in buffet furniture from 1922 stayed in place during our remodel construction. If there were air leaks within the built-in buffet furniture or tiny cracks between the framing and the porch, Taylor couldn't get to them. We were hoping the careful attention he paid to other parts of the house would make up for any possible air leaks from these places.

As the intrepid homeowners attempting a rigorous remodel for the first time, we were approaching this with the beginner's mindset that anything was possible. We were firm on meeting this target. This was done with carrots and a stick. We hired an experienced air sealing consultant to help Taylor. We planned for an interim blower door test and paid a bonus for meeting the target. The stick was spelled out in the contract. The final draw (last contract payment) for the project was contingent on passing the airtightness test performed by a third party using the blower door equipment when the construction was complete. Airtightness was to be taken seriously.

Final test scheduled

It had been twelve months since construction work started. If we hadn't stopped construction for two months to decide on the solar thermal system, we would have been done. As the year 2012 drew to a close, we called George Nesbitt to come out and do the final blower door test.

The date was set: January 3, 2013. I got ready for the event by preparing food. Not that I thought it was going to be a picnic in the park. I thought of it more as preparing fuel for a marathon. In endurance events athletes can "bonk" if they have not been fueling themselves properly during the race. They become fatigued and disoriented when their body uses up the energy. I eat when I'm stressed, but not everyone does. When my husband is stressed he forgets to eat. From what I know of Taylor, he too forgoes eating when he's under stress. Not knowing how long this day would last, I wanted to make sure our team didn't bonk.

Setting up the test

George Nesbitt of Environmental Design/Build is a home performance contractor in Oakland with a lot of different green credentials, and he is also a Passive House consultant. He's a talented guy with lots of knowledge and passion around building science and home performance construction. When George arrived, he unloaded his gear and I eyed his computer nervously. The software on his computer works with the blower door equipment from Energy Conservatory. It launches a series of automated tests to gather multiple data points and averages out the measurements. It measures air leakage in both pressurized and depressurized settings. The software produces a report with test results in a format compliant with the German National Standard for determining air permeability of buildings, fan pressurization method (DIN EN 13829 protocol). We need this report for Passive House certification.

George fitted the red door into the opening of the front door and calibrated the equipment. Taylor walked around the house making sure the windows and doors were closed properly. He poured water into the bathtub and sinks so that the P-traps were filled with water as in a normally operating house.

We were ready. Then George asked us for the air volume of the house.

"It's a 1,569-square-foot house with 9 foot ceilings," I muttered as I entered the numbers on my phone calculator. "That's 14,121 cubic feet. Minus 75 for the lower ceiling height in the master bathroom and closet area." Tap, tap, mutter, mutter. "That will be 14,046 cubic feet." I showed him the numbers on my phone.

George wasn't certain about my calculations; he'd rather have the air volume number from Graham, our Passive House consultant.

"You mean what I just gave you is not right?"

"Certain dimensions on the interior are discounted, like the walls and mechanical area."

My nervousness increased. "Oh, right. Let's input 14,046 for now and we'll confirm with Graham."

Darn it! If the denominator gets smaller, then the numerator needs to get smaller too. Maybe the 151 CFM number Taylor hit back in August was not quite enough.

Detecting air leaks

The quiet whirl of the fan filled the room. The program on George's computer automatically ran successive tests to collect 100 data points. The test was measured at 50 Pascals, a unit of measure that is equivalent to having 20 mph winds blowing outside.

We hit between 160 and 166 CFM and it wasn't getting any lower. Taylor asked George to crank up the pressure so he could hear the leaks. George cranked up the pressure from 50 to about 180 Pascals.

When Taylor did the interim blower door test with Terry, they ran the fan at a higher speed and listened for air leakage with their ears and felt it with their hands. Some people use a small draft detector device that gives off smoke at the end of a stick to make a visual diagnosis of the air movement to find the leaks. Like Terry, Taylor preferred to use his body as a sensor.

Taylor walked around the house methodically and put his hands on the likely suspects—light switches, electrical sockets, and seams along the wall where two different materials came together. Every once in a while he would open up the facing that covered a light switch box and delicately spray the interior of the box with a can of spray foam with a straw attachment on the nozzle. Over the next few hours this meticulous exercise resulted in dropping the air leakage measurement on George's computer by 10 CFM or so. That was still too high to meet the airtightness test.

Looking for 16 CFM

It was a lovely, sunny, winter afternoon and George took a break on the back deck to eat his lunch. I didn't worry about him bonking because he brought his own food. Taylor meanwhile put on his jumpsuit and went into the crawlspace to look for possible leaks under the floor. The blower door equipment was still running, providing pressure needed to detect leaks. As expected, there were no gaping holes under the floor. By this time we got the interior volume number from Graham. Our target air leakage number in cubic feet per minute (CFM) was 131. We were at 147. Pressure was mounting though no one in the room dropped their professional demeanor. No cursing. Tempers remained in check.

"We're now at the point in a marathon where glycogen is nearly depleted," I thought. "We're not going to bonk." I got food for Taylor and Kurt. They ate out of practicality. I'd been grazing out of nervous habit. About six hours into the test, Taylor suggested we check to see if there were leaks in the HRV ducts. We covered up all of the supply registers and the exhausts in the rooms. Taylor said he didn't see any cracks in the Zehnder ComfoDucts, but if we ran the fan again, we'd know if there were leaks in the ducts if the air leakage dropped.

Found the leak!

Whirrrrrrrl hummed the blower door fan as it began the test. We watched over George's shoulder to get a glimpse of the numbers flicking through the screen: 98, 99, 101, 103, and it kept ticking up. Then it stopped and stabilized around 128. Holy cow! This meant there was a leak in the ventilation duct. Thirteen tubes of ComfoDucts poked out of the ceiling into the attic. Penetration through the ceiling sheetrock was tightly sealed with tape and foam. The leaky duct could be in the attic or in the worst case, in the wall.

"Let's go check the attic." Taylor's tone was crisp as he removed the taped-up plastic sheets covering the supply register and the exhausts of the ventilation system. Our access to the attic was from the exterior, through a small door above the windows in the middle of the east wall. We propped up our tall, rickety extension ladder against the wall and Taylor climbed the ladder and crawled into the attic opening. I followed with my flashlight and iPhone. The sea of cellulose conjured up an image of all the clothes dryer lint from the entire city dumped in one space. "What do you see? I yelled.

"Tell George to...wait!"

I held my breath.

"I found it!" cried Taylor, "There's a big gash on this duct."

I cheered. Taylor sent me down the ladder to get the Siga tape from his tool bag in the kitchen.

"He found it!" I screamed as I raced through the house to grab the tape. I wore the roll of Siga tape like a bracelet on my wrist and grabbed a pair of scissors too. Phooey on the admonition to not run with scissors.

Taylor called out the hazards to help me make a safe passage along the two-inch-wide ceiling joists. I didn't want to step through the sheetrock and poke a hole. Or crush a duct. That would defeat the purpose of this exercise. I was careful, but really excited.

When I reached Taylor, he had dug up the cellulose to reveal a group of ducts sprouting above the HRV distribution box. Each duct ran in different directions.

He showed me a big gash in one of the ducts. I took a picture of it.

"It looks like the split was caused by a hot item burning a hole in the plastic," assessed Taylor. He grabbed a long piece of tape from me and patched up the leak. There weren't any other gashes, just this one.

"How did you find it?"

"I saw some movement in the cellulose and then I felt the air coming through here."

Finished with the repair, we went down to find Kurt and George. I showed them the photos I took. George also thought it looked like a burn. There were lots of possibilities for how it got damaged, but no way to know for sure.

"Well, regardless of who caused it, it's now fixed. Let's run the test," I said.

The fan of the blower door whirled one last time. "It's looking good," George said. "About 129 CFM for depressurized and 131 for pressurized, an average of 130 CFM."

I jumped up and down screaming "Woo hoo!" and high fived everyone in the room.

"Thank you, Taylor," said Kurt with a relieved and grateful expression on his tired face. "You are amazing."

Interior air volume

Nine hours after the start of the final blower door test we all packed up and left. We felt satisfied that we'd cleared the highest hurdle of the project. Some people we had talked to in the Passive House community had missed air sealing target by a fraction and could not be certified. We were so proud of the team and slept soundly that night.

When we saw the email from Graham next morning, we thought it would be a round of 'atta boy recognition. It wasn't. The house air volume calculation that meets DIN EN 13829 was very specific about what is included and excluded from this internal measurement of the house dimensions. In so many words, he told us that the 130 CFM blower door test result we achieved yesterday was not 0.6 ACH_{50}. The denominator had shrunk so the numerator needed to come down.

"Oh crap! We don't want to do this over again," I thought. But before we could answer Graham's email, Taylor responded: The windows are installed on the outside and the walls are nine inches thick and the air space created by the windows must be accounted for. He said he'd check the measurements and get back with them.

Later when Taylor replied with the precise measurements of the volume represented by the windows mounted on the outer edge of the wall, the denominator came back up—just enough to meet 0.6 ACH_{50}. All was well again.

And we didn't bonk.

What we learned during the final test

The final blower door test can be a tense time. We learned a valuable lesson that it's not enough to say 0.6 ACH50 for the target. The target number expressed in CFM is important.

❖ Confirm the internal volume of the house early in the project to get the exact target number in CFM from the Passive House consultant.

❖ Be prepared for a long, stressful day. Take breaks when you can and don't forget to eat.

❖ Test for duct leakage by covering up the HRV registers. If the air leakage number drops, then there is a leak in the duct.

16
The Proof Is in the Utility Bills

We learn by living in a Passive House

Switching from construction mode to operation mode meant we began to put our experience into perspective and formed new practices. We had to overcome a few hitches before moving in, and found benefits from altering our habits. The big questions wouldn't be answered immediately: would our energy use meet our expectations, and would we get certified by the Passivhaus Institut.

Getting ready to move in

The heat recovery ventilator went through a quality assurance step of commissioning to make sure that it was operating as planned. For Passive House certification, Midori needed a commissioning report showing the actual ventilation measurements. A specialist came by with the equipment used to measure airflow to do the commissioning work. He placed the balometer, a large black capture hood shaped like a very large megaphone, over the HRV register to measure the amount of air coming into the room or extracted out of the room. I saw the display screen on the hood showing low flow measurements of 8 or 10 or 11 CFM. If the measured flow did not meet the specification, he adjusted the baffles inside the register for proper balancing. When he was done balancing the ventilation system, he gave us a report that showed the airflow measurements of each register matching the design specification.

The final green building inspection by the city's building inspector took place on January 22, 2013. Throughout the construction phase, there were several city inspections to ensure code compliance, such as shear nailing, rough plumbing, insulation, and others. We never knew when they were scheduled, so we never got to observe them. However, for the green building final inspection, we got to see the interaction between Jennifer, the green building specialist with the City of Santa Cruz, and Taylor.

Jennifer spread the green building scoring matrix over the kitchen counter and ticked off each of the items listed on the plans we submitted a year and a half earlier. Stamps indicated either "documentation required" or "inspector to verify" next to most of the items listed on the matrix. In an efficient, business-like manner, she asked Taylor to show her proof of the green features installed. Taylor was just as efficient as he pulled out receipts from his folder or photos of construction details on his phone. Points verified totaled up to 305, more than three times the number of points needed to receive the green building plaque at a public ceremony in front of the city council members.

But more important than certification and plaques, this meant we could move into Midori. We started with the basic kitchen supplies. Utensils, plates, cups, and silverware went into the cabinets. Then we placed some temporary furniture in the dining room and living room and threw a party to thank the team for a job well done. I got to use the steam oven and the induction cooktop to make a lot of food. It was a fun evening of food, drink, and stories.

We were eager to move in immediately after the final inspection, but our noses and lungs didn't let us do so. The smell of various stains lingered even with the HRV running on the highest setting full time. The fiberglass doors, baseboards, bead board under the kitchen counter, Murphy bed, refinished French door and the buffet continued to off-gas. Opening the windows and running the fans during the cold month of February wasted heat energy, but it had to be done.

Given the burglary incident, we dared not to leave the windows open overnight. For a while we had a daily routine of coming into the house to do the airing out and shutting it up in the evening. We wiped down the surfaces a number of times and waited to breathe. We met with the people who make custom blinds locally and had them take measurements, but we didn't want these up until the off-gassing was complete. We busied ourselves with various tasks while we waited to move into the dream house we'd carefully planned and transformed. We felt like kids running around in a candy store waiting for mom to come and buy the candy. It was March when we moved into the house full time.

Expected and unexpected benefits

We knew from our little experiment at our condo that simply turning off the heater resulted in only 35 percent energy reduction, and I was cold and grouchy when we did this. I expected better from Midori. We'd been told that homes built to the Passive House Standard use 80 percent less energy compared to conventionally built homes, and the house stays at a comfortable temperature.

Did Midori perform as advertised? The short answer is yes. The most energy intensive month for Midori was January 2013 when her gas boiler turned on for the very first time to bring the house up to temperature in the dead of winter when the average low temperature was 39°F. She used 25 therms of gas. Similarly sized homes in the neighborhood used more than three times more gas than Midori, about 83 therms in the same month.

Once Midori was up to temperature, she used an average of 9 therms of gas on a winter month. This bumped up to to 12 therms a month when rainy weather prevented the sun from heating water. It was comfortable inside with consistent temperature range: 68°F at the middle of wall, 67°F at the ceiling, and 66°F on the floor.

To be fair, most of the houses in the neighborhood used gas for cooking and clothes drying. Midori used electricity. So for an apples-to-apples comparison, we would need to compare the total annual energy by adding electricity and gas together using a common unit of measure. Even without doing this conversion exercise, I knew that our lower gas bill was not due to a higher electricity bill. By looking at the graph of similar homes on our energy usage dashboard at PG&E, I could see our electricity usage to be much lower than average. We were pleased that expected benefits of significant energy savings and comfortable temperature were realized.

Then we discovered an unexpected benefit. On a sunny Sunday afternoon we chatted with our neighbor. She was upset with the neighbors on the other side of the backyard fence. They'd had a loud party around the fire pit with music and loud conversation that went on way too long. Kurt and I looked at each other and said, "We didn't hear anything." Our neighbor said, "Oh, that's right, you guys are living in a hermetically sealed house and missed out on the racket that was going on. Our bedroom windows open in that direction, and we couldn't sleep until 3:00 a.m."

Wow. The bonus of having a well-insulated, tightly air-sealed house is that you don't hear noise from loud parties. Come to think of it, I've noticed seeing cars passing by on the street but did not hear them as I sat in my living room. We feel more than hear the low-frequency sounds of the rumbling garbage truck. The high pitch of the siren wailing down the street is muted. Cars pass by our front window soundlessly.

But while sounds outside the house don't travel much to the inside of the house, the sounds inside the house do travel and reverberate. It's like being inside a guitar. Kurt is an avid consumer and collector of classical music, which he plays on his analog stereo system. He had the four speakers pre-wired under the floor to be placed in the four corners during construction. When he finally sat down and played his favorite classical music CD, he was stunned.

At the condo, he played this many times on the same equipment. Yet he heard details he'd never heard on that recording. He was a little amped when he said, "This room is amazing!" Then he added, "You know, I now realize that the room itself makes a huge difference in the listening experience. I could have bought much more expensive high fidelity stereo equipment. It could have sounded really good in the showroom, but it just would not have been the same if it was placed in a room where you couldn't hear it." The amazed look on his face said he was happy to have made the choice of spending money on the house rather than on an expensive gadget. This is another unexpected benefit.

We realized a third unexpected benefit by having another conversation with a neighbor. They mentioned rats in the neighborhood. I gave a blank look and asked, "Rats?" They replied, "You guys are hermetically sealed. I guess you wouldn't know." This is when I appreciated the benefit of meticulous air sealing. Years ago when I lived in a brand new condo in San Jose, I saw a mouse scamper across my kitchen floor. My dad told me to check the wall to see if the opening made for plumbing would allow the mouse to squeeze through. Sure enough, I found the wall opening for the gas line to the stove was more than twice the diameter of what it needed to be and the tiny mouse could easily enter and exit. With Midori we won't worry about rodents coming in. If air can't come in, neither can they.

The fourth unexpected benefit changed our laundry behavior. We heard that passive house can be a bit on the dry side with the HRV removing moisture. When we measured and compared the relative humidity when the indoor and the outdoor temperatures were the same, we did indeed find the indoor to be a touch drier. Rather than get a humidifier to add moisture back into the house, we decided that we'd simply hang our laundry indoors on collapsible laundry racks near the wall-mounted HRV supply registers to moisten the air a bit. This worked quite well and the side benefit from this was even lower energy usage because the clothes dryer went unused. How did we measure the humidity? We installed temperature and humidity sensors connected to a data logger.

Gathering data

Early on we knew we wanted to capture information but we didn't choose the system to do this with until we were ready to move in, way after the wiring had been done. Taking manual measurements and writing them down is tedious and inconsistent, so we spent time and money to have a data logger system installed. Not only did this satisfy our curiosity, but this voluntary act is a way for us to give back some data to the community that provided us with information and help during Midori's transformation. It also is a way to share our data with those who have questions when embarking on their own journey.

We chose WELserver for measuring temperature, humidity, and VOCs in different rooms. We were curious about the performance of the house over time. We had to back pedal a bit to make it work because WELserver operates on a 1-wire bus where one wire runs from the WELserver base unit to sensor A, then to sensor B, then to sensor C, and so forth. During the rough electrical stage, we had the wires laid out in a star configuration (similar to the home run plumbing layout) where dedicated wires ran from a central location to each of the sensor location. It wasn't ideal but it worked fine.

A friend introduced us to a graduate student at the local university studying network engineering. He managed to physically connect all the components over a few weekends between his studies, and we were pleased with the outcome. The system using a 1-wire bus made it economical to add different sensors from different manufacturers.

The WELserver gives us a snapshot of the temperatures in the rooms inside the house as well as on the front porch and the deck that overlooks the backyard (for indoor and outdoor comparison). A few of the sensors measure relative humidity as well as the temperature. This data is logged on a server every minute, and we can download the monthly file from the WELserver website and analyze the data in a large spreadsheet. Kurt was keen on having this measurement for his office where he carefully stored his photographic prints, slides, and camera equipment. The ideal temperature and relative humidity targets in art museums are 70°F (plus or minus two degrees) and 45–60 percent relative humidity. We are within that range for temperature, much to Kurt's satisfaction.

We deliberately chose the placement of the WELserver sensors to be on the interior walls (walls between rooms) rather than on the exterior walls (walls of the building envelope). We thought the room temperature taken at the interior wall would better reflect the true temperature of the room because the interior wall is less susceptible to outside weather. In general, we avoided the exterior wall for running pipes and ducts because they took away space from Midori's sweater, the cellulose insulation in the wall cavity. Also, anything installed on the interior wall was less problematic for air sealing. Our preference of favoring the interior wall also applied to the placement of HRV supply vents. By the time we avoided the spots for the furniture, the temperature sensor and the HRV supply registers ended up near each other. This skewed the temperature reading a little by measuring the temperature near the source of heat for the room. Not a huge difference, perhaps a degree or two. Looking back, we wished we placed the temperature sensor and the HRV ducts farther apart from each other.

Managing ultra-fine particles

As we eased into our new life with Midori, we noted how we behaved in response to Midori's performance. We were pleased with the thermal comfort, low energy usage, quiet interior, and not having to worry about rodents. Once we got over the drama of the off-gassing of materials, we enjoyed the continuous fresh air that was filtered and delivered at a comfortable temperature. What we weren't ready for were ultra-fine particles.

One day Kurt smelled smoke in the house. He sniffed a few times and concluded it was not the smell of burning food, but rather a fireplace smell.

"I thought the HRV filter would have taken care of that," I said.

"Smoke particles are really small. We've got MERV 13 HRV filters. They're pretty good, but smoke particles are much, much smaller than what these filters capture."

Ugh. We unplugged the HRV. We left it off for a few hours and did a sniff test outdoors before we started up the HRV again. Most of our neighbors have fireplaces in their houses and some have fire pits in their backyards. If the wind direction happened to be toward our HRV intake, then when they burn wood we smell smoke inside our house. Because the HRV moves stale air out as well as brings in fresh air, the smell of smoke eventually goes away.

Ultra-fine particles also come from some of our other neighbors—skunks. If they are frightened and spray near our HRV intake, we notice it inside the house. So we started our practice of manually unplugging and plugging back in the HRV based on the sniff test.

When we learned that Zehnder offered a charcoal filter that can be installed near the HRV intake, we jumped on it. This cuts down on the ultra-fine particles coming into the house. If the smell is severe, we still unplug the HRV, but we've been doing this much less after we installed the charcoal filter.

We generate VOCs too

Malodorous smell doesn't have to come from the outside. We can easily generate it inside the house. We now know that cooking odor can easily travel throughout the house and stick around. Sure, we have a range hood above the cooktop, and it is capable of sucking up the cooking fumes at the rate of 400 CFM. The range hood's charcoal filter screen traps odors and it exhausts near the ceiling. In theory the hot air exhausted from the range hood would hug the surface of the ceiling while it makes its way over to one of the two the HRV exhaust outlets in the kitchen. In most homes the exhaust fumes from cooking would be carried outside, but we chose to have a recirculating vent hood for airtightness as well as for heat recovery. The limited capacity of the recirculating vent hood to trap cooking odor was duly noted on the first time I fried some bacon in the cast iron skillet on the induction cooktop. The smell of bacon is pleasurable only up to a certain point, peaking at the first bite, then it slowly degrades. At a certain point it becomes annoying, like when the whiff of bacon is present in the bedroom when I'm trying to fall asleep.

Fortunately we had a simple solution to migrating cooking odors: doors between the rooms. The simple solution works really well and it was pure luck that we kept the original design and the doors and had the ability to isolate each room. Our design runs contrary to trends we saw in home magazine photos, those airy kitchens that open up to the living room and dining room in an expansive "great room." We liked how the dining room felt when we closed the doors—the room hugged us. We had pocket doors between the kitchen and the dining room, French doors between the dining room and the living room, and there was a door between the hallway and the living room. In other words, each of the rooms in the house could be somewhat sealed off. We used these physical barrier layers for containing cooking odors after our bacon lesson.

With our practice of cooking in a closed-off kitchen where the smell, humidity, and temperature is quarantined in one space, we've noticed that the rooms can sometimes feel like different climate zones. For example, when I'm cooking a lot, the kitchen feels like a tropical jungle. The window fogs up from pasta boiling in a stockpot, a cake baking in the oven, sauce simmering in the saucepan, veggies sautéing in the skillet. On the other side of the pocket door the dining room is ten degrees cooler and it has lower humidity. In the winter, much desired heat is redistributed throughout the house via the HRV. In the summer, when we don't want the heat redistributed, we can simply open the windows in the kitchen and let the outdoor air dilute the smell, humidity, and temperature in the room. The nighttime temperature in the summer is often mild with coastal fog so we don't worry about overheating here in Santa Cruz.

We have one of the VOC sensors in the space shared by the mudroom and kitchen. The other one is in the master bedroom. The master bedroom VOC reading shows a constant, very low level throughout the day whereas the VOC readings in the mudroom spike up whenever cooking odors permeate the kitchen. The VOC sensor detects a number of compounds in the air such as alcohol, aldehydes, ketones, organic acids, amines, and more.

Because the sensor reports an aggregate number, we never know what specific compound is spiking.

We're learning these operational details as we live in our Passive House. We're not complaining. We're just learning new routines to make our experience of living in a Passive House better.

Managing temperature

The climate in Santa Cruz is mild. Hardly any air conditioners are installed in homes in this area. But this does not mean that it doesn't get hot around here. We do have heat waves coming through the area and the daytime high temperature reaches near 100°F. What makes it tolerable is the cool air from the ocean that keeps the nighttime temperature in the low 60s. Most people manage the heat by night cooling, by opening windows to let the cool ocean breeze in. We do that too.

Our summer cooling strategy is a pretty simple manual system that doesn't cost much. The first part is managing the sun. The arbors above the deck facing the backyard and the deck facing the driveway are covered with a shade cloth. The original plan was to grow some plants like kiwI or grapes on the arbor and have them provide shade during the summer when the leaves are fully grown. In the winter, after the plants dropped their leaves, the sun would come through to warm the space. Since the plants wouldn't be mature enough to provide summer shading for the first summer, we decided to create our own shade cloth using inexpensive materials from the local hardware store and tied them onto the arbor. The shade cloth was installed in May and taken down in October. This worked so well that we decided to forego planting vines and avoid the extra maintenance of sweeping plant debris off the deck.

The second part of the summer cooling strategy is night cooling. We limit this to opening windows early in the morning since we don't feel comfortable leaving the windows open all night, and it works well. If we know a heatwave is coming, we cool the house down to about 68°F by opening the windows early in the morning. Then we shut all the blinds in the house and turn down the HRV to a low setting. Even Taylor was surprised by how well this worked. On one of the heatwave days when the external temperature was about 100°F, he came by the house at around 4:00 p.m. He said, "Wow, your house is cold!" when he stepped inside. The thermostat read 73°F.

During our second winter with Midori, we adopted a new heating strategy. While many people would find 68°F to be comfortable in the winter, I liked it better if the ambient temperature was 72°F. Kurt made a brilliant change in the thermostat setting to make me happier. He set the thermostat to 73° between 10:00 a.m. and 4:00 p.m. During this time the sun is heating the hot water so the heat energy is free and just a small amount of electricity is used to power the pump to circulate the hot water through the hydronic coil. In the evening we let the house temperature drift down to 68°. This works really well. Even if the low angle of the sun warms up the south facing rooms to around 77° in the afternoon, it doesn't feel too hot. I like this routine we adopted to manage our internal temperature in the range we like.

We learn through incidents

There were two incidents with our solar thermal system. We could have saved time, energy, and frustration if there were alarms flashing on some screen to indicate a malfunction. We kept our system simple without any remote displays or controls. The first incident happened in November 2013. All summer long the solar thermal system produced enough hot water that the backup gas boiler never turned on. Only when the rain came in November did we notice that the backup boiler was not firing when needed. We noticed it when the shower was lukewarm after a few rainy days.

I checked the gauges in the mech room after a lukewarm shower. The temperature in the tank was only 100°F, much lower than the set point of 120°F. It turned out that the aquastat sensor in the hot water tank was corroded and failed to trigger the signal to fire up the backup boiler. When Duane came out to take a look, he found the dielectric coupler had a pinhole leak which sprayed a fine mist and corroded the aquastat sensor. "They don't make them like they used to. I'll order a replacement one," Duane said. Dielectric couplers are used to separate two dissimilar metals in close proximity to prevent electric charge passing between them. He showed me how to temporarily connect the wires to trigger the backup boiler. The weather forecast showed rain for the upcoming week (meaning no sun) and we needed the boiler to work. Hot wiring the boiler was my daily task for a week or so until we got the replacement part. There's nothing like having a breakdown to learn the system.

Another incident happened seven months later in the summer. This time the problem was harder to detect because we did not suffer inconvenience from the system not working. It was Kurt's sharp hearing that caught the problem. He heard a humming, and we went to investigate. It was good thing we did. We found that the backup boiler was kicking on daily during the summer when there was ample sunlight, but the tank was not heating the water with the sun. Why? The glycol loop wasn't functioning. The pressure gauge that measures the flow rate of glycol circulating was not moving even when the solar pump was on. When Duane came out to take a look, he found a small leak from a 90-degree elbow joint in the mechanical room. Half of the glycol leaked out so slowly over time that we didn't notice any drips or puddles. This meant glycol, the heat-exchange fluid, didn't make it up to the roof to harvest heat and bring it back down to deposit heat in the tank. Our solar thermal tank was operating like a regular hot water tank at this point. We used as much gas in the month of June as we did in the rainiest month of February. This was only 12 therms, which is about the amount of gas used by other homes in the area that month. With the leak fixed and glycol refilled, we were back in operation.

A solar thermal system is very efficient and works well when everything is in working order. But it is a system that moves fluids with pumps and sensors, so we've needed the installer to come by to diagnose the problems and fix them. Each time we encountered an issue, we learned more about the system. These incidents provide perfect examples for documenting how the system works. Right before we moved into the house Taylor told me, "You have a complex system here. You should create a manual of how it works for future reference." He was right. I have a running log of notes from these incidents that help me understand and keep track of the solar thermal system.

First year energy use

The big question in March 2014 was, "How much energy did we use during our first year of living in Midori Haus?" Did Passive House deliver the low energy along with the comfort we've been enjoying? Let's see.

PG&E makes it easy for us to figure this out by simply downloading the usage data from their website. We used a scant 2,869 kWh of electricity and 51 therms of natural gas during the first year of living at Midori Haus (March 2013 to February 2014). Converting 51 therms of gas to kilowatt hours and adding it to the annual electricity total, it comes out to 4,389 kWh. If someone threw those numbers at me five years ago I would have blinked and asked, "So is that good, bad, or average?" because without context, it's hard to derive meaning from a set of numbers. The most useful numbers to provide context comes from the energy bill from the prior occupant of the house.

The seller of the house kindly ordered a set of duplicate bills from previous years so that we could do a comparison. Since the number of occupants is similar and the square footage of the house is the same, the difference is mostly attributed to the performance of the house. The previous occupant's energy usage was on par with similar homes in the neighborhood.

Midori went from 21,938 kWh per year to 4,334 kWh per year, an 80 percent reduction in total energy use for the house. Hurray!

Recognition and awards

We received the Green Building Award from the City of Santa Cruz in a little recognition ceremony at the City Council meeting. We invited the team to come join us for this short ceremony where we received a certificate and a plaque from the mayor and took pictures with the team. We celebrated with a beer at the nearby pub.

Thousand Home Challenge is another voluntary program we participated in. The goal of the Thousand Home Challenge is to demonstrate the potential to reduce total annual site energy consumption of existing North American homes by 70 percent or more. These reductions will be achieved through a combination of energy efficiency, renewable resources, community-based solutions, and behavioral choices. This program requires the proof of a year's worth of utility bills to show that this deep energy retrofit target was met. At a gathering of program participants in Northern California, Midori became the twenty-second house in the country to receive the Thousand Home Challenge Award.

There are people who build to the Passive House Standard but don't get their building certified. It's a voluntary certification process that costs time and money. For some people it's enough to live in a comfortable, ultra-low energy home without having a certification plaque on the wall. We chose to go through with the certification process because I felt that we would regret it if we didn't.

While there are various certifiers of Passive House Standards, we decided to go to Passivhaus Institut, the mother ship in Darmstadt, Germany. Their email correspondence was cordial and their requests for information seemed to go on for a long time. Fortunately we were not in a hurry to get it done quickly. We didn't know what to expect.

About eighteen months after we began the certification process, we received an email from Germany. Midori became the first house in Santa Cruz County to receive the Passive House Certification. We felt validated. Our official certification from Germany came with a surprise. Midori happened to be the house that crossed the threshold of millionth square meter of certified Passive House around the world. This made us giggly and we celebrated by having a recognition ceremony. Representative from Passivhaus Institut presented us with a certificate award. The Mayor of Santa Cruz, who happened to be our neighbor across the street, came over to congratulate us. Bill Monning (our state senator) sent a representative to present us with a California Senate Award recognizing Midori Haus for an outstanding commitment to residential energy efficiency and engaging local and international communities in green building design and renovation. We were featured on the front page of the local newspaper, the *Santa Cruz Sentinel*. It felt surreal.

What we learned about data: the proof is in the utility bills

There is nothing like living in the house to experience the benefits, resolve issues, and create new routines. Our learning shifted from learning from other people to learning from living with Midori.

❖ See before and after photos of Midori at: http://midorihaus. com/house-transformation-photos/

❖ Passive House is quiet and we enjoy an acoustic quality we've not experienced before.

❖ With rigorous air sealing, we don't have to worry about rodents.

❖ The heat recovery ventilator lowers the humidity. We adapted by hanging laundry on drying racks inside the house for dual benefit of energy savings and adding humidity.

❖ A charcoal filter helps reduce the quantity of ultra-fine particles coming into the house.

❖ Cooking smells can be contained by closing the door to the kitchen, and that's an important design consideration.

❖ We learn about the details of the systems when we encounter issues and keep a log for future reference.

❖ The combination of utility bills and the measurements captured by a temperature data logger proved the Passive House Standard works.

❖ We were building our dream, not looking for applause. When Midori achieved her certification, her recognition became a beacon. Other people in the region were very interested in what we did and how we did it.

17
Rainwater System

Rainwater system intention

Rainwater is another natural resource falling freely on our roof. Just as our solar system enabled us to harness sun energy and reduce our purchased energy, rainwater system infrastructure could reduce our purchased water. We felt we could make wise use of rainwater inside the house. We chose a phased approach to implementing a rainwater harvesting system for indoor non-potable use, and we intentionally kept the design simple.

Vision for a rainwater harvesting system

We waited more than a year after we moved in to fully install the rainwater harvesting system. We'd installed some parts of the system in 2012 when the yard was already dug up. We could have had Taylor install the rainwater tank in a corner of the yard and collect the rainwater for landscape irrigation while we waited for our vision of the rainwater system to be feasible. We chose not to do that because our landscape irrigation need was so small. The mature fruit trees seemed to be doing fine without us watering them. Most of the yard was mulched and the few plants we placed in the front yard didn't need much water.

Our vision was to use rainwater inside the house for flushing toilets and cold water laundry. About 20 percent of household water goes down the toilet in an average home. Just think, the water department does a good job of gathering and purifying water to make it drinkable. Then it's pumped into the house and we simply flush about a fifth of it down the toilet every day. Another 20 percent of drinking water is used for laundry. Do we need this to be drinking water quality? We certainly would not buy bottled water to do laundry or to flush the toilet.

We had an idea for what we wanted to do. In 2011 we toured the San Francisco Zen Center at Green Gulch and were impressed with their rainwater system. They collected rainwater from the roof of the dormitory and stored it in large tanks. They had a leaf filter, primary sediment filter, secondary sediment filter, and a UV light device to sterilize the water. This produced water so clean it was almost drinking water quality. The system appealed to us as a way to reduce our consumption of the region's precious water, as a way to use a resource that fell on our house for free, and as a way to up our degree of "green."

Our ideas for a rainwater system were ahead of the curve in 2011 because of regulations.

Feasible system

Regulation for rainwater use varies from state to state. In some states, rainwater harvesting is forbidden. In others, rainwater can be collected for drinking water. The plumbing code in California did not specify rainwater for indoor non-potable use prior to 2013. This meant each of the building departments in different cities and counties had to make their own decision on what was safe, and they tended to be overly cautious. In Santa Cruz, when we asked the city's building department about this type of system, they said we'd have to get clearance from the Health Department in the County of Santa Cruz. That would be on top of building department codes and regulations. When the California Plumbing code was updated in 2013, Chapter 17 clearly spelled out the requirement for indoor, non-potable use for rainwater. It did not require a clearance from the health department.

As the year 2013 came to a close, an opportunity to fulfill our rainwater system vision presented itself. A local environmental nonprofit organization was looking for a handful of participants to take part in a study to measure the effect of using a rainwater harvesting system for indoor non-potable use. They were implementing a California State Proposition 84 Stormwater Planning and Monitoring grant from the State Water Resources Control Board, the Monterey Bay Regional LID Planning and Incentives Program. The goals of the monitoring program were to determine the most cost-effective treatment options for meeting water quality standards for indoor, non-potable rainwater harvesting systems and to evaluate the potential of such systems to reduce potable water demand from surface and groundwater resources. In short, they wanted to see how much potable water could be saved by using rainwater for flushing toilets and doing cold water laundry and what treatment was needed, if any, to meet the water quality standard for indoor non-potable use. The study period spanned eighteen months.

Receiving technical assistance in designing the system and receiving a $10,000 rebate was an incentive. We just needed to have some skin in on the game by paying at least 20 percent of the system cost and allowing them to take samples and measurements during the study period. We applied for this program and became one of the seven sites in the study in Santa Cruz and Monterey Counties. Of the various types of buildings with varying degrees of water-efficient fixtures, Midori's profile stood out as being a recently renovated house with water efficient appliances, fixtures, and distribution plumbing. Our program manager was curious. How much potable water would such system save in a water-efficient home?

Choosing the rainwater contractor

After we were accepted into the rebate program in January 2014, we immediately started looking for contractors who could design and build this rainwater harvesting system for indoor non-potable use. This time the selection criteria was a bit more stringent because the program stipulated minimum qualifications for the contractor including the accredited professional certification from American Rain Catchment System Association (ARCSA) and having more than five systems under their belt with tanks sized 1,000 gallons or more. This eliminated lots of good contractors, including Taylor.

We reached out to two companies that were pre-screened by the program. Both of their estimates hovered around $30,000. Which meant our out-of-pocket cost would be twice the amount of the rebate. Ouch!

California was two years into what would ultimately be a record drought, and homeowners were getting serious about water conservation. The drought naturally increased the demand for the certified rainwater contractors, which meant we didn't have leverage in negotiating a lower price. Plus complexity was a concern. One of the homeowners we talked to during a reference call was an early adopter of the system we wanted to install. When we asked her, "What would you do differently if you were to do this over again," she said she wished she understood the control systems better. That was encouragement enough for us to keep the system simple. Fancy control systems complicate things and they could be expensive to maintain.

We looked through the ARCSA member directory to see if there were other contractors in the area who met the criteria. Fortunately we found a contractor who would install a simple system without any fancy control system. Jon Ramsey of AquaSoleil was from Carmel, about an hour drive away. Eager to add our project to his growing portfolio of rainwater systems, he gave us a bid that was about half the amount bid by the other guys. His contractor license was active and he had good references. We chose to work with him.

Sizing the tank

Not too small, not too big, but just right is what we were looking for in tank capacity. There's a sweet spot for sizing the tank,
and we looked at the range of tank sizes to see what made sense
for our goal of laundry and toilet flushing. A small tank, let's say
a 50-gallon rain barrel wouldn't do the job because it would be
too small. It would fill up and start spilling over in less than one
day, and we would use it up in less than a week of toilet flushing.
During the summer, when we have less than a quarter inch of rain
per month, it wouldn't help at all. Plus smaller tanks are relatively
expensive: $72 for 50 gallons; $300 for 200 gallons; $400 for 500 gal-
lons; $1,200 for 2,500 gallons; $3,000 for 5,000 gallons. Larger tanks
are more cost effective.

Another reason why a larger rainwater storage tank is important is because of the variability of rainfall where we live. It's wet
during the winter and dry during the summer, but our indoor
rainwater usage would be pretty constant throughout the year.
I estimated this to be between 600 and 700 gallons per month. The
larger the storage tank, the longer we could stretch the rainwater
into the dry season. A while back we spoke to a couple who did
a stealth installation of rainwater harvesting for flushing one of
their toilets. They have a 600-gallon tank and the rainwater lasts
through the year.

If a larger tank is better, what if we tried to capture every single drop of rain falling on our roof in the tank? How large would
it need to be? With the average annual rainfall being thirty-one
inches, we would need a very large tank, about 30,000 gallons.
That would be too much because our water bills showed that we
used only 27,000 gallons of potable water for everything (drinking, cooking, bathing, laundry, toilets, landscape irrigation) in one
year. We were also in a drought. We'd only received an annual
average of seventeen inches of rain the past three years, nearly half
of what we usually receive in an average year.

Not too small, not too large, but just the right-sized tank was
what we were looking for. For us the 5,000-gallon tank was the

sweet spot—not too big, not too small, and it felt right. The pecu-
liar thing about this size tank is that it's advertised and sold as having 4,995 gallons of capacity. Why would manufacturers do that? It
turns out that is the maximum legal capacity of a tank that can be
installed above ground on a simple bed of gravel. Anything larger
than 5,000 gallons requires a sturdy foundation which bumps up
the cost of the system. So the 5,000-gallon tank reflects the sweet
spot where we maximize rainwater harvesting and we keep the
system simple and cost effective.

A few good rainstorms in the winter will fill our 5,000-gallon
tank easily. For every inch of rain, we can store about 900 gallons of
rainwater in the tank. We use about three-quarters of the roof area
(1,503 square feet) to collect and feed the rainwater tank. The rain
falling on the remainder of the roof is routed into the storm drain.

Simple design

Our rainwater system has a simple design. The tank is gravity-fed.
Rain falling on the roof runs into the gutter and then through the
downspouts that connect to the underground pipe that feeds the
rainwater tank. When the tank is full, the overflow goes into the
rain garden next to the tank. We manually operate the two valves
controlling the flow of rainwater going into the tank at the beginning and end of the rainy season. The valves controlling the flow
of water into the tank are sturdy agricultural grade valves so we
know they will last a long time.

Water coming out of the bottom of the tank first goes through
a small 100-micron filter before it reaches the pump. This filters out
small debris to prevent problems with the equipment down the
line. Next to the filter is the water meter that measures how much
rainwater flows out of the tank as required by the program to track
our rainwater usage. The only automatic feature of the system is
the pump. When it senses moving water from a toilet being flushed
or the washing machine drawing water, the pump turns on to push
the water into the house, providing the pressure (about 60 psi)
that the washing machine and toilets need to operate. When the

water stops moving after the toilets or the washing machine stops demanding water, the pump turns off.

The design proposed by Jon was plain and simple. No control systems. No excessive filters. Everything was understandable. He advised us of two things that were different from our original idea. One was the shape of the rainwater tank. Originally we thought we wanted a soup-can-shaped tank, basically taller than wider shape, but ended up choosing a tuna-can-shaped tank. The tuna can takes up more yard space, but it would sit sturdier. The other advice we took was to install a Rhino gutter guard so that we never have to clean the gutter. We love low-maintenance features, especially when they're reasonably priced.

Jon's wife Cindi is an architect, and she drew up this simple plan. I took the plan down to the building department and hoped for an over-the-counter permit, but I was told it needed review from different departments. Two weeks later when we received the plan check response there were twenty-one comments. Since we wouldn't be receiving any rain for the next six months or so, we weren't in a hurry. Our team assembled a response and resubmitted the plans. The permit was issued on May 27, 2014, after we paid a fee of almost $900.

Tank installation

The tuna-can-shaped tank from Bushman was back-ordered. We had to schedule around vacation plans. By the time the tank appeared on site, it was late July. Jon and his crew rolled the tank down the driveway and guided it toward the corner of the yard on 2x4 skids. When they tilted the tank down on its final spot, it was perfectly placed.

It took them three days to install the fittings and flush out the stagnant water in the rainwater conveyance pipe between the roof gutter and the tank. Indoor plumbing was already done. Taylor had installed the rainwater plumbing while the walls were open. The rainwater lines were colored purple to clearly distinguish them as being the non-potable water source. Taylor had put in two cold water outlets on the wall next to the toilet. One marked "city water" was the potable water source and the other, "rainwater," would be for the non-potable source. The wall box behind the washing machine had similar markings for the cold water lines.

Rainwater system test

Since there were two different contractors involved in the installation of the rainwater system, we asked both to be present for the system test. Jon was responsible for the elements outside of the house and Taylor for the elements inside. On a warm day in August 2014 both Jon and Taylor came over to test the system.

The test consisted of three parts: 1) filling the tank, 2) clearing the pipe, 3) making sure toilets and washing machine worked properly. Filling the tank was easy. Jon placed the garden hose into each of the downspouts and turned on the water. Eventually when the pipes filled up, the water started pouring into the tank. Gravity feed works as long as the starting point of the water flow is higher than the entry point into the tank. So far so good.

Clearing out the pipe was necessary because the pipe that ran from the tank to inside the house sat dormant for more than two years before the tank was installed. After turning off the city water valve, Taylor removed the flexible toilet supply line from the toilet tank and connected the line to the rainwater valve. He pointed the end of the supply line toward the toilet bowl and turned on the rainwater valve. Sputtering dirt and small pieces of mulch and dirty water started to flow into the toilet. At one point the flexible supply line became clogged, so Taylor dug out the debris using a bamboo skewer.

After the rainwater line ran clear for several minutes, it was time to test the toilet. Jon said to me, "You can have the honor of the first flush." Without ceremony I pressed the button. The 0.8 gallons per flush Niagara toilet relies on water pressure to create a vacuum to assist the low-flow flush. Will the automatic flow-sensing pump do the job? Yep. The water flushing down the toilet looked no different than when it was connected to the city water line. After a while the faint humming sound of the pump heard through the open window stopped. I flushed again and the pump ran for a about a minute. Good, it worked as expected.

The toilet we tested was the first point of rainwater plumbing coming into the house. From there it branched off to the clothes washer and to the other toilet. Accessing the water valves behind the clothes washer took two strong guys lifting the stackable clothes dryer off the washing machine. The valves were nestled into the wall in a box behind the clothes washer. The HRV was located right next to it, so it wasn't easy for a little person with short arms like me to switch the lines over. Following a procedure similar to the one Taylor used with the toilet, he disconnected the cold water supply line and connected it to the rainwater line. This time the initial flush of water was sent into a bucket. When the water ran clear, it was time to connect the rainwater line to the Bosch Axxis+ clothes washer. Will it work? Did we get all the debris out of the line? Yes. The quick wash cycle that uses only cold water ran perfectly.

The last test was the toilet in the master bathroom. We followed the same procedure as the first toilet. And the result was the same. It worked. With smiles on their faces, the contractors cleaned up, packed up, and left after switching the cold water lines back to the city water supply. This was August and we didn't expect the rain to come for another two to three months.

Backflow prevention

While waiting for the rain, we got a visit from an inspector with the city's water department. He wanted to know if we had a backflow prevention device installed on our rainwater system. This device ensures the water delivered to customers is untainted from private property sources. If there is a pump at the customer's site with a potential for tainting the potable water supply through some cross connection, the city wants to eliminate that possibility, however remote, by having a device at the front yard to prevent the backflow. Interesting.

Once we learned about this, we started to notice backflow prevention devices in front of various buildings around town. At a strip mall there were thick fat pipes protruding a couple of feet above ground with valve shut-off wheels the size of a car steering wheel painted in bright red. There are much smaller ones painted green in front of some houses. In front of every commercial building there is almost always a backflow prevention device.

We didn't want to have that in front of our yard. It's an eyesore. I'm sure we would stop noticing it after a while, but it costs a few hundred dollars to install, and we would have an inspection charge every year. The idea of paying a third party more than our annual water bill just to have the privilege of saving water was annoying. We were doing the right thing to save water during the drought. We wanted to be a demonstration site where people could come by and see what's possible. Could we get by without having the backflow prevention device?

Fortunately, others in this rainwater system study had already encountered this situation. They told us we could avoid installing a back flow prevention device if we could clearly show an air gap between the city's potable water supply and the rainwater. That meant we needed to run a potable water line from the house to the rainwater tank. The potable water would be operated by a valve attached to a float.

It works the way a toilet tank valve works. When the level of the rainwater falls below the length of the float line, the valve opens and the city water pours into the tank until the water level reaches the point where the float relaxes tension on the string that triggers the float. With this setup we would never have to switch the water supply line for our toilets or the washing machine when the rainwater ran out. If we didn't have to fiddle with the supply line between city water and rainwater, the probability of cross connection is near zero.

The inspector from the water department was a stern and polite man who never cracked a smile. When he came out to check out the system after the air gap was installed, he was satisfied. This ended up being a $730 change order with Jon, but it brought us the benefit of never having to worry about whether there would be enough water in the tank at the end of the dry season to flush the toilet, so it was worth it. All was well again.

Results of water savings

With the one inch of rainfall in October 2014, we switched one toilet to the rainwater. At the beginning of January 2015, we switched out the cold water source for our washing machine to rainwater. At that point, we were fully using the rainwater for indoor non-potable use. Once a month a representative from the nonprofit visited our backyard to take measurements and collect samples from our rainwater system. From measurements taken during these visits, we know that we use an average of 625 gallons of rainwater per month or 7,500 gallons per year. This is more than a quarter but less than a third of all the water we use.

The best part is that we didn't run out of rainwater. Because we chose to keep our system simple, we didn't install an external gauge to show how much water was in the tank. We used a very simple sensor, our ears. We placed our ears on the tank wall and knocked at different levels. If the knock rang through the tank like a knock on a hollow door, there was no water at that level. When the knock sounded like a dull thud we knew there was water. When we wanted to know the water level in the tank, we simply knocked ourselves out up and down the tank. Our 5,000-gallon tank captured enough rainwater between October 2014 and May 2015 so that we could use it to flush our toilets and do cold water laundry for an entire year. We still had a bit of rainwater in the tank to spare when the rain came in November 2015.

The water samples were taken to measure E. coli and total coliform levels. Sterile cups like those used for urine tests at the doctor's office are used to take water samples and sent to the lab for analysis. Our water is pretty clean. During the first twelve months the level of total coliform, a useful indicators of pathogens in the water, stayed below the EPA water quality standard for indoor non-potable use.

Our utility bill from Santa Cruz Municipal Utilities won't show a significant reduction in water usage or the dollars billed.

Most of the utility bill is for sewer and garbage services. The water connection fee is about $20 per month and each unit of water consumed is $1.91. Water is billed in units of hundred cubic feet or CCF, which is 748 gallons. It's very cheap. Prior to installing the rainwater system, our water usage was already low. It ranged from 1 to 4 CCF per month. The restriction set by the Santa Cruz Municipal Utility for single family homes is 10 CCF per month. Even when I was watering a lot of vegetables I was growing in the backyard, our highest usage topped out at 6 CCF.

Our cost for tap water is $0.00255 per gallon, and we save 7,500 gallons a year by using rainwater. That saves us $19.13 per year. We paid a little over $16,000 for our rainwater system. The payback time for this is over 800 years. Financial savings was clearly not our motivation for installing this rainwater system. We did this because we feel it's the responsible thing to do in drought-prone California. Why should I flush hundreds of gallons of clean drinking water down the toilet each month? Water is a valuable natural resource we need to survive, and the price if water is kept artificially low to service everyone. Kurt and I value water and we have made significant improvements in our own infrastructure to use less water—thin three-eighths inch PEX pipes for distribution, water-efficient appliances and fixtures, gray water from the soaking tub to water our plants. The rainwater system is the next step for us in conserving water. The bottom line is that we chose to install this system based on our personal values, not on financial payback.

What we learned about creating a rainwater system

We chose to use rainwater for indoor non-potable use to further conserve water supplied by the utility. We were able to do this in a phased approach by installing dual plumbing during the main construction of the house.

❖ Asking the question, "Do we need to flush the toilet with clean drinking water?" put our indoor water use in perspective.

❖ After changing the appliances, plumbing fixtures, and distribution pipes to be water efficient, the next step toward water conservation inside the house was to use rainwater for toilets and laundry.

❖ Even during a drought year our 5,000-gallon rainwater tank provided us with ample rainwater for toilet flushing and laundry year round.

❖ Regulations pertaining to rainwater use vary across the country. Anyone contemplating this step should check the requirements of local building, water, and health departments.

18
Hindsight Perspective

What we learned from Midori

In the beginning of our dream green house journey, we had a desire to co-create a space that reflected our personal values of "green." We embraced this umbrella term of green by choosing materials, methods, and practices that would make us feel good. On the journey we learned about the various facets of green and about making choices based on our personal values. Aesthetic choices were important. We didn't want to settle for something that had green properties but was ugly. We wanted to love the place we created with our hearts and we wanted to validate the performance with data.

We chose a focus for our green efforts: reducing energy in our home that also reduces the input energy at the power plants. Passive House Standard opened our eyes. The track record of 80 percent or more energy reduction for heating and cooling the house seemed too good to be true. We learned that the reduction is possible when we shifted our thinking from the conventional, "Given this house with this type of enclosure, what should the heating, cooling, and ventilation system be?" to "Given this tiny annual energy budget, what enclosure will enable a tiny heating, cooling, and ventilation system to keep the people living in the house comfortable?" This is a powerful mindset.

When this powerful mindset is aided with a software tool (Passive House Planning Package) to model the performance of the house, it shapes the plan for success. We've gained immense respect for builders and construction crew who apply their skills meticulously to bring the plan to life. Third-party testing to ensure airtightness heightens quality assurance. Our final test—which evaluated all our efforts—had tense moments, but we're glad and amazed by the outcome.

Working with an older house in an established neighborhood allowed us to explore the relationship with the local environment and history. Living in this house made with wood harvested from our local forest and lime harvested from a local quarry almost a century ago made me feel more connected with the place.

We made lots of decisions along the way. At the outset, had we known about the amount of decision-making required, we may have been overwhelmed. Having a beginner's mind, not knowing what to expect, helped us. We simply learned as we went along and used our personal values as a guide to navigate our choices. We made mistakes along the way too. That's part of the process and added color to our journey.

Comfort is mentioned liberally in this book, but the actual feeling of being comfortable inside the house is difficult to convey. Being an early adopter of Passive House Standard in our area, we have opened our doors for public tours and classroom tours for local schools. We share our experience and answer questions from those who are looking to embark on their own journeys.

A new phase of learning began when we started living in our Passive House. The house is indeed comfortable and she operates on the principle of long time constant. Once a comfortable temperature range is achieved, it's kept there by minimizing heat transfer rather than moving heat quickly by mechanical means to achieve instantaneous comfort in an drafty environment. Now we pay attention to the weather forecast to make manual adjustments on the days we have extreme weather in our local climate spectrum.

We look forward to adding PV on the roof. It will get us to net zero and very likely a net positive house that will enable us to start making our car transportation greener by having an electric vehicle. Passivhaus Institut has updated their Passive House Standards since Midori was certified. Midori's certification level is now referred to as "Classic" and there are two more levels: Plus and Premium. While the criteria for heating demand of a Passive House may not exceed 15 kWh/m² per year will continue to apply, for the new higher certification levels the demand for renewable primary energy level is used.

Midori taught us a lot about the house as a system. She was in a perfect state to demonstrate what is possible and was a willing patient for teaching us many things. How she breathes and how it affects us. How wearing the right clothing, hat, and shoes makes her and us comfortable. She taught us how to reuse heat and how to reuse water. She taught us about working well with the sun. She taught us about resiliency. By thinking through our needs and wants, connecting them to the place where we live, keeping focus on what is important to us and why, and having a team of committed and talented people, Midori's transformation was successful. We are grateful for these dedicated people who made this possible: http://midorihaus.com/resources/

Thank you for taking the time to read this extended case study. I hope it provided food for thought for a green future for you and *your* house.

Acknowledgments

I owe many thanks to Karen Strauss and her team at Hybrid Global Publishing for the collaboration and support for making this book. Thank you Penny Hill for tuning my voice and editing my work. I am thankful for the cover design by Daniel Cook. Special thanks to Harmoney Laurence for prompting me to take a leap of faith. I am glad I chose to pursue my green building dream.

I am grateful to those who read earlier versions of this manuscript and provided valuable comments. Early readers include Merna Richardson, Susan Wright, Teri Ichiriu, Chris Stratton, Graham Irwin, Nickie Irvine, Andy Pavis, Gary Ransone, Bronwyn Barry, Walker Kellogg, Adele Talmadge, Hiromi Kelty, Laurie Clark, Anne Hull Seales, Tom Nedelsky, Linda Wigington, Taylor Darling, Alex Wilson, Larry Weingarten, Mary Nipper, Debra Little, Mohan Mahal, Jacquie Low, Scott Heeschan, Andy Couturie, Colin Smith, Mary Lastra, Barbara McBane, Allison Anthony, Jo Flemming, Pamela Moriarty, Elva Castanda de Hall, Carola Bernstein, and Jennifer Ruby Privateer.

I received inspiration and support from many people in the Passive House California community. Thank you for your encouragement, advice, and support.

I am grateful for the team of people who made Midori's transformation a success. Not only did they physically transform an old house, but they also transformed the way I look at houses. I thank Taylor Darling and the team at Santa Cruz Green Builders for excellent work and their commitment to Green Building. Graham Irwin was instrumental in guiding us down the Passive House path with unwavering belief of combining performance and aesthetics.

To my husband, Kurt Hurley, without you Midori would not be the same. I truly appreciate your intelligence, compassion, and discipline as we journeyed together on this adventure.

I am also extremely grateful to each one of you who chose to pick up this book. Thank you all so much.

CPSIA information can be obtained
at www.ICGtesting.com
Printed in the USA
LVHW02s2343060318
568948LV00007B/305/P